Institutional accommodation and the citizen: legal and political interaction in a pluralist society

This publication has received political and financial support from the Directorate General of Employment, Social Affairs and Equal Opportunities of the European Commission

Trends in social cohesion, No. 21

Council of Europe Publishing

French edition:
Accommodements institutionnels et citoyens: cadres juridiques et politiques pour interagir dans des sociétés plurielles
ISBN 978-92-871-6739-2

The opinions expressed in this work are the responsibility of the authors and do not necessarily reflect the official policy of the Council of Europe.

All rights reserved. No part of this publication may be translated, reproduced or transmitted, in any form or by any means, electronic (CD-Rom, Internet, etc.) or mechanical, including photocopying, recording or any information storage or retrieval system, without prior permission in writing from the Public Information and Publications Division, Directorate of Communication (F-67075 Strasbourg Cedex or publishing@coe.int).

Cover design: Documents and Publications Production Department (SPDP), Council of Europe
Layout: Editions européennes, Brussels

Council of Europe Publishing
F-67075 Strasbourg Cedex
http://book.coe.int

ISBN 978-92-871-6740-8
© Council of Europe, December 2009
Printed in France

Titles in the same collection

No. 1   **Promoting the policy debate on social exclusion from a comparative perspective** (ISBN 978-92-871-4920-6, €8/US$12)

No. 2   **Trends and developments in old-age pension and health-care financing in Europe during the 1990s** (ISBN 978-92-871-4921-3, €8/US$12)

No. 3   **Using social benefits to combat poverty and social exclusion: opportunities and problems from a comparative perspective** (ISBN 978-92-871-4937-4, €13/US$20)

No. 4   **New social demands: the challenges of governance** (ISBN 978-92-871-5012-7, €19/US$29)

No. 5   **Combating poverty and access to social rights in the countries of the South Caucasus: a territorial approach** (ISBN 978-92-871-5096-7, €15/US$23)

No. 6   **The state and new social responsibilities in a globalising world** (ISBN 978-92-871-5168-1, €15/US$23)

No. 7   **Civil society and new social responsibilities based on ethical foundations** (ISBN 978-92-871-5309-8, €13/US$20)

No. 8   **Youth and exclusion in disadvantaged urban areas: addressing the causes of violence** (ISBN 978-92-871-5389-0, €25/US$38)

No. 9   **Youth and exclusion in disadvantaged urban areas: policy approaches in six European cities** (ISBN 978-92-871-5512-2, €15/US$23)

No. 10   **Security through social cohesion: proposals for a new socio-economic governance** (ISBN 978-92-871-5491-0, €17/US$26)

No. 11   **Security through social cohesion: deconstructing fear (of others) by going beyond stereotypes** (ISBN 978-92-871-5544-3, €10/US$15)

No. 12   **Ethical, solidarity-based citizen involvement in the economy: a prerequisite for social cohesion** (ISBN 978-92-871-5558-0, €10/US$15)

No. 13   **Retirement income: recent developments and proposals** (ISBN 978-92-871-5705-8, €13/US$20)

No. 14   **Solidarity-based choices in the marketplace: a vital contribution to social cohesion** (ISBN 978-92-871-5761-4, €30/US$45)

No. 15   **Reconciling labour flexibility with social cohesion – Facing the challenge** (ISBN 978-92-871-5813-0, €35/US$53)

No. 16   **Reconciling labour flexibility with social cohesion – Ideas for political action** (ISBN 978-92-871-6014-0, €35/US$53)

Contents

Part D – Overview and conclusions

Foreword

This edition of "Trends in social cohesion" – *Institutional accommodation and the citizen: legal and political interaction in a pluralist society* – looks at ways of encouraging and promoting changes to institutions and individual behaviour to enable citizens of our increasingly pluralist societies to live together in harmony. It forms part of a project funded jointly by the Council of Europe and the European Commission on the development of intercultural skills in the social services.

The articles in this volume are concerned with "accommodating differences" from both the European and Canadian perspectives. Part A looks at the potential contribution of the law on both sides of the Atlantic to changes in our societies. Part B then raises the highly relevant question of whether we are concerned with reasonable accommodation or mutual accommodation, that is how to coexist at a time of growing diversity. The answer is far from simple since what is implied is acceptance of cultural interaction and an evolution towards something new, which is still to be created.

Since we also wish to place the question of accommodation in the context of intercultural dialogue – which the Council of Europe, with its White Paper, has made a priority – and training in intercultural skills and competences, Part C goes on to look at the various forms of resistance to this approach and the anti-pluralist position, and then at ways of ensuring that the "exceptions" established for minorities also benefit the rest of the population and can serve as vehicles of progress. This volume will be followed by one more specifically focused on education and training in intercultural competences aimed at social agencies, local authorities and civil society, but it already highlights a number of challenges that such an approach poses for public services.

For example, in addition to the debate on legal options, we look at policies and practices for dealing with plurality in a democratic society faced with hitherto unprecedented rapid change.

This edition of "Trends in social cohesion" is thus an opportunity for the Council of Europe to contribute to a major social issue and outline a vision of the future that allows us to set aside mutual suspicion and develop institutional arrangements and forms of social interaction capable of making diversity a factor for progress and well-being. In particular, this vision should enable each of us to benefit from the presence of others, and discover a world in which identities will not in any case remain fixed but will evolve and accommodate to each other.

Alexander Vladychenko

Director General of Social Cohesion
Council of Europe

Introduction

The papers appearing in this edition of "Trends in social cohesion" are part of a broader reflection on the ways in which public institutions – primarily social services, health-care services, employment services and others – can adapt their conduct and service provision in response to the plural identities of European populations while at the same time ensuring due regard for human rights. These contributions are part of a project co-financed by the Council of Europe and the European Commission.

This project asks the key question how – that is, by what voluntary or mandatory means – do institutions incorporate the skills, knowledge and practices enabling them to respond to the specific needs of individuals caused by the "rift" between identity and territory.[1] There is a danger that these specific needs, if overlooked or disregarded on the pretext of uniform equality, will turn into factors of exclusion arising from discriminatory or stigmatising practices.[2] From the point of view of social cohesion, incorporating at institutional level a concept of plurality accommodating difference is one of Europe's most important challenges.

Accordingly, this project analyses the value of a reasonable accommodation obligation as an inclusive and proactive approach for the integration of cultural diversity, using as a reference its application in Canadian law. In Canada, this obligation seeks to correct the discriminatory effects of a norm, either by exempting the individual concerned from its application or by adapting the norm itself.

"Accommodating" difference is an exercise in social and political discernment which should be part of "common sense" and "reasonableness", but which unfortunately comes up increasingly against such impassioned emotions and opposition that it often has to be implemented by legal imposition or, discreetly, out of goodwill.[3] The transformation in the concept of "nation", as described in Article 7 of Resolution 1735 (2006) of the Parliamentary Assembly of the Council of Europe, "from a purely ethnic or ethnocentric state into a civic state and from a purely civic state into a multicultural state where specific rights are recognised with regard

---

1. Text by Lidija R. Basta Fleiner.
2. Text by François Fournier.
3. Text by Emilio Santoro.

not only to physical persons but also to cultural or national communities", presupposes a long learning curve on the part of institutions and citizens requiring reference frameworks, training in skills, the transformation of language and legitimised political spaces for interaction and exchange between "diverse cultures".

However, the idea of a pluricultural or intercultural state in itself gives rise to profound resistance among populations whose national identity is synonymous with loyalty, conquest, freedom and discipline forged over the course of history. While plurality presupposes that rights to express themselves and to decision-making powers are granted to minorities on an equal footing with majorities,[4] and acceptance of the principle of mutual influence by interaction, then tension on the part of the host society over values, symbols, ways of occupying spaces, etc., could damage the calmness of the debate on the institutional changes to be made. This resistance could become all the more manifest given that it is frequently stirred up and exploited by the political class presenting "plurality as an embarrassment in itself" as A. Sen (2002) critically observed in another context. Such tension may lead to the formulation of false equations, giving the impression that restricting the freedoms of the "new arrivals" or "minorities" would lead to an increase in the freedoms of the majority. The opposite is true: when one interferes with the freedom of conscience of one section of society, it is everyone's freedom that is affected.[5]

Public facilities and services – which are supposed to comply with the principle of equality in access to rights and services – inevitably reflect the national culture in both the application of norms and in behaviour vis-à-vis citizens, institutional language and the evaluation of problems and satisfaction levels. It is generally assumed that these facilities do not give rise to psychological barriers, mistrust, incomprehension or fear since they are in response to the public interest. It is only very recently that the "ethnic" composition of administrative staff in Europe has been taken into account as a factor contributing to equality: it is not that long since multicultural cities such as Amsterdam and Berlin introduced multi-ethnic or multiracial staff recruitment policies.

The texts included in this edition present legal "options" which have been adopted in Europe and in Canada (particularly Quebec) to combat both direct and indirect discrimination and to produce guidelines to

---

4. Text by Eduardo Ruiz Vieytez.
5. Text by Tariq Ramadan.

ensure that "acknowledgement" of specific features is not undermined by stigmatising practices; consequently, institutions have been obliged to analyse the facilities they offer. Moreover, these texts raise questions concerning the possible political and legal choices (reasonable accommodation through legal procedures or through the development of institutional competences? Reasonable accommodation for minorities or for everyone? What type of intercultural dialogue can support the adaptation of regulatory frameworks, services and policies? How can one accommodate the "Islamic question" when Islam is so different from – or indeed incompatible with – the laws of secular countries?). Lastly, they describe the actions and steps – of varying degrees of political legitimacy – taken to accommodate difference in public services.

The contributions also address the question of the explicit or latent "resistance" encountered by any type of transformation.[6] Some authors believe that "ha da passa' 'a nuttata" (the night will soon be over) quoting the Neapolitan writer Eduardo de Filippo. Our societies are bound – despite resistance – to find the most appropriate ways to re-establish balances in contexts of rapid cultural change.[7] Others ask how far a democratic society must go in recognising differences.[8] The challenge is a considerable one especially as this gives rise to a highly emotive debate, particularly concerning the belief that any identity must remain unchanging and unchangeable in order to survive. In the "Invisible Cities" of Italo Calvino, we find Zora: in order to preserve its identity, this imaginary city banks on immobility, languishes and ultimately disappears. The Earth has forgotten it. There is no trace of its existence. Nonetheless, since the question of "to what extent should we change" persists, in order to avoid it becoming a source of sterile confrontations, the answer should take into account the fact that interaction also enables "the others" to change: migrants and minorities too have no desire to see their culture "calcified" or to live on the sidelines of democracy, rather they want to ensure that what makes them different does not turn into discrimination.

On another register, these texts explore – by comparing two different legal traditions – whether it would be appropriate for Europe to incorporate the North American concept of reasonable accommodation (over and above the provisions of Directive 2000/78/EC for the employment of

---

6. Text by François Fournier.
7. Text by Emilio Santoro.
8. Text by Marie-Claire Foblets and Pierre Bosset.

people with disabilities) to encourage the adaptation of rules and practices, public and private facilities and services so that difference does not become a barrier to the full enjoyment of rights and opportunities.[9] This measure also concerns both the procedures for identifying the obstacles (of a cultural, psychological or other nature) to equal access to services and the preventive and proactive conception of their operating rules and, lastly, the provision of personalised solutions where obstacles persist because of organisational constraints (cost, availability of relevant staff, etc.).[10] A number of questions are raised in this connection. If applied to the European context, would this legal measure provide additional protection for rights? Could it constitute a new means of recognising diversity? Would it make it possible to overcome hitherto unimagined obstacles to integration? Above and beyond the value of this legal measure in the fight against all forms of discrimination, what contribution could it make to more harmonious coexistence for the well-being of all which takes due account of our differences?

This comparative exercise in the legal field raises a number of questions, discussed by the authors themselves: an analytical summary is presented in the conclusion. And here, by way of introduction, are some of these questions to whet the reader's appetite.

To what extent are European legal frameworks (human rights, non-discrimination and protection of national minorities) effective in ensuring that the adaptation of facilities, social services, health care and other establishments can put into practice the principle of equality in diversity, in comparison to the reasonable accommodation obligation, as applied in Canada (bearing in mind that this does not relate to minority issues, which are regulated in the context of relationships between provinces)? Furthermore, how do these frameworks lay down the limits of what is reasonable (or the margin of appreciation) to ensure the desired results?

By granting courts the entire responsibility for deciding whether some individuals or groups should enjoy special regulations, does reasonable accommodation lead to exceptional treatment being the rule? Is exceptional treatment able to provide the right approach for social and citizenship learning in contexts where accommodating differences gives rise to conflict?[11] Does the accommodation obligation have the potential to

---

9. Text by Jennifer Jackson Preece.
10. Text by Myriam Jézéquel.
11. Text by Emilio Santoro.

adapt collective rules in the interest of all citizens, by devising new inclusive rules, rather than exceptions to the rules targeting the majority?

Is the right not to suffer indirect discrimination a suitable legal instrument for guaranteeing respect for ethnic, religious and cultural diversity in Europe? Does it oblige social structures to go beyond appearances of equality, to take a fresh look at themselves and if necessary to adapt in order to meet the needs of new groups of citizens?[12]

How can reasonable accommodation, as a legal technique, supplement the European legal framework regarding indirect discrimination in order to encourage our democracies to develop from a mere question of majorities towards the necessary incorporation of minorities from an equality perspective?[13]

In the light of certain best practices developed in Europe, can one claim that accommodations in Europe are the result of "common sense" rather than impositions by the courts? What can be gained from court proceedings?

Is reasonable accommodation a relevant approach to rectify the discrimination suffered by the "more vulnerable groups" or is it more appropriate to acknowledge specific aspects of identity, considered as essential for the integrity of individuals, separately from a situation of social or economic disadvantage?[14]

Above and beyond the debate on legal options, this edition includes discussions on political concepts and practices to address the question of plurality within democratic societies, in the context of rapid unprecedented change. Several texts emphasise the fact that reasonable accommodation – like the legal instruments for the recognition of human rights in Europe – does not replace policies of intercultural dialogue, interaction and participation aimed at building up a feeling of belonging, of shared projects. These policies seek to encourage – by fostering a sense of citizen empowerment – the creative management of differences and a sustainable accommodation-oriented approach in society, as indicated by one of the authors.[15] It is therefore not simply a matter of institutionalising a

---

12. Text by Frédérique Ast.
13. Text by Eduardo Ruiz Vieytez.
14. Text by Jennifer Jackson Preece.
15. Texts by Christoph Eberhard and Lidija R. Basta Fleiner.

new practice, but of ensuring that mutual and dynamic accommodations become an integral part of changes in society.[16] To this end, the Council of Europe is suggesting that the development of a vision and of progress indicators in well-being for all and in the communities be based on deliberative processes in which citizens representing social, cultural, religious and other "differences" all participate on an equal footing. Seeking out a shared vision is a means of overcoming dividing lines and possibly moving towards defining common understandings and projects.

Public institutions, more than any other organisations, have a responsibility to offer high-quality services, which are accessible and tailored to a pluralist population and to reflect this diversity in its programmes, practices and action.

The uncertainty focuses on the extent (and the binding aspect) of the necessary and reasonable adjustments to be made to institutions in a spirit of equity and inclusion. With due regard for the rights (legal benchmarks) and responsibilities (organisational constraints and remit) of everyone, how much adaptation should we agree to? What principles should guide us in this respect?

At a practical level, the search for equitable solutions, excluding the creation of a parallel network of services, requires institutions to think about their practices and transform their organisational culture.

In other words, the accommodation obligation refers to a question of managing diversity and reconciling rights which goes far beyond intercultural education in tolerance and harmonious coexistence. How can one encourage the integration of diversity in equality without adversely affecting social cohesion or democratic values? How can one strike a fair balance between competing interests? In order to respond to the needs of its immediate environment, should the institution accept the reasonable accommodation obligation by moving beyond the search for ad hoc solutions towards structural solutions? Should one extend the concept of diversity to include any distinctive feature which might make someone vulnerable? How can one avoid the situation in which consideration of diversity is regarded only in a conflictual context and one for which a judicial solution is required?

---

16. Text by Jane Wright.

In this context, promoting equal access by users to these services (without their difference being a disadvantage to them) also depends on the operators themselves having access to a series of conceptual reference points and means of action. What are the best strategies to enable professionals to solve conflicts of norms, evaluate their margin for manoeuvre and negotiate reasonable adjustments?

Over and above political arguments (integration of minorities), ideological arguments (enhancing difference), legal arguments (application of the right to equality) or social arguments (the demographic necessity for adjustment), consideration of diversity requires the building up of new professional skills incorporating diversity.

Diversity sensitisation tools are no longer adequate for stakeholders who want legal benchmarks and professional reference points (intercultural mediation techniques, social and procedural guidelines) to find a practical solution to conflicts of norms, values and rights. They wonder how they can adapt the legal obligations of non-discrimination to the particular terms of reference of their institution. Furthermore, these conflicts have not risen solely because of immigration. Individual freedom and the individualisation of deeply held convictions multiply the diversity of personal values and the individual ways of applying common values. Any rigidity in the application of rules can put people in a dilemma: should they forego their rights or go against their convictions. Liberal societies find it intolerable that society interferes in the intimate beliefs and convictions of individuals. Nevertheless, what forums for expression are provided for such beliefs and convictions when they are in conflict with common norms?

In this area, there are many questions going beyond the scope of the stakeholders involved, calling on the whole of society to reflect on the choice of its collective values. What reasonable limits can society impose on individuals who want to live according to their personal convictions but whose convictions run counter to the rules or common values? To what extent should institutions attempt to make their rules compatible with these minority differences? Can a society or an institution transform its rules without giving up its identity?

How is one to decide whether or not the harmful effects of a rule for certain individuals outweigh the beneficial effects of making the rule universal in nature? Assuming that the advantages of a rule having general application weigh heavier on the scales of a particular right than the disadvantages for a group, is the solution to create an exemption? How can we be sure in weighing up individual rights on the one hand and public order on the other that we are not overestimating (exacerbating the difference) or underestimating (diluting the difference) the impact of the hardship that may be caused? How can we avoid criticism of "excessive concessions" or, on the contrary, "excessive restraint"? How can we guard against cultural claims being presented as claims for acknowledgement of a right?

Clearly, the doctrine of reasonable accommodation has pushed back the frontiers of exclusion and made it possible to relax the rules of general application. But it raises the crucial question of the degree of flexibility of our common rules and the "excesses" of particular demands and the latitude that institutions have in managing this diversity. From this perspective, each society must strike what it regards as the right balance to incorporate diversity while ensuring social cohesion, legal stability, reliability of the system and the viability of the organisation.

These contributions are an attempt to discuss together whether the institutional adjustments and new social balances should take place by means of a citizenship-based, legislative or judicial approach. In this way, it sheds light for policy makers on the multiple facets of incorporating diversity in our public institutions. A key question in this connection relates to clarifying and promoting the advantage for the majority of the institutional accommodations introduced to incorporate diversity.[17] Moreover, even though mediation is an indispensable practice to be introduced in all public services, accommodating differences necessitates changes in the organisational conception of structures themselves. Should one therefore consider other institutional ways of functioning, for example in networks or by creating cross-sectoral support facilities, so as to introduce a degree of sharing of difficulties which is inherent in accommodation? Experiments under way in Europe highlight some of the avenues to be explored. In the town of Prato (Tuscany), schools are networked in order to share the taking in of immigrant children throughout the school year. The Dutch Equality Commission – an independent organisation set up in 1994 to promote and monitor the application of non-discrimination legislation – advises and provides information on the standards to be applied. Any citizen or institution may contact this commission to obtain free of charge an opinion on a specific situation of inequality or discrimination.

To conclude, the questions raised in these papers call for calm, collected political reflection – in consultation with citizens – on the frameworks to

---

17. Texts by Francine Saillant and Fabrizia Petrei.

be drawn up and the skills to be acquired in order to "live, interact and develop together" in our pluralist societies.

Gilda Farrell

Head of the Social Cohesion Development and Research Division
DG Social Cohesion
Council of Europe

Myriam Jézéquel

Consultant in diversity management, Ph.D.
(Sorbonne-Paris IV)

PART A – THE CONCEPT OF REASONABLE ACCOMMODATION: ITS POTENTIAL AGAINST EUROPEAN FRAMEWORKS OF CITIZENSHIP AND COMBAT AGAINST DISCRIMINATIONS TO MEET THE NEED FOR INSTITUTIONAL CHANGE, PARTICULARLY IN SOCIAL SERVICES

The reasonable accommodation requirement: potential and limits

Myriam Jézéquel[1]

In a pluralist society, accepting, integrating and managing cultural diversity is a challenge to the community and to public institutions, from the standpoint of both service to clients and personnel management. Public establishments have to respond to the needs of and growing demands for change from users and employees. Sometimes, these varied needs take the form of demands for changes to or exemptions from institutional norms. Some users want services provided in their own language, special diets for religious or moral reasons, the right to wear forms of dress or symbols prescribed by their religion and forms of service provision compatible with their values or traditions. In Canada, and in Quebec, public institutions have practised accommodation when these demands or requests relate to rights or freedoms guaranteed by charters and confirmed by the courts. In practical terms, the right to equality requires institutions to make specific accommodations to permit the integration or participation of persons with special needs. Such establishments must make adjustments to avoid inequalities in access to or the provision of services. They may only be excused from this obligation if they can show that any adjustment that might be contemplated would place excessive constraints on the institution's capacities, or its ability to fulfil its mandate

---

1. Consultant in diversity management, Ph.D. (Sorbonne-Paris IV). Author of several articles and handbooks on reasonable accommodation and conflicts of rights and values in intercultural relations.

or protect the rights of others. The management of reasonable accommodation is based not just on law but also on a willingness to acknowledge diversity and respect differences, in the interests of living in harmony.

To identify the legal content of this notion the article will start by drawing a distinction between voluntary adjustment measures and the statutory obligation of accommodation. We shall then look at how this obligation emerged in Canada and consider the legal definitions of this rapidly developing concept and the responsibilities of public institutions. Finally, although the duty to accommodate is rich in potential, in terms of solidarity, protection and respect for human dignity, its legal development has been accompanied by considerable uncertainty, which will also be discussed.

Voluntary effort or legal obligation?

In one sense, service providers' efforts to adjust to users' demands were already an integral aspect of their everyday practice and simply reflected their institutions' responsibility to provide the same standard of service equally and fairly to all. However, in certain cases they are required by legal charters to pay particular attention to situations that could lead to discrimination against persons from minorities and ones who are particularly vulnerable. Examples include failure to provide interpretation facilities and single menus in cafeterias. The law requires institutions some of whose norms or practices may have detrimental effects to rectify them by making necessary and reasonable adjustments, meaning that these are no longer simply dependent on the goodwill of those concerned.

The courts' interpretation of equal rights has created a legal duty to accommodate that requires institutions to make more than just voluntary adjustments. Thus, while some users ask for voluntary adjustments that the staff or institution concerned can choose whether or not to implement, other demands legally oblige institutions to review their rules of operation. However, the suppliers of goods and services to the public and first-line staff do not always master these legal aspects. As one lawyer has observed, when cases arise that require an accommodation, it is difficult for staff to identify precisely what elements might be applied. "Have I the right?" and "what are my obligations?" are clearly relevant questions that require answers. And she points out that in dealing with requests for accommodation, the organisational context has to be considered if the measure adopted is to be successfully applied.[2]

In response to public concern about the scope of and limits to the duty to accommodate, in February 2007 the Quebec Prime Minister, Mr Jean Charest, set up a consultative committee on accommodation practices to deal with cultural differences. It was co-chaired by Gérard Bouchard, a sociologist, and Charles Taylor, a philosopher. The public consultations that followed revealed a great deal of confusion about the notion of reasonable accommodation, involving considerable misunderstanding and over-simplification, such as seeing it purely in terms of religious accommodation or as a means of assimilating new arrivals to the country and a failure to differentiate between reasonable accommodation and concerted voluntary adjustments. In response to media exaggerations, the notion's legal underpinnings were forgotten and it became equated with any form of negotiated arrangement. In its conclusions, the consultative committee, also known as the Bouchard-Taylor Commission, clarified the meaning of the duty to accommodate and recommended that steps be taken to remove accommodation requests from the scope of the law by encouraging a more citizen-based approach, with preference being given to agreed adjustments and harmonisation of practices.[3]

The committee thus adopted a pragmatic and conciliatory approach that reflected developments in the law itself, which is tending to extend the scope of the accommodation requirement beyond that of simply combating discrimination. Quite apart from any individual cases, the Supreme Court has invited employers and others "in all cases to accommodate the characteristics of affected groups within their standards, rather than maintaining discriminatory standards supplemented by accommodation for those who cannot meet them".[4] Since 1999, the requirement to make accommodations has taken on a broader scope than purely individual adjustments and exceptions to the general rules, in response to specific requests.

---

2. Caroline Dubé, "Gestion de l'accommodement: un défi d'application au-delà du droit", *Gestion, Revue internationale de gestion*, summer 2008, Vol. 33, No. 2, HEC Montreal, p. 52.

3. www.accommodements.qc.ca.

4. *British Columbia (Superintendent of Motor Vehicles) v. British Columbia (Council of Human Rights)*, [1999] 3 S.C.R. 868 (Grismer judgment).

The judgments of the Supreme Court of Canada reflect a continuing battle against all insidious forms of exclusion. The effect has been to reformulate the accommodation requirement in more positive terms, involving a more proactive and institutional approach that gives the right to equality a more collective dimension. It is thus developing a more progressive standard of equality, increasing our awareness of individual differences and establishing a process for managing requests in which institutions can contribute to a more egalitarian model of society and more inclusive practices. In other words, this obligation is not just a legal constraint but also offers guidelines on what accommodation measures to adopt to manage diversity.

The origins of the duty to accommodate

The reasonable accommodation requirement was introduced into Canadian law in 1985 in the *O'Malley v. Simpsons-Sears Ltd* decision.[5] A saleswoman, a member of the Seventh Day Adventist Church, asked her employer to excuse her from working on Saturdays because it was incompatible with her religious beliefs. The Supreme Court acknowledged that the employer was entitled to open its store on Saturdays. However this "normal" employment requirement had a discriminatory effect on this employee because of her religious practice. In the absence of excessive constraints or major disadvantages, the employer was not entitled to prevent the employee from practising her religion. It must therefore try to accommodate her personal needs by adjusting her working hours. The same year, in the Big Mr Drug Mart case,[6] a company challenged the Sunday observance legislation that required all shops to close on Sundays, in accordance with the tenets of the Christian faith. As such this Sunday legislation required non-Christians to accept this rule of the majority. The Supreme Court recognised that the effect of this law was to create an inequality between Christians and non-Christians, that is between the dominant religion and religious minorities.

In these two judgments, the court indicated clearly that persons could not be prevented from acting or obliged to act against their beliefs and contrary to the spirit of the charters and personal dignity. They also showed that "the same rules for everyone" could have different conse-

---

5. *Ontario Commission of Human Rights and Theresa O'Malley (Vincent) v. Simpsons-Sears Ltd.*, [1985] 2 S.C.R. 536.

6. *R. v. Big M. Drug Mart Ltd.*, [1985] 1 S.C.R. 295.

quences for individuals, according to their personal characteristics. Rules and policies that at first sight seem neutral, justified and equally applicable to all may have detrimental effects on certain persons because of one or more specific characteristics or special needs. These collective rules based on majority characteristics reflect a sort of "implicit norm". This norm need not be unfair or discriminatory in itself. Even if there is no intention to exclude, where in practice such norms result in exclusion that is judged to be discriminatory this is sufficient for them to be considered a source of injustice. Intention is not a necessary element of discrimination.[7] The Supreme Court therefore invites individuals and organisations to consider the repercussions of their rules on their employees and users. For example, serving the same single menu in an establishment's only cafeteria, with no consideration for religious dietary requirements or restrictions linked to moral convictions, such as vegetarianism, or allergies, can create distinctions between individuals who have no alternative to using that cafeteria. Thus, the duty to accommodate applies with even more force to so-called "captive" clienteles.

The duty to accommodate therefore places us first and foremost in the field of law.[8] It derives from the right to equality and was initially conditional on the existence of discrimination (Article 10 of the Quebec and Article 15 of the Canadian charters).

For there to be discrimination within the meaning of Article 10 of Quebec's Charter of Human Rights and Freedoms, a practice must generate a distinction, exclusion or preference that has the effect of nullifying or impairing a right protected by the charter:

> 10. Every person has a right to full and equal recognition and exercise of his human rights and freedoms, without distinction, exclusion or preference based on race, colour, sex, pregnancy, sexual orientation, civil status, age except as provided by law, religion, political convictions, language, ethnic or national origin, social condition, a handicap or the use of any means to palliate a handicap. Discrimination exists where such a distinction, exclusion or preference has the effect of nullifying or impairing such right.

---

7. *British Columbia (Public Service Employee Relations Commission) v. BCGSEU*, [1999] 3 S.C.R. 3

8. Myriam Jézéquel (ed.), *Les accommodements raisonnables: quoi, comment, jusqu'où? Des outils pour tous*, Yvon Blais, Cowansville (Quebec), 2007.

From a strictly legal standpoint, therefore, requests for accommodation will only be admissible if (1) the contested rule or standard is discriminatory; (2) the discrimination is prohibited by the charter; (3) the obligation to abide by the rule or standard is detrimental to the applicant.

These grounds for discrimination are specified in Article 10 of the Quebec and Article 15 of the Canadian charters and include race, colour, sex, pregnancy, sexual orientation, civil status, age except as provided by law, religion, political convictions, language, ethnic or national origin, social condition, a handicap or the use of any means to palliate a handicap. The list of grounds shows that the need to adjust rules and practices is not dependent on the presence of immigrants or confined to religious or cultural diversity. Apart from the grounds enumerated in the charter, the Supreme Court may recognise "analogous" ones. According to its reasoning in the Corbière judgment,[9] "these grounds have in common the fact that they often serve as the basis for stereotypical decisions made not on the basis of merit but on the basis of a personal characteristic that is immutable or changeable only at unacceptable cost to personal identity". In support of this argument, it appears that an individual may exhibit vulnerability without being a member of a vulnerable group, that is one that is "historically disadvantaged". Even persons who do not belong to groups identified by their ethnic origin, sex, colour, age, religion, social class and so on may be deemed to be vulnerable if they have personal characteristics, and a degree of social fragility, that expose them to the risk that their interests will be neglected and their rights abused. This means that the grounds of discrimination are no longer interpreted solely in accordance with parliament's original understanding of the term. They have to be considered in the context of contemporary values and existing social reality. The outlawing of discrimination must work to the benefit of all.

Finally, the courts penalise not just refusal but also failure to accommodate, resulting in exclusion through inertia. This results from not taking practical measures to enable disadvantaged persons or groups to enjoy equal access to services for the population at large. The ban on discrimination also covers the subjective dimension of discrimination based on perceptions, that is where people are excluded on the basis of prejudice.[10] Accommodation requires greater flexibility in rules that uninten-

---

9. *Corbiere v. Canada (Minister of Indian and Northern Affairs)*, [1999] 2 S.C.R. 203.

10. *Eaton v. Brant County Board of Education*, [1997] 1 S.C.R. 241.

tionally create distinctions. The rules should be modified or their effects on certain persons should be attenuated by establishing exceptions to generalised practices, exemptions from operating rules or specific adaptation of the rules that apply. If such rules are not adjusted to eliminate their discriminatory elements, individuals with particular characteristics or from minority groups may be disadvantaged or excluded by rules adopted by and for the majority. Such initially corrective measures are intended to produce a level playing field. For example, schools or hospitals should be able to offer interpretation services for persons who are deaf or who speak a minority language to guarantee them full access to the services offered.

This obligation is recognised in all Canadian human rights legislation. It should be noted that the Canadian Charter of Rights and Freedoms only applies to relations between individuals and the federal and provincial public authorities. The Quebec charter applies equally to relations between citizens and the state and to private relations between individuals.

Quite apart from the Canadian law context, this legal instrument is based on the democratic values of Canadian society, its policy of multiculturalism and Quebec's intercultural policy. To support the notion's application, there is a series of government documents and institutional policies that together form a common public culture. They include a so-called moral contract on the integration of persons of immigrant origin, involving reciprocal rights and duties, the principle of social justice and solidarity for persons with special needs, to ensure full and universal participation in society, the right to preserve minority cultures (Articles 43 of the Quebec and 27 of the Canadian charters), and the Canadian Multiculturalism Act, to support multicultural pluralism. At another level, the reasonable accommodation requirement is fully consistent with all the legislation governing public institutions in Quebec, including the laws on the health and social services, youth protection, young offenders and public education. These different departments aim to improve the quality of public services by collaborating with members of local and other communities and by fostering such collaboration in order to take action on aspects that are socially critical for vulnerable groups.

The obligation to provide the necessary resources to make equality a reality

Canadian society defends an ideal of itself as one in which each and everyone can be sure that the law recognises them as human beings who deserve the same respect, deference and consideration. Everyone must have access to the same opportunities and benefits, and must be treated with dignity and respect. Up to a certain point, this equality of consideration calls for difference of treatment. Equal treatment of persons in a group or in an institution sometimes means treating them differently. As one of the Supreme Court judges has put it, "difference in treatment between individuals under the law will not necessarily result in inequality and ... identical treatment may frequently produce serious inequality".[11]

The duty to accommodate necessitates both the establishment of a new standard of equality and the means to make that equality a reality in all its domains. In contrast to formal equality, this new concept of differential equality requires differences between individuals to be taken into account so that forms of action can be adapted to their legally protected characteristics. In the words of another Supreme Court judge, "to the extent that a standard unnecessarily fails to reflect the differences among individuals, it runs afoul of the prohibitions contained in the various human rights statutes and must be replaced. The standard itself is required to provide for individual accommodation, if reasonably possible. A standard that allows for such accommodation may be only slightly different from the existing standard but it is a different standard nonetheless."[12]

This differential, material and inclusive form of equality sometimes calls for changes to existing rules that may go as far as destabilising certain well-established customs or posing a challenge to benefits enjoyed by the majority.

However, the duty to accommodate is not accompanied by any obligation to secure results. To be acceptable, the accommodation must be reasonable. Restrictions on fundamental rights may be authorised, subject to the application of the first article of the Canadian charter, namely "subject only to such reasonable limits prescribed by law as can be demonstrably justified in a free and democratic society", or of Article 31 of the Quebec charter, having "proper regard for democratic values, public order and the general well-being of the citizens of Quebec". There can also be exceptions to and grounds of defence against the duty to accommodate such as normal professional requirements, exemptions for religious and political organisations and one relating to equality access programmes.

---

11. *Andrews v. Law Society of British Columbia* judgment.
12. *British Columbia (Public Service Employee Relations Commission) v. BCGSEU*, [1999] 3 S.C.R. 3.

The duty to accommodate is not absolute, therefore, but depends on the context. Grounds for refusing an accommodation can include excessive costs, serious risk, the size of the organisation, the likelihood of infringing the rights and well-being of others and organisational problems connected to the interchangeability of staff or democratic values. In determining whether a form of reasonable accommodation is relevant or realistic, institutions can refer to these legally established criteria, which are not exhaustive.

However, "more than mere negligible effort is required to satisfy the duty to accommodate. The use of the term 'undue' infers that some hardship is acceptable; it is only 'undue' hardship that satisfies this test."[13] What constitutes undue constraint has to be assessed in terms of the institution's characteristics, such as its terms of reference and type of clientele, and the specific context – whether there is adequate staffing, the cost of the operation and so on. Each case must be considered on its merits. Arguments that it would infringe the rights of others or damage staff morale must be based on more than just impressions or fears to outweigh employees' or clients' right to accommodation. The judgment continues: "The employer must establish that actual interference with the rights of other employees, which is not trivial but substantial, will result from the adoption of the accommodating measures. Minor interference or inconvenience is the price to be paid for religious freedom in a multicultural society."

Accommodating measures must always strike a certain balance between employees' or users' right to equal treatment and the right of an employer or institution to manage its organisation efficiently. The introduction of such measures must not therefore become unmanageable for the organisation or interfere with democratic values. Those concerned must do everything to show that they have made real and adequate efforts and have acted in good faith. The duty to accommodate implies a reciprocal obligation to negotiate to find a mutually satisfactory solution. Such solutions are generally the result of a compromise and their success depends on mutual respect and a sharing of responsibilities. The practical lesson to be drawn is that the framing of fair rules necessitates, firstly, acceptance of the rules of discussion.

---

13. *Central Okanagan School District No. 23 v. Renaud*, [1992] 2 S.C.R. 970.

From reactive to proactive measures

Initially, this legal obligation was concerned with corrective measures, allied to a pragmatic approach, to ensure that majority practices did not exert pressure to conform on persons of minority background. Today, following a series of court decisions, the duty to accommodate requires individuals and institutions to take preventive action by assessing the difficulties faced by persons who are not part of the majority culture. The Supreme Court now urges all concerned to be more vigilant and more proactive. This active and proactive obligation has considerably broadened the scope of the duty to accommodate.

There is no longer a requirement simply to remedy exclusion and re-establish equality in individual discriminatory situations. Since 1999, the courts have called for additional efforts beyond that of merely ending discrimination. They urge employers and institutions not just to consider individual complaints but also to incorporate the notion of equality into their employment rules and policies, in order to remove, as far as possible, structural and institutional barriers.

> Employers designing workplace standards owe an obligation to be aware of both the differences between individuals, and differences that characterize groups of individuals. They must build conceptions of equality into workplace standards. By enacting human rights statutes and providing that they are applicable to the workplace, the legislatures have determined that the standards governing the performance of work should be designed to reflect all members of society, in so far as this is reasonably possible. Courts and tribunals must bear this in mind when confronted with a claim of employment-related discrimination. To the extent that a standard unnecessarily fails to reflect the differences among individuals, it runs afoul of the prohibitions contained in the various human rights statutes and must be replaced. The standard itself is required to provide for individual accommodation, if reasonably possible. A standard that allows for such accommodation may be only slightly different from the existing standard but it is a different standard nonetheless.[14]

The exception, in the form of responses to individual cases of discrimination at the request of isolated persons whose rights have been breached,

---

14. Source: *British Columbia (Public Service Employee Relations Commission) v. BCGSEU*, paragraph 68.

is no longer the rule. Accommodation must now be incorporated into the rules themselves, to ensure that they are no longer discriminatory. As one arbitrator has put it, employers must now see the right to equality, not as an exception to the rule but as a means of accepting differences.[15]

Exceptions now constitute waivers of the rules. However, rather than invalidating such rules this strengthens their legitimacy. Acknowledging exceptions both limits and confirms rules. This reformulation of the duty to accommodate establishes that rules are now valid not in so far as they admit exceptions but in that they incorporate the equality requirement, which is at the heart of the duty to accommodate. Refusal or failure to review rules of operation would serve to perpetuate their discriminatory effects on certain persons.

Another lesson to be drawn is that, to a certain extent, rules and standards must reflect the development of a pluralist society by taking account of differences between people. Standardising rules is incompatible with the composition of a pluralist society. According to the Supreme Court in the Grismer judgment, employers are now required "in all cases to accommodate the characteristics of affected groups within their standards, rather than maintaining discriminatory standards supplemented by accommodation for those who cannot meet them".[16]

The main protagonists, both lawyers and non-lawyers, have not so far drawn all the consequences from this change in the law, which is extending the scope of this legal notion beyond historically stigmatised groups ("analogous" grounds for discrimination), traditional forms of discrimination (the ban on discrimination in all its forms) and the right to equality (with a generous interpretation of the exercise of these rights). This new formulation is very broad in scope because it represents a change of perspective and dimension.

This enlarged and remodelled definition of accommodation has a number of consequences:

- it shifts the burden of demanding equality from persons suffering discrimination to society as a whole;

---

15. The arbitrator François Blais in *Soleno inc. v. Métallurgistes unis d'Amérique*, 2005 Canlii 55297, paragraph 196 (2005T-1114).

16. *British Columbia (Superintendent of Motor Vehicles) v. British Columbia (Council of Human Rights)*, [1999] 3 S.C.R. 868.

- it goes beyond banning discrimination by incorporating equality into rules and standards, thus creating an inclusive environment where there are no obstacles to integration;

- institutions are invited to initiate the accommodation process, since it is they better than anyone who understand how their organisations function. Adaptation becomes the main responsibility of the institution, as guarantor of respect for the right to equality.

The reformulation of the duty to accommodate creates new responsibilities for institutions, which raises certain questions: (1) does the regular application of a rule have the same general impact on everyone or does it disadvantage certain groups with specific characteristics?, and (2) what forms of discrimination might emerge in a particular institution, in connection with the needs of current clients or possible future ones?

More than ever, reasonable accommodation creates a duty to act, associated with a positive obligation to establish in advance inclusive rules and practices of benefit to all.

The scope of reasonable accommodation and the scale of the task

Much thought and action is required before we can achieve a genuinely pluralist and egalitarian society. The duty to accommodate creates not only legal requirements but also a vision of a country where everyone has a role to play in society and an equal opportunity to participate in that country's community, political and economic life, and where institutions can help to make society more inclusive through greater acceptance of differences. This implies a vision of social justice and community life in which everyone can consider him- or herself to be a full citizen sharing certain common values.

Here, the courts play a critical role. According to the President of Quebec's Human Rights Court, the courts must incorporate the expression of this diversity into their legal reasoning, bearing in mind such fundamental social values as universal equality before the law, the right to dignity and the right to life and security. The challenge is to strike a fair balance between changes in society and a level of legal stability that guarantees respect for these fundamental values. Our approach to pushing back the frontiers of exclusion and promoting cultural diversity must take account of the needs of law and justice, but above all it requires great openness and a willingness to listen.[17]

The way that this legal measure has expanded gives some idea of the size of the outstanding task:

- identifying obstacles to eligibility for and equal access to institutional services;

- identifying all the rules of operation, standards and facilities in terms of the new equality rule and reflecting the diversity representative of society;

- establishing personalised solutions for users when the obstacles persist and cannot be eliminated, bearing in mind health and safety and cost requirements.

According to the Canadian Supreme Court, this is the price to be paid for pursuing the ideal of equality. The social justification for reasonable accommodation within our institutions has also been illustrated as follows: "Inequality is likely to erode social capital, including the sense of trust and citizen responsibility that is key to the formation and sustainability of sound public institutions" (United Nations Development Programme report, 2001).[18]

Progress and matters for concern

Judicial interpretations of this legal concept have had a number of social and organisational consequences.

In Quebec, media coverage of certain minor improvised compromises has raised fears that a *laissez-faire* approach to accommodation practices may place certain shared values at risk, disrupt the balance between majority and minority rights and pose a threat to the fundamental values of society, or even Quebec's identity. According to this view, the increased use of this legal measure opens the door to the tyranny of minorities. The fear is that the duty to accommodate will lead to excessive identity-related or opportunistic demands, which paradoxically are also discriminatory and which ultimately divert this legal notion away from its real purpose of securing

---

17. Michèle Rivet, "Introduction", in *La justice à l'épreuve de la diversité culturelle*, Yvon Blais, 2007, p. 15.

18. www.undp.org/annualreports/2001/undpar2001.pdf.

equality, in favour of obtaining privileges. These challenges to the duty to accommodate are explicitly concerned with the expression of freedom of religion in the public sphere. Various court decisions have given rise to a more subjective, and thus more protective, interpretation of the rights of believers. The subjective criterion of belief, namely sincerity of the faith, now takes precedence over the objective criterion of religious doctrine. This means that consideration of requests for accommodation must be based primarily on the believer's sincerity, even if the individual's belief is based on a purely personal interpretation of his or her religion (Amselem judgment).[19] To ensure that legal flexibility is not transformed into legal elasticity, members of the public and voluntary associations are urging the authorities to reaffirm that equality of the sexes places limits on freedom of religion. These concerns reflect a question asked by the Supreme Court in 1985: "The question [of accommodation] is not free from difficulty. No problem is found with the proposition that a person should be free to adopt any religion he or she may choose and to observe the tenets of that faith. ... Difficulty arises when the question is posed of how far the person is entitled to go in the exercise of his religious freedom. At what point in the profession of his faith and the observance of its rules does he go beyond the mere exercise of his rights and seek to enforce upon others conformance with his beliefs?"[20] The judges of the Supreme Court have recently sought to clarify the interpretation of this right embodied in the Canadian Charter of Rights and Freedoms. The case[21] concerns members of the Hutterian Wilson Colony, who believe sincerely that the Second Commandment of their religion prohibits them from having their photograph willingly taken. They therefore objected to the Alberta government requiring them to be photographed in order to obtain a driving licence. On 24 July 2009, in a judgment delivered by four judges to three and drafted by Chief Justice Beverley McLachlin, the Supreme Court reaffirmed the reasonable limits to the duty to accommodate. She stated that "because religion touches so many facets of daily life, and because a host of different religions with different rites and practices co-exist in our society, it is inevitable that some religious practices will come into conflict with laws and regulatory systems of general application. As recognized by the European Court of Human Rights in *Kokkinakis v. Greece*, judgment of 25 May 1993, Series A no. 260-A, cited by my colleague Abella J., this pluralistic context also includes 'atheists, agnostics, sceptics and

---

19. *Syndicat Northcrest v. Amselem*, 2004 CSC 47, [2004] 2 S.C.R. 551.
20. O'Malley judgment, op. cit.
21. *Alberta v. Hutterian Brethren of Wilson Colony*, 2009 CSC 37.

the unconcerned' (para. 31). Their interests are equally protected by s. 2(a): *R. v. Big M Drug Mart Ltd*, [1985] 1 S.C.R. 295, at p. 347. In judging the seriousness of the limit in a particular case, the perspective of the religious or conscientious claimant is important. However, this perspective must be considered in the context of a multicultural, multi-religious society where the duty of state authorities to legislate for the general good inevitably produces conflicts with individual beliefs." Clearly then, the debate on the duty to accommodate, its boundaries and how to reconcile it with acquired rights is far from over, and we may yet require further guidance on how to apply this notion, so rich in potential.

Accommodating diversity in Quebec and Europe: different legal concepts, similar results?

Pierre Bosset[1] and Marie-Claire Foblets[2]

Introduction

Regulating multiculturalism, Cotterell and Arnaud recently wrote, requires those who practise different cultures that are in contact with each other to accept responsibility for a common approach.[3] The concept of reasonable accommodation is tied up with such an approach. It is particularly concerned with indirect discrimination in contemporary democratic societies where numerous groups and communities coexist, based on a substantive notion of equality, or real equality. This entails appropriate measures to prevent superficially neutral rules or standards from being discriminatory in effect, because their application is detrimental to particular categories of person.

The main idea underlying reasonable accommodation is that democratic states must allow everyone to participate fully in society on an equal footing, as far as possible while continuing to respect diversity. The aim is equality in diversity. In certain circumstances, achieving this aim may make it necessary to take account of individuals' specific features, such as their religion, language or culture, by treating them differently. Promoting the social inclusion of the maximum number of members of the community may sometimes entail a different approach that takes account of differences.

Whereas the notion of reasonable accommodation is already firmly rooted in the legal systems of the United States and Canada, where it originated, it has only very recently appeared in Europe, where it appears to be making an impact, albeit discreetly. The present publication is an illustration of this.

---

1. Professor of Public Law, University of Quebec at Montreal (UQAM) (Canada).
2. Professor of Law and Anthropology at the universities of Louvain and Antwerp (Belgium).
3. Roger Cotterell and André-Jean Arnaud, "Comment penser le multiculturalisme en droit?", *L'Observateur des Nations Unies* (special edition: "Le Multiculturalisme", 2007, 2 (Vol. 23), p. 24.

The European and North American approaches do nevertheless differ. This is what we shall be describing, very briefly, in the following pages. The aim is to compare experience on either side of the Atlantic and the specific characteristics of each of the legal systems concerned.

In the first two parts we assess the notion of reasonable accommodation in its North American context, taking Quebec as the starting point. In particular we consider the contribution of Canadian and North American courts to the development of reasonable accommodation, especially its application to the public services. In the third part we look at the situation in Europe.

We hope that this comparative exercise will lead on to a much broader enterprise requiring more far-reaching research, namely a general debate on the possible benefits that European countries might gain from the systematic application of the principles of reasonable accommodation in their own domestic environments. Such a debate remains for the future. We confine ourselves in our conclusions to a number of questions that we feel should be the subject of such a debate.

1. The concept of reasonable accommodation in Quebec

It is unusual for concepts created by and for lawyers to find their way into everyday language, but this is the case with reasonable accommodation in Quebec. The original, modest legal aim was to find a practical way of dealing with certain problems of discrimination, but the concept was suddenly propelled into the heart of the debate on Quebec's identity, and the so-called "reasonable accommodation crisis".[4] As was to be

---

4. The "reasonable accommodation crisis" reached its peak in 2006-07, a period in which the Quebec media published frequent attacks on "unreasonable accommodations" (see: Maryse Potvin, *La crise des accommodements raisonnables: une fiction médiatique?* Editions Athéna, Montreal, 2008). By winter 2007, it had become a political issue. As the election campaign loomed, the Quebec Government set up a consultative committee on accommodation practices to deal with cultural differences, the Bouchard-Taylor Commission. The commission's mandate was to conduct consultations on accommodation practices and make recommendations to ensure that they were compatible with the values of Quebec as a pluralist, democratic and egalitarian society. The commission held hearings in Quebec's 17 regions. They were broadcast live on television. The commission received no fewer than 901 submissions.

later established, this was much more a "crisis of perception"[5] than a real crisis.

At a time when Europe is casting curious and questioning glances at the notion of reasonable accommodation as it is practised in North America, particularly Quebec (see Part II), the Quebec experience highlights the need to dispel certain conceptual ambiguities. There was a certain confusion in the Quebec public debate on the possible meanings of reasonable accommodation, which at times could lead to misunderstanding. In the interests of an informed European debate, it is helpful to present the various levels of meaning of the notion in the form of concentric circles. As we shall see, the confusion is mainly the consequence of the different meanings that lawyers and non-lawyers give to it.

Reasonable accommodation: overlapping meanings

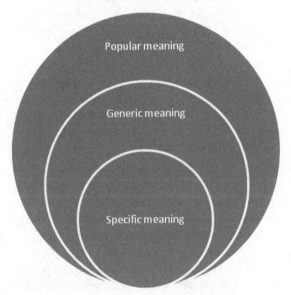

The popular meaning is the broadest in scope. It encompasses both legal and non-legal dimensions of the concept. It signifies any arrangements to which the management of conflicts – cultural, religious or other – might give rise. The case of a Montreal YMCA offers a symbolic illustration of this

---

5. See the report of the Bouchard-Taylor Commission, *Building the Future: A Time for Reconciliation,* Montreal, 2008. The word "crisis" appears frequently in the report, but generally in inverted commas.

popular meaning of reasonable accommodation. In this incident, which became headline news during the reasonable accommodation "crisis", in order to "accommodate" the faithful at a neighbouring synagogue, who were apparently disturbed by the sight of women in sportswear, the YMCA agreed temporarily to frost some of its windows. This cannot be considered to be reasonable accommodation in the legal sense of the term. There was no discrimination or breach of human rights in this case, whether it be the right of the synagogue faithful to observe their religion or of members of the sports centre to use its facilities. Whether or not it was advisable, the decision to frost the windows was essentially aimed at maintaining good relations with the synagogue.[6] In the absence of any discrimination this type of "accommodation" does not reflect any legal obligation.

In a second, more restricted, sense, the term is sometimes used – incorrectly – to refer to adaptations or adjustments to legal rules, particularly legislation. We believe that this is often an abuse of language, since the legal grounds for such "accommodation" measures as constitutional exemptions[7] or cultural defence[8] are not necessarily the same as those applicable to reasonable accommodation in the legal sense, which is essentially based on the right to equality. Some have pushed this generic meaning of reasonable accommodation still further by associating it with certain demands for recognition of the existence and validity of parallel systems of rules to that of the state, particularly religious legal systems. This can be illustrated by reference to the controversy surrounding the possible application of religious law by the Ontario courts in family

---

6. Bouchard-Taylor report, p. 70. The YMCA finally retracted and reinstalled transparent windows.

7. The possibility of a constitutional exemption as a remedy for a violation of a constitutional right was raised by the Supreme Court of Canada in *Osborne v. Canada (Treasury Board)*, [1991] 2 S.C.R. 69. The court now seems to be more reluctant. *R. v. Ferguson*, 2008 CSC 6.

8. Cultural defence may be a ground of defence in the true sense or a basis for reducing the penalty. In both cases its use is controversial, because of the abuses that can arise. See: Pascale Fournier, "The Ghettoisation of Difference in Canada: 'Rape by Culture' and the Danger of a 'Cultural Defense' in Criminal Law Trials", *Manitoba L.J.*, 29, 2002, p. 81; Marie-Pierre Robert, *La défense culturelle: un moyen de défense non souhaitable en droit pénal canadien*, Coll. "Minerve", Yvon Blais, Cowansville (Quebec), 2004. More recently, for a comparative study: Marie-Claire Foblets and Alison Dundes Renteln (eds), *Multicultural Jurisprudence. Comparative Perspectives on the Cultural Defense*, Hart, Oxford and Portland (Oregon), 2009.

arbitration cases.[9] However, this problem, which is linked to that of legal pluralism, must be distinguished from that of reasonable accommodation. Recognition of legal systems parallel to those of the state raises much more fundamental questions. It inevitably raises questions about the relationship between the law of the state and other systems of laws that also aspire to regulate social relations.[10] Even in the attenuated form of a simple dialogue between state and religious systems of rules, the issues raised by legal pluralism are quite distinct from those connected with the duty to accommodate, which in principle simply requires institutions' rules and practices to be adjusted in individual cases to redress established forms of discrimination. This does not imply the incorporation of the principles of religious law into the law of the land.

We are more concerned here with the specific, or technical, meaning of reasonable accommodation. In a contribution to this work, Myriam Jézéquel clarifies this technical meaning with a legal definition of the duty

---

9. In 2004, a report to the Attorney General of Ontario was sympathetic to family arbitration based on the principles of religious law, though subject to various legal safeguards. See: Marion Boyd, *Dispute Resolution in Family Law: Protecting Choice, Promoting Inclusion*, 2004. The Ontario government finally opted for the opposite approach, and made the conditions under which family disputes could be submitted for arbitration much stricter. Family Statute Law Amendment Act, S.O. 2006, c. 1. In Quebec this debate has always remained purely theoretical since Article 2639 of the Civil Code excludes family matters from the subjects that can be settled by an arbitrator.

10. See in this context: Pierre Bosset and Paul Eid, "Droit et religion: de l'accommodement raisonnable à un dialogue internormatif?", in *Actes de la XVIIe Conférence des juristes de l'État*, Yvon Blais, Cowansville (Quebec), 2006, pp. 63-95; Douglas Farrow (ed.), *Recognizing Religion in a Secular Society: Essays in Pluralism, Religion and Public Policy*, McGill-Queen's University Press, Montreal/Ithaca, 2004; Pauline Coté and T. Jeremy Gunn (eds), *La nouvelle question religieuse: régulation ou ingérence de l'État?/The New Religious Question: State Regulation or State Interference?*, PIE-P. Lang, Brussels/New York, 2006; Harm Goris and Marianne Heimbach-Steins (eds), *Religion in Recht und Politischer Ordnung heute/Religion in Law and Politics Today*, Ergon, Würzburg, 2008. These are only a few of the many titles on this subject. Many of them have been published only very recently.

of reasonable accommodation.[11] Reasonable accommodation in the technical sense stems from laws that in Canada prohibit discrimination both in the private sector and in the activities of the state.[12] The granting of religious holidays[13] and changing the duties of disabled persons[14] are typical examples of reasonable accommodation. In the Bergevin case, the Supreme Court said that the duty of reasonable accommodation in the technical sense was an integral part of the right to equality.[15] As we will see later, this often leads the court to require employers and others governed by human rights legislation in all cases to accommodate the characteristics of affected groups within their standards. Incorporating accommodation into the standard itself is meant to ensure that each person is assessed according to her or his own personal abilities.[16]

Depending on who is concerned, reasonable accommodation may be concerned with the rules laid down by private undertakings, legislation or quite simply practices connected with interpersonal relations or good neighbourliness. It is not always easy to say whether those taking part in the public debate on reasonable accommodation are referring to the concept in its popular, generic or technical sense, or a combination of all three. These debates are by no means always characterised

---

11. Myriam Jézéquel, "Reasonable Accommodation: Potential and Limits for Reconciling Different Norms and Values in Societies Faced with Managing Diversity". Other theoretical contributions to this subject include José Woehrling, "L'obligation d'accommodement raisonnable et l'adaptation de la société canadienne à la diversité religieuse", *R.D. McGill*, 43, 1998, pp. 325-401, and Pierre Bosset, "Les fondements juridiques et l'évolution de l'obligation d'accommodement raisonnable", in Myriam Jézéquel (ed.), *Les accommodements raisonnables – Quoi, comment, jusqu'où?* Yvon Blais, Cowansville (Quebec), 2007, pp. 3-28.

12. See Quebec's Charter of Human Rights and Freedoms, R.S.Q., Chapter C-12, and, at federal level, the Canadian Human Rights Act, R.S.C. 1985, Chapter H-6, with modifications. There is equivalent legislation in all the Canadian provinces and the federal territories.

13. For example, *Commission scolaire régionale de Chambly v. Bergevin*, [1994] 2 S.C.R. 525 (hereafter Bergevin).

14. See: *Commission des droits de la personne du Quebec v. Emballages Polystar*, [1997] 28 C.H.R.R. D/76 (T.D.P.).

15. Bergevin, op. cit., p. 544.

16. *British Columbia (Superintendent of Motor Vehicles) v. British Columbia (Council of Human Rights)*, [1999] 3 S.C.R. 868, paragraph 19.

by exemplary intellectual rigour.[17] However, they do highlight the importance, if the debate is to continue in Europe, of separating the non-legal definitions of reasonable accommodation from those that are properly legal. It is the latter we will concentrate on here.

2. Reasonable accommodation in the public services: the North American experience

Although it is Quebec where debates on reasonable accommodation seem to have extended furthest beyond the legal fraternity, the concept first emerged elsewhere in North America. Reasonable accommodation made its first legal appearance in the early 1970s in American civil rights legislation. Title VII of the Civil Rights Act 1964 was amended to include specific reference to a duty of reasonable accommodation, applicable to both private and public employers, in matters of religion.[18] A similar obligation was later created in connection with discrimination on grounds of disability.[19] When it introduced the notion of reasonable accommodation into Canadian (and Quebec) law, the Supreme Court of Canada initially acknowledged this historical pre-eminence of American law.[20] Very quickly though, as we shall see, Canadian practice started to diverge from that of the United States.[21]

---

17. For an attempted clarification see the Bouchard-Taylor report, pp. 63-65. For a criticism of this exercise: Stéphane Bernatchez, "Un rapport au droit difficile – La Commission Bouchard-Taylor et l'obligation d'accommodement raisonnable", in *Droits de la personne – Éthique et droit: nouveaux défis. Actes des Journées strasbourgeoises 2008*, Yvon Blais, Cowansville (Quebec), 2009, pp. 69-92.

18. 1972 amendments to the Civil Rights Act 1964, 42 U.S.C., Section 2000e(j): "The term 'religion' includes all aspects of religious observance and practice, as well as belief, unless an employer demonstrates that he is unable to reasonably accommodate to an employee's or prospective employee's religious observance or practice without undue hardship on the conduct of the employer's business."

19. Rehabilitation Act 1973, Public Law 93-112 93rd Congress, H.R. 8070; Americans with Disabilities Act (1990), 42 U.S.C., Section 12111(10).

20. *Ontario Commission of Human Rights and Theresa O'Malley (Vincent) v. Simpsons-Sears Ltd.*, [1985] 2 S.C.R. 536.

21. For a comparative study: Emmanuelle Bribosia, Julie Ringelheim and Isabelle Rorive, "Aménager la diversité: le droit de l'égalité face à la pluralité religieuse", *Rev. trim. D.H.*, 2009, 78, p. 319, at pp. 325-348.

We will consider here the impact of reasonable accommodation on North American public service provision, where necessary showing how Canadian and United States law and legal practice differ.

2.1. Reasonable accommodation and public services

In the United States, a certain generic duty to accommodate derives from the freedom of religion protected by the first amendment to the constitution. "Accommodation" then takes the form of an exemption from the application of a rule of law, when the beneficiary of the exemption is the "recipient" of the law in question.[22] The legislative exemption, based on freedom of religion, highlights a possible overlap between the latter and the right to equality in the proper sense, an aspect to which we shall return when we consider Canadian law. However, such exemptions are now governed by legislation,[23] and are only possible if there is a "substantial burden" on the exercise of religion. Moreover, such exemptions may not stand in the way of "a compelling governmental interest", which is a potentially significant restriction on any exemptions likely to be granted.[24]

When there is no threat to religious freedom, the concept of reasonable accommodation is of fairly limited relevance for the delivery of American public services. Outside the employment relationship, United States anti-discrimination legislation does not impose any specific obligation on its public services to accommodate cultural diversity. The duty to accommodate only applies to two grounds of prohibited discrimination: disability and religion, and in the latter case, only in connection with employment.[25]

In contrast, reasonable accommodation is considered to be an integral part of the right to equality in Canadian and Quebec law, which has significant consequences for public services. As a result, the duty to accommodate also applies to relations between the state and users of public services, since the latter are also covered by anti-discrimination

---

22. See, for example, *Sherbert v. Verner*, 374 U.S. 398 (1963) (refusal to award unemployment benefit to a Seventh Day Adventist, because she was unavailable for work, for religious reasons); and *Wisconsin v. Yoder*, 406 U.S. 205 (1972) (exemption, on religious grounds, from the obligation to attend school to the age of 16).

23. Religious Freedom Restoration Act, 42 U.S.C. Section 2000bb (1993).

24. Bribosia, Ringelheim and Rorive, op. cit., pp. 327-332 (and the jurisprudence cited).

25. See above notes 18 and 19.

legislation. Moreover, in principle the obligation is transversal, in other words reasonable accommodation is not confined to religious diversity (as is sometimes made out) and disability but can apply to all the grounds of discrimination, including particularly sex, pregnancy, age, civil status and national origin.[26]

Canadian public services' legal duty to accommodate applies to all decisions, practices and rules that have a discriminatory effect on the exercise of a human right or freedom. Schools, hospitals,[27] courts,[28] municipalities[29] and other public services[30] are therefore legally bound to reasonably accommodate members of the public who use their services. Although accommodation generally takes the form of individual and specific exemptions from rules or standards, in the Meiorin and Grismer cases the Supreme Court required the institutions concerned to take account of the situation of the affected groups when actually drawing up standards.[31] Incorporating accommodation into the standard itself ensures that each person is assessed according to her or his own personal abilities. To avoid discrimination proceedings, therefore, Canadian public institutions should, in principle, adapt their rules and standards even before receiving any individual requests for adjustments or exemptions. Thus, by influencing the actual formulation of standards, accommodation

---

26. See the cases cited in Bosset, op. cit., pp. 13-14.

27. *Eldridge v. British Columbia (Attorney General)*, [1997] 3 S.C.R. 624 (medical services must provide sign language interpreters for the deaf). The accommodation of deaf people is generally seen to be based on disability. Within the deaf community, however, there are those who think that failure to provide sign language interpretation is a form of discrimination based on language. This brings us within the sphere of cultural difference. See in general: Mary Ellen Maatman, "Listening to Deaf Culture: A Reconceptualization of Difference Analysis under Title VII", *Hofstra Labor L.J.*, 1996, 13, p. 269.

28. *Centre de la communauté sourde du Montréal métropolitain v. Régie du logement*, [1996] R.J.Q. 1776 (T.D.P.).

29. *Morel v. Corporation de Saint-Sylvestre*, [1987] D.L.Q. 391 (C.A.): "in certain circumstances, the Quebec Charter requires public bodies, including municipalities, like other bodies, to adjust aspects of their organisation and operating methods to the needs of persons with various forms of disability, to alleviate the consequences and facilitate their life and activities" (p. 393 of the judgment).

30. *Canadian Association of the Deaf v. Canada*, [2007] 2 F.C.R. 323 (access to government services).

31. *British Columbia (Superintendent of Motor Vehicles) v. British Columbia (Council of Human Rights)*, [1999] 3 S.C.R. 868 paragraph 19 (Grismer); *British Columbia (Public Service Employee Relations Commission) v. BCGSEU*, [1999] 3 S.C.R. 3 (Meiorin).

becomes less reactive and more structural.[32] It now plays a preventive and even proactive, rather than purely corrective, role and as such may take on a collective dimension that bears witness to the increasing importance of reasonable accommodation since its introduction into Canadian law in the mid-1980s.

Schools, where requests for accommodation are fairly frequent, offer a practical illustration of how the functioning or organisation of Canadian public services may be the target of such measures. They may concern standards and practices in such areas as:

- pupil admissions;[33]

- course assessments;[34]

- leave on religious grounds;[35]

- dress rules;[36]

- access to premises;[37]

- documents required to enrol for a course.[38]

---

32. See: Jean-Yves Brière and Jean-Pierre Villaggi, "L'obligation d'accommodement de l'employeur: un nouveau paradigme", *Développements récents en droit du travail*, Yvon Blais, Cowansville (Quebec), 2000, p. 219.

33. *Commission des droits de la personne du Québec v. Collège Notre-Dame du Sacré-Cœur*, [2002] R.J.Q. 5 (C.A.) (admission of a disabled pupil capable of completing the school's academic syllabus, despite the latter's emphasis on sports).

34. *Commission des droits de la personne et des droits de la jeunesse v. Commission scolaire des Draveurs*, J.E. 99-1061; REJB 1999-12851 (T.D.P.) (recognition of stuttering as a form of disability).

35. *Commission scolaire régionale de Chambly v. Bergevin*, op. cit. (leave taken by Jewish teachers over and above the days off specified in collective agreements).

36. Quebec (Commission des droits de la personne et des droits de la jeunesse), *Le port du foulard islamique dans les écoles publiques*, Montreal, 1994 (Islamic headdress in public schools).

37. Quebec (Commission des droits de la personne et des droits de la jeunesse), *Réflexion sur la portée et les limites de l'obligation d'accommodement raisonnable en matière religieuse*, Montreal, 2005, pp. 11-12 (how far premises might be made available for religious purposes).

38. *Commission des droits de la personne et des droits de la jeunesse v. Collège Montmorency*, J.E. 2004-966 (T.D.P.) (need to take account of immigrants' potential difficulties in producing official documents from their country of origin).

However, the Supreme Court of Canada placed significant limits on the duty of reasonable accommodation in the Hutterian Brethren of Wilson Colony judgment of 24 July 2009, where it said the duty did not apply to parliament.[39] The case derived from regulations requiring all persons holding a driver's licence in the province of Alberta to have a photo attached. Members of the Wilson Hutterite Colony, who are forbidden by their religion from being photographed, challenged the constitutionality of this provision on the grounds that it was an unjustified breach of their freedom of religion and forced them to choose between the latter and their ability to move around autonomously by car. The lower courts[40] had upheld their challenge, and included a duty to accommodate in the proportionality test applicable to violations of constitutional rights.[41] However, a majority of four judges to three in the Supreme Court rejected this approach. The majority drew a distinction between the situation of the legislature and that of the parties subject to the duty to accommodate ("most commonly an employer and employee").[42]

> By their very nature, laws of general application are not tailored to the unique needs of individual claimants. The legislature has no capacity or legal obligation to engage in such an individualized determination, and in many cases would have no advance notice of a law's potential to infringe Charter rights. It cannot be expected to tailor a law to every possible future contingency, or every sincerely held religious belief. Laws of general application affect the general public, not just the claimants before the court.[43]

The stance taken by the majority in this case means that the nature of measures breaching the right to equality or freedom of religion must first be established. The duty of accommodation will apply when applicants can show that a government action or administrative practice infringes a fundamental right. However, if the validity of a law is being challenged, only the proportionality test can be applied, and according to the court this involves not an individualised assessment of the sort applicable to reasonable accommodation, but a general assessment that takes account

---

39. *Alberta* v. *Hutterian Brethren of Wilson Colony*, 2009 CSC 37 (24 July 2009) (Wilson Colony).
40. See: 57 Alta. L.R. (4th) 300 (Q.B.); 77 Alta. L.R. (4th) 281 (C.A.).
41. See *R. v. Oakes*, [1986] 1 S.C.R. 103.
42. Wilson Colony, paragraph 68.
43. Ibid., paragraph 69.

of "the broader societal context".[44] This represents a change of perspective but – as the court stresses – the legislature is still required to show that any particular law is rationally connected to a pressing and substantial goal, minimally impairs rights and is proportionate in its effects, which will involve a consideration of its impact on certain persons.[45]

A final comment should be made on the application of the duty of reasonable accommodation to Canadian public services. Despite the transversal nature of the duty to accommodate, there are very few court decisions where this duty is relied on in conjunction with such grounds of discrimination as ethnic or national origin, language, race or colour, even though these grounds are also associated with "cultural diversity". It is as if cultural diversity was confined in some ways to religion. There are reasons to think that the omnipresence of religious grounds in applications for accommodation reflects, at least in part, Canadian courts' reluctance to require genuinely objective evidence to support demands based on religion, the test being rather that of the applicant's (subjective) sincerity.[46] This "subjective" approach to religion is open to dispute. Although in principle it shows due regard for individual autonomy (and the limitations of the courts, which are perhaps ill-equipped to settle disputes on such matters as the interpretation of sacred texts), it can be exploited in furtherance of political,[47] or quite simply opportunistic or fraudulent requests. The Bouchard-Taylor Commission considered this problem in its report but concluded that, all things considered, the courts were qualified to judge the sincerity of accommodation applications and that there was no need to re-examine the sincerity test.[48] At all events, we believe that the potential for reasonable accommodation to promote cultural diversity in the public services is far from being fully explored. Sooner or later, the courts are likely to be called on to consider requests for accommodation

---

44. Ibid., paragraphs 66-67. In this case, the court considered that the regulation in question, which was aimed at minimising identity theft associated with driver's licences, met the proportionality test.

45. Ibid., paragraph 71.

46. *Syndicat Northcrest v. Amselem*, [2004] 2 S.C.R. 551, 2004 SCC 47. The American courts show the same reluctance; see *Thomas v. Review Board of the Indiana Employment Security Division*, 450 U.S. 707 (1981).

47. See Sébastien Lebel-Grenier, "La religion comme véhicule d'affirmation identitaire: un défi à la logique des droits fondamentaux", in P. Eid et al. (eds), *Appartenances religieuses, appartenance citoyenne – Un équilibre en tension*, Presses de l'Université Laval, Sainte-Foy, 2009, pp. 123-139.

48. Bouchard-Taylor report, pp. 176-178.

based on grounds of discrimination other than religion, particularly ethnic or national origin and language.

2.2. Undue hardship in the public services

Undue hardship, a notion inherent in the concept of reasonable accommodation, constitutes a limit on the duty to accommodate.[49] The notion exists in both Canadian and American law, but has been interpreted in significantly different ways in the two countries. This is reflected in a legal duty to accommodate that, as we shall see later, is much more demanding in Canadian law.

The notion of undue hardship reflects a principle. As stated in the preamble to the Quebec Charter of Human Rights and Freedoms, the rights and freedoms of the human person are inseparable from the rights and freedoms of others and from the common well-being. The Canadian Supreme Court also stated when it gave the duty of reasonable accommodation its formal stamp of approval:

> In any society the rights of one will inevitably come into conflict with the rights of others. It is obvious then that all rights must be limited in the interest of preserving a social structure in which each right may receive protection without undue interference with others.[50]

The notion of undue hardship therefore calls for a balance to be struck between the right to accommodation and the interests of those concerned.

In the Trans World Airlines case, the United States Supreme Court applied the principle that anything more than a *de minimis* cost could be deemed excessive.[51] In this case, the Court considered it excessive to require an employer to waive unilaterally the provisions of a collective agreement to enable an employee to take leave for religious reasons. The notion of undue hardship is therefore interpreted fairly generously in American law,

---

49. The idea according to which accommodation should be "reasonable" and that according to which accommodation should not lead to "excessive constraints" are two different ways of expressing the same concept: *Central Okanagan School District No. 23 v. Renaud*, [1992] 2 S.C.R. 970, p. 984.
50. Simpsons-Sears, op. cit., pp. 554-555.
51. *Trans World Airlines v. Hardison*, 432 U.S. 63 (1977).

or at least in an accommodating way for the individual or body with the duty to accommodate.

In the Renaud case, the Canadian Court thought that the *de minimis* test applied by the American Supreme Court reduced the required hardship threshold to a minimum and virtually removed the duty to accommodate. The court opted for a more rigorous test: "more than mere negligible effort is required to satisfy the duty to accommodate. The use of the term 'undue' infers that some hardship is acceptable; it is only 'undue' hardship that satisfies this test."[52]

What in practice does the undue hardship test add up to in the public services context?

Hitherto, the Canadian courts have applied three types of test to determine whether an accommodation request entails undue hardship: financial costs, impact on the organisation's functioning and infringement of other rights.[53] These tests have been developed in the very specific context of employment relationships but they do offer a useful basis for applying the notion of undue hardship to the public services, a distinctive feature of which is their responsibility towards the entire community.[54] We will attempt here to explain what undue hardship means in the specific public service context.[55]

The financial costs

The financial test uses a simple indicator, namely how many dollars are involved, but its application is more complex. The size of the institution necessarily affects the judgment of what constitutes excessive cost.[56] The Supreme Court also accepts that what might be a reasonable financial

52. *Central Okanagan School District No. 23 v. Renaud*, [1992] 2 S.C.R. 970, p. 984.

53. Christian Brunelle, *Discrimination et obligation d'accommodement raisonnable en milieu de travail syndiqué*, Yvon Blais, Cowansville (Quebec), 2001, pp. 248-252.

54. Pierre Bosset, "Limites de l'accommodement raisonnable: le droit a-t-il tout dit?", *Éthique publique*, Vol. 9, No. 1, spring 2007, pp. 165-168.

55. We have based this on: Pierre Bosset, "Les pratiques d'accommodement en éducation au Québec: aspects juridiques" (Legal aspects of accommodation practices in Quebec), to be published by Presses de l'Université Laval in 2010 in a joint work entitled *La diversité ethnoculturelle en éducation: contexte, tendances et réalités* (edited by Pierre Toussaint).

56. *Central Alberta Dairy Pool v. Alberta (Human Rights Commission)*, [1990] 2 S.C.R. 489.

cost at a time of prosperity could become excessive when budgetary restrictions are applied.[57]

In the Bergevin case, for example, the court allowed the request of three Jewish teachers who had taken a day off to celebrate Yom Kippur to receive a day's pay from their employer, the respondent school board. The court stated that no evidence had been presented that payment for this day, which represented 1/200th of the teachers' yearly salary, would place an unreasonable financial burden on the school board.

The functioning of the institution

To paraphrase the Supreme Court in the Simpsons-Sears case, what needs to be determined here is whether the reasonable accommodation requested would interfere with the smooth running of the organisation, which sometimes depends on fairly down-to-earth considerations. For example, tests of the smooth running of a school entail such factors as:

- the interchangeability of staff, for example when teachers request leave of absence for religious reasons;

- the availability and adaptability of premises, for example, when the accommodation would require a room to be made available;

- the number of persons affected;

- the length of the accommodation;

- the time of the school year concerned, etc.[58]

However, these are not the only factor to be taken into account under the functioning of schools. Other, more substantive characteristics also need to be taken into account, relating to schools' actual purpose. In its opinion on religious pluralism, Quebec's Human Rights Commission identified various aspects that fell outside the scope of reasonable accommodation because of their fundamental nature, both in law and in accordance with

---

57. Bergevin judgment, op. cit.

58. Similarly, see the criteria applied in work places considered in: Brunelle, op. cit., pp. 250-251.

the educational curricula in force, including compulsory school attendance, the number of school days and curriculum content.[59]

Infringement of other rights

The tests for infringement of rights take account of safety, compliance with collective agreements, the possible detrimental effect of accommodation on others and conflict with other fundamental rights.[60]

As shown by the Multani case, which concerns the wearing of the kirpan in school, the application of the safety criterion must take account of the nature of each specific environment.[61] In this case, the Supreme Court ruled that the administrative ban on the kirpan, rather than subjecting it to conditions allowing it to be worn safely, was not proportional to the safety objective. The court contrasted wearing kirpans in aircraft, a closed environment where emergency services are not immediately available, or courts, where the parties are opposed to each other in an adversarial setting, from wearing it in school, an environment where staff and students collaborate over a long period in furtherance of the school's educational aims. The court considered that school was a unique environment that permitted relationships to develop among students and staff, which "make it possible to better control the different types of situations that arise".[62] To summarise, in this case the court acknowledged the importance of safety but also recognised that schools were living communities, which meant that it could place the safety debate in a specific institutional context.[63]

The adverse effect test, initially discussed in the Central Alberta Dairy Pool judgment, was reformulated in the Renaud judgment. The court emphasised that this test must be applied "with caution". Legitimate fears that there will be interference with the rights of others need to be taken into

59. Quebec (Commission des droits de la personne et des droits de la jeunesse), *Legal Pluralism in Quebec: a Legal and Ethical Challenge,* Montreal, 1995, p. 12. (See also the Bouchard-Taylor report at p. 163.)
60. Brunelle, op. cit., p. 250.
61. *Multani v. Commission scolaire Marguerite-Bourgeoys,* [2006] 1 S.C.R. 256.
62. Ibid., paragraph 65.
63. The Multani judgment was concerned with constitutional provisions rather than the anti-discrimination legislation. However, the court made it clear that "the analogy with the duty of reasonable accommodation is helpful to explain the burden resulting from the minimal impairment test". This is a good illustration of the possible overlap between freedom of religion and the right to equality.

account but attitudes inconsistent with human rights are irrelevant.[64] This principle is particularly applicable in the school context, in view of schools' educational role and, in particular, their responsibilities concerning education in human rights and freedoms. The court has stressed this role, stating that "schools are meant to develop civic virtue and responsible citizenship, to educate in an environment free of bias, prejudice and intolerance".[65] In Multani, it drew this practical consequence:

> Religious tolerance is a very important value of Canadian society. If some students consider it unfair that Gurbaj Singh may wear his kirpan to school while they are not allowed to have knives in their possession, it is incumbent on the schools to discharge their obligation to instil in their students this value that is ... at the very foundation of our democracy.[66]

The potential conflict between reasonable accommodation and other fundamental rights, which is the final component of the test for infringement of rights, is sometimes the subject of furious debate. The charters of rights do not give precedence to reasonable accommodation if this is incompatible with other fundamental rights, such as the right to equality. More specifically, the relationship between religious accommodation and equality of the sexes can take the form of peaceful coexistence, and not raise any particular problems, tension, which calls for dialogue and vigilance, or finally conflict, which necessitates the mediation of the law.[67] In the last-named case, the notion of undue hardship and the limits generally applicable to freedom of religion[68] would probably suffice to refuse

---

64. Renaud, op. cit., pp. 987-988.

65. *Trinity Western University v. College of Teachers*, [2001] 1 S.C.R. 772 (paragraph 13).

66. Multani, op. cit., paragraph 76.

67. Pierre Bosset, "Accommodement raisonnable et égalité des sexes: tensions, contradictions et interdépendance", in *Appartenances religieuses, appartenance citoyenne – Un équilibre en tension*, op. cit., p. 184.

68. See Article 9.1 of the Quebec charter: "In exercising his fundamental freedoms and rights, a person shall maintain a proper regard for democratic values, public order and the general well-being of the citizens of Québec. In this respect, the scope of the freedoms and rights, and limits to their exercise, may be fixed by law."

the granting of an accommodation that would interfere with another person's fundamental right or freedom.[69]

2.3. A positive interim assessment

The Bouchard-Taylor report sought to place the legal duty of reasonable accommodation in a more ambitious social and political context, namely "the sociocultural integration model established in Québec since the 1970s".[70] The commission concluded – correctly we believe – that if reasonable accommodation is understood in its more specific or technical sense, it remained a concept whose legal limits were established or could be deduced from more general principles, and which could be adequately managed at ground level by those concerned, particularly if they were supplied with the relevant technical resources, with an emphasis on shared information on tried and tested practices.[71]

The commission's extensive discussions led to a whole series of recommendations on learning diversity, harmonisation practices (not restricted to reasonable accommodations), the integration of immigrants, interculturalism, inequality and discrimination, the status of the French language and secularism.[72] This ambitious approach did not receive unanimous support, including among lawyers, particularly in view of the risk of trying to take on too much and losing sight of accommodation practices properly speaking. With hindsight, though, we think that this approach has helped to defuse the reasonable accommodation "crisis" by showing that while such practices can be incorporated harmoniously into a cultural or multicultural approach to diversity,[73] reasonable accommodation cannot,

---

69. For instance, in *Commission des droits de la personne et des droits de la jeunesse v. Hôpital général juif Sir Mortimer B. Davis*, TDPQ Montréal 500-53-000182-020, 2007 QCTDP 29 (CanLII), a case where jobs had been specified as being reserved for men and others for women, the Human Rights Tribunal stated that the employer had not shown sufficient evidence to support the measure. The tribunal referred to Article 9.1 of the Quebec Charter of Human Rights and Freedoms and stressed that female staff were entitled to measures of accommodation. It was up to the hospital to show that this would involve undue hardship. The judgment can be interpreted as confirming the need to balance freedom of religion with women's right to equality.

70. Bouchard-Taylor report, p. 17.

71. Ibid., pp. 251-253.

72. Ibid., pp. 263-272.

73. See Pierre Bosset and Paul Eid, "Droit and religion: de l'accommodement raisonnable à un dialogue internormatif?", op. cit.

of itself, constitute a diversity policy. A genuine diversity policy must involve much more than simply managing individual examples of discrimination, the original objective of reasonable accommodation, and attack the institutional and systemic elements of racism and discrimination. By influencing the framing of standards, the Canadian version of reasonable accommodation undoubtedly goes beyond the reactive management of discrimination. It has acquired a collective dimension that it lacked at the outset, so long as it does not pose a challenge to the legislative process itself. Nevertheless, reasonable accommodation as currently practised in Canada in general, and Quebec in particular, is no panacea for dealing with all the social relationships linked to cultural diversity. For example, the affirmative action or positive discrimination programmes, which offer collective remedies to persons from discriminated against groups by granting their members temporary preferential treatment,[74] do not come under the reasonable accommodation umbrella. Likewise, the reasonable accommodation approach has still failed to extend to the fundamentally political problem of the relationships that have always existed between the national groups that form Quebec: indigenous peoples, French-speaking majority and English-speaking minority. Because of the historical nature of these relationships, in Quebec they continue to be managed mainly through the political process.[75]

Reasonable accommodation and its fundamentally pragmatic underlying approach reflect the Anglo-Saxon judicial philosophy and its inductive method. It is therefore understandable that there may be certain reservations about it in civil law jurisdictions, because of its casuistic and apparently un-Cartesian nature. It is perhaps not surprising that the concept emerged in a common law country, the United States, before migrating to Canada, where it has since seen major developments.[76] Nevertheless,

---

74. In connection with these programmes, see Articles 86-92 in Part III of the Quebec Charter of Human Rights and Freedoms. See also paragraph 15(2) of the Canadian Charter of Rights and Freedoms.

75. In any case, the Bouchard-Taylor report excluded such relationships from its terms of reference (p. 34).

76. The expansion of the reasonable accommodation concept in Canadian law, in terms of grounds of discrimination and the areas of activity covered, and the different definition of undue hardship to that applied in American law, bear eloquent witness to the "acculturation" that may follow the migration of a legal notion from one country to another. Pierre Bosset, "Droits de la personne et accommodements raisonnables: le droit est-il mondialisé?", *Revue interdisciplinaire d'études juridiques*, 2009, 62, pp. 1-32.

we should not exaggerate the importance of legal cultures in the way a concept such as reasonable accommodation is received. Despite its civil law tradition, Quebec has adopted the notion without difficulty and incorporated it into its anti-discrimination legal armoury. We can perhaps hypothesise that legal systems' receptiveness to concepts such as reasonable accommodation may depend less on legal culture than on institutional factors, particularly the level of discretion of the courts in interpreting legislation or their powers to make reparation or impose sanctions.

3. The European context: a varied approach to reasonable accommodation

This brief overview of the situation in Canada and the United States has shown that lawyers have rapidly become convinced of the value of the jurisprudential concept of reasonable accommodation as a means of promoting pluralism in isolated situations. It now seems to be accepted that reasonable accommodation as a particular means of applying the equality principle may, in certain cases, entail an obligation to take various measures on such grounds as religion, ethnicity or sex. It is clear, as we have shown, that it is in Canadian law that the concept has been developed the furthest in practical terms, since all categories of protected persons may, in principle, benefit from it. Nor do the courts confine such obligations to public authorities/services. The whole of the economic community/actors, including the private sector, is covered. It is reasonable to speak of a general right to reasonable accommodation, as a corollary of the right to equality and religious freedom.

In Europe, setting aside the employment sector in the case of disabled persons,[77] there is no general right to reasonable accommodation. The situation cannot therefore be compared with Canada, where recognition of such a right greatly strengthens individuals' situation vis-à-vis authorities or institutions faced with a duty to accommodate. They have no choice but to consider all requests for accommodation they receive and can only refuse them on grounds specified in law or by the courts. Nor is there any suggestion that such a broad interpretation is currently under

---

77. Cf. *infra* (note 80).

consideration in Europe for grounds other than disability.[78] In fact, the issue remains largely unexplored.

Nevertheless, this does not mean that less attention is being paid to the challenge – sometimes posed dramatically – of how to respond legally to the growing diversity of groups and cultures in European society. This has led to a variety of approaches, some of which do resemble that of reasonable accommodation but all of which have their own distinctive features. How law in the different European countries offers the necessary legal guidelines to enable practitioners faced with practical situations requiring a balance between the obligation to treat people equally and respect of specific forms of diversity, varies according to whether these guidelines are in the European Convention on Human Rights, the legal system of the European Union or the domestic legal systems of the various countries. In an excellent recently published article three Belgian legal specialists, Emanuelle Bribosia, Julie Ringelheim and Isabelle Rorive, turned their attention to reasonable accommodation and offered a detailed comparative analysis of its role in Canadian, American and European law, particularly in connection with the religious field.[79] The main focus of their analysis is the question that also concerns us here, namely whether the approach adopted in Canada and the United States offers the same potential in a European context and whether the concept of reasonable accommodation can be used to deal with indirect discrimination as effectively as the methods currently used. The article looks at the legislation and case law in the different European countries that are currently the main points of reference in the religious and philosophical field and in connection with cultural affiliations. It is a very valuable piece of work. Following their analysis, we consider here the European context from the standpoint of (A) European Union law; (B) the rights embodied in the European Convention on Human Rights; and (C) the situation in different countries' domestic legal systems. Inevitably, we must be very brief.

---

78. Some remain very sceptical and issue warnings about what they see as the potential risks of reasonable accommodation, such as the non-negligible risk of a fragmentation of society based on each individual's cultural affiliations. Nadia Geerts, "'Raisonnables', les accommodements?", La Libre Belgique, 18 May 2009.

79. Bribosia, Ringelheim and Rorive, op. cit.

3.1. European Union law

In 2000, the European Union issued a directive obliging employers to provide reasonable accommodation for people with disabilities.[80] In practice, the courts must decide on the extent of this obligation. The relevant case law is not sufficiently developed at this stage to offer an initial assessment. It is not yet therefore possible to draw any lessons from European Union law about the possible shape of a policy for strengthening the equal treatment principle for disabled persons.

Nevertheless, in anticipation of clarification from the courts, several authors have expressed disappointment that the scope of the duty to accommodate is restricted to the employment sector and to disabled persons alone.[81]

Bribosia, Ringelheim and Rorive share this regret. However, they do not exclude the possibility that the Court of Justice of the European Communities or the domestic courts of member states might interpret the ban on indirect discrimination as justifying, in certain cases, a requirement that the authors of a general provision or standard amend it to avoid discriminating indirectly against certain individuals on account of their religion.[82] The court is to some extent dependent on actual complaints eventually reaching it for a ruling on such a requirement. However, the three authors point out that, even before the directive was issued, the court had implicitly acknowledged the reasonable accommodation principle in its Vivien Prais judgment.[83] The case, under the European public service disputes procedure, concerned a candidate in an open competition organised by the Council of the European Communities. The date of the examination coincided with a holy/religious day, which prevented the candidate from sitting it. Her request to sit the test on another day was rejected. She alleged discrimination. The court did not accept this

---

80. Council Directive 2000/78/EC of 27 November 2000 establishing a general framework for equal treatment in employment and occupation. The directive draws substantially on the American legislation described in Part II.

81. Dajo De Prins, Stefan Sottiaux and Jogchum Vrielink, *Handboek Discriminatierecht*, Kluwer, Malines, 2005, pp. 538-541, 553-555, 1249-1269 and 1440; Christian Bayart, *Discriminatie tegenover differentiatie. Arbeidsverhoudingen na de Discriminatiewet. Arbeidsrecht na de Europese Ras- en Kaderrichtlijn*, Larcier, Brussels, 2004, p. 896 ff.

82. Cf. *supra* (note 21), p. 371.

83. CJEC, 27 October 1976, case 130/75.

argument but instead considered that "it is desirable that an appointing authority informs itself in a general way of dates which might be unsuitable for religious reasons, and seeks to avoid fixing such dates for tests" (paragraph 18). Such a reasoning is surprisingly close to the concept of reasonable accommodation. This position was undoubtedly a precursor for its time.

3.2. The European Convention on Human Rights: the proportionality test

Any attempt to provide an accurate description, with reference to reasonable accommodation in the specific sense given in Part I, of how the rights enshrined in the Convention for the Protection of Human Rights and Fundamental Freedoms (hereafter the Convention) can be used to enhance diversity and the specific differences on which it is based, in accordance with the equality principle, is likely to lead to confusion. This is because of the way the Convention promotes these values.

There are currently very few cases that offer an unequivocal parallel with the notion of reasonable accommodation. Bribosia, Ringelheim and Rorive refer to the *Thlimmenos v. Greece* judgment[84] of 6 April 2000, in which the Court held that, in accordance with the non-discrimination principle in Article 14 of the Convention, in certain circumstances states might be required to introduce appropriate exceptions into legislation to avoid penalising, with no objective or reasonable justification, persons practising a particular religion. The applicant, Mr Thlimmenos, had previously refused to perform military service on the grounds that, as a Jehovah's Witness, it would be contrary to his beliefs. He then received a criminal conviction. Several years later, this conviction was the ground for refusing to appoint him to a post of chartered accountant, since Greek law prohibited persons convicted of a serious crime from such appointments. The Court upheld Mr Thlimmenos' complaint. It stated that the Greek authorities should have provided for appropriate exceptions to ensure that persons such as Mr Thlimmenos were not discriminated against on account of their religious beliefs. The fact that he had exercised his freedom of religion did not make him a "dishonest" person. The ground of refusal specified in the legislation resulted in his suffering discrimination. The Court considered that provision should have been made for exceptions.

---

84. European Court of Human Rights (Grand Chamber), *Thlimmenos v. Greece*, 6 April 2000.

To achieve a better understanding of the ways in which Convention-based rights can be used to remedy the effects of direct or indirect discrimination, it is necessary to take a broader approach, by means of a more general examination of how the courts have interpreted the various provisions of the Convention over the years, in order to identify circumstances in which states party to the Convention might be required to take account of certain specific situations. In practice, it is the judicial authorities that are called on to find viable solutions. Such an approach is not without its problems.[85] In principle, the traditional notion that each individual should be free to demand respect for the exercise of his or her freedoms and be guaranteed equal treatment does not raise any difficulties. This might be interpreted as a right to be different. However, problems do arise when, in actual cases, it has to be decided just how far persons demanding equal treatment can go in exercising their freedoms.[86] Of necessity, court involvement in such matters requires them to consider a specific context. The courts are then required to adopt an approach based on the obligation to protect rights and freedoms without unduly impinging on the rights and freedoms of others.[87] They must therefore determine the limits of the freedom in question. There are considerable variations in how courts define these limits. These differences of approach, and by extension treatment, in turn lead to considerable legal insecurity. They highlight the difficulties of securing the principle of equality in diversity by applying human rights standards. In certain areas, changes in case law have made it possible to refine the applicable tests or criteria and clarify their extent, but hitherto it has not proved

---

85. See, in particular: Gérard Gonzales (ed.), *Laïcité, liberté de religion et la Convention européenne des droits de l'homme* (proceedings of the colloquy organised on 18 November 2005 by the Institut européen des droits de l'homme), Nemesis/Bruylant, Brussels, 2006; Christelle Landheer-Cieslak, *La religion devant les juges français et québécois de droit civil*, Yvon Blais, Cowansville (Quebec), 2007; Thierry Masis and Christophe Pettiti (eds), *La liberté religieuse et la Convention européenne des droits de l'homme* (proceedings of the colloquy organised on 11 December 2003 by the Institut de formation en droits de l'homme du Barreau de Paris and the Ordre des avocats à la Cour de Paris), Nemesis/Bruylant, Brussels, 2004.

86. For a practical illustration see Sandrine Plana, *Le prosélytisme religieux à l'épreuve du droit civil*, L'Harmattan, Paris, 2006.

87. Emmanuel Tawil, *Norme religieuse et droit français*, Presses universitaires d'Aix-Marseille, Aix-en-Provence, 2005; Renata Uitz, *Freedom of Religion in European Constitutional and International Case Law*, Council of Europe Publishing, Strasbourg, 2007.

possible to incorporate the principle of equality in diversity into a clear line of argument that offers those concerned unambiguous guidelines.

In several cases, particularly ones concerning freedom of religion under Article 9 of the Convention, alone or in combination with Article 14, the European Court (and before it the Commission) have taken the position that if a law or regulation with an objective and legitimate purpose nevertheless restricts the liberty of certain individuals and that changes to it would avoid such interference without undermining this lawful aim, then this option should be chosen. In other words, in such cases, the least restrictive means should be adopted. This approach seems to us to resemble the arguments sometimes put forward by the American and Canadian courts when they apply the reasonable accommodation concept.[88] However, these resemblances should be considered in more detail. There is every reason to believe that the Court's requirement for proportionality between the means applied and the purpose sought when supervising the application of the Convention plays a role similar to that of reasonable accommodation. It determines the compatibility with the Convention of depriving someone of their liberty.[89] In several cases the European Court of Human Rights has had to rule on measures introduced by governments to restrict liberties. When the restriction is general in application and in principle neutral, but may cause particular hardship for certain people, the question of indirect discrimination may arise and will then be subjected to the proportionality test. The proportionality test must prevent unjustified differences of treatment. At first sight therefore it shares the same objective as reasonable accommodation in Canadian and American law.

In practice, though, the European Court of Human Rights appears to adopt a much more cautious approach than the Canadian Supreme Court to states' commitments and responsibilities with regard to equal treatment. As already seen, the latter has not hesitated on a number of occasions to infer from a specific case that a reasonable accommodation would help to avoid differential treatment and that government and/or the competent

---

88. See the use of reasonable accommodation by the Canadian Supreme Court in the kirpan case (Multani, see above, section 2, footnote 61).

89. See Eva Brems, "The Margin of Appreciation Doctrine of the European Court of Human Rights: Accommodating Diversity within Europe" in David P. Forsythe and Patrice C. McMahon (eds), *Human Rights and Diversity: Area Studies Revisited*, University of Nebraska Press, Lincoln/London, 2003, pp. 81-110.

authorities had a duty to remedy the situation by altering the relevant rule or standard. The case law of the European Court reveals a much more cautious position, with states being given a considerable margin of appreciation. The discretion granted to states party to the Convention reflects the Court's respect for the principle of democracy within a plural Europe. But offering states this margin means that the Court's ability to oversee governments' policies generally remains limited. In addition, the systematic application of the margin of appreciation principle also means that the effects of a Court judgment in a particular case will not necessarily be of any help to persons in a similar situation who have the misfortune to live in a country with a different policy. The example often cited concerns Muslim women and Islamic headdress, which has been the subject of various cases before the Court.[90] So we can only draw very limited lessons on this subject from the Strasbourg case law, as situations have to be considered on a country-by-country basis and the Court scrupulously avoids any interference in countries' policy decisions. Restrictions on freedom of religion that are justifiable in one country and not necessarily so in another.[91] At first sight, therefore, it is difficult to compare the uncertain case law of the European Court of Human Rights with the situations in Canada or the United States. This would require much more detailed analysis.

3.3. The national systems of various countries

Finally, European countries have the option of introducing into their domestic law, on their own initiative, a duty to accommodate and/or specific arrangements for ensuring fully equality in the different sectors of society, with no distinction of race, religious, sex, ethnic affiliation and

---

90. Malcolm D. Evans, *Manual on the Wearing of Religious Symbols In Public Areas*, Council of Europe Publishing/Nijhoff, Leiden/Boston, 2009; Marianne Hardy-Dussault, "Le port de signes religieux dans les établissements publics d'enseignement: comparaison des approches québécoise et française", in *Appartenances religieuses, appartenance citoyenne*, op. cit., pp. 75-121; David Koussens, "Le port de signes religieux dans les écoles québécoises et françaises. Accommodements (dé)raisonnables ou interdiction (dé)raisonnée?", *Globe – Revue internationale d'études québécoises*, 2008, pp. 115-131; Françoise Lorcerie (ed.), *La politisation du voile en France, en Europe et dans le monde arabe*, L'Harmattan, Paris, 2005.

91. Among the many commentaries on this issue, see Dominick McGoldrick, *Human Rights and Religion: the Islamic Headscarf Debate in Europe*, Hart, Oxford and Portland (Oregon), 2006.

so on. In fact, legislation to impose accommodations in specific areas remains proportionally fairly rare.

The only real obligation that binds the European Union member states and requires them to pass legislation granting a right to reasonable accommodation derives from the aforementioned directive of 27 November 2000 establishing a general framework for equal treatment in employment and occupation.[92] The Flemish Parliament has extended this obligation. Employers' responsibilities are not confined to persons with disabilities but apply equally to all forms of discrimination. We are not aware of any other European legislation extending the requirements of the directive beyond disability.[93]

More generally, there has been growing awareness of these issues over the years and governments are now much more prepared to introduce relevant legislation or regulations in certain areas. For example, several countries have passed laws or introduced regulations on adjustments to working hours and/or annual leave. Others have changed their legislation on the slaughtering of animals to allow religious communities to comply with the rituals by which they are bound. Space prevents us from presenting here an exhaustive list of such laws and regulations in the different countries of Europe. We believe that such an inventory has not yet been drawn up. This could be an extremely interesting exercise as it would cast much more light on which areas legislators in European countries have considered to require some form of intervention in recent years to limit the risks of indirect discrimination and to offer more legal security to some of the most vulnerable individuals in Europe. It would also be interesting to consider the particular wording of such legislation or regulations to see how, in different real-life settings, the relevant authorities ensure that the principles of law underlying reasonable accommodation are effectively applied.

This would necessitate a very thorough examination of the various European countries that took account both of the obligations imposed in legislation and regulations and adjustments that have been conceded on the ground, as a result of either court decisions or new practices

---

92. Cf. *supra* (note 80).

93. Decree of 8 May 2002 on proportional participation in the labour market (*Moniteur Belge*, 26 July 2002), on which the authors cited in note 80 have commented. See also the decree of 10 July 2008 on the Flemish equal opportunities and treatment policy (ibid., 23 September 2008).

arising from decision-making powers conferred on a particular authority, in accordance with democratic and previously laid down criteria. Such an inventory would undoubtedly provide a rich and varied source of information.

Conclusion: the lessons to be drawn from a comparison of the Canadian and American situation and European experience

Reasonable accommodation is based on a legal approach to diversity that transfers or shifts, at least in part, individual responsibility to society and institutions, in other words not just the state but also all the bodies with the power to manage diversity, whether these be businesses, government departments or other types of establishment. As such, up to a certain point reasonable accommodation frees individuals whose personal characteristics prevent them from benefiting from a particular job or service from the need to adapt or integrate and places the duty of adaptation on the shoulders of society as a whole. Underlying the notion of reasonable accommodation is the idea that the factors that together form an obstacle to individuals' access to certain services or jobs are to be sought in the social environment rather than in those individuals themselves. Clearly, such an approach has great potential. So long as it is properly applied, it can make society more inclusive vis-à-vis persons whose minority status and/or personal characteristics leave them particularly vulnerable. Now perhaps more than ever, the role of the law in a pluralist society is to establish the necessary parameters to ensure a unified society while continuing to encourage diversity.

Could Europe adopt the concept of reasonable accommodation, with all that that implies from a legal standpoint? Possibly, but the right questions need to be asked. As already noted, one key difference between the Canadian and European situations is that in Europe, setting aside disabled persons' employment, there is currently no general principle governing reasonable accommodation for the whole of society. The result is that there are far fewer requests for its application or assessments of its potential. However, Canadian experience shows how hard it is in practice to determine where the responsibilities lie in specific cases. It is very likely therefore that reasonable accommodation as a concept will undergo further changes in the years to come. Before any decision is taken to introduce into Europe a genuine right to reasonable accommodation, which signifies acceptance of its wide-scale application, it needs to be determined how exactly it could offer significant advantages over the proportionality test, by offering ways of overcoming some of the shortcomings in that test.

We have outlined in Parts I and II some of the problems that the application of reasonable accommodation, as it has been developed by the American and Canadian courts, has encountered in real life. Certain pitfalls may emerge when it becomes necessary to respond to individual requests by identifying the responsibilities of each of the parties and determining their boundaries. There is no shortage of such difficulties. For example, what actually constitutes a compelling governmental interest (United States) or a legitimate and compelling objective (Canada) that is sufficient to justify refusing a request for an exception? What is meant by "undue hardship" and how to decide whether the cost to the individual or body asked to make a particular accommodation is too high or that an exception would unduly infringe the rights of others? How far should the duty to accommodate extend to the legislative power? All these questions show that in each individual case implementing reasonable accommodation in the technical sense of the term requires all interests involved to be weighed in the balance and that the challenge for the courts is to draw up a more precise definition of accommodation that is consistent and yet sufficiently flexible and open to reasonable requests. Diversity is daily becoming an increasing feature of life and the demands that accompany it are giving a new significance to the possible role the law can play in this process. The challenge is enormous. Reasonable accommodation and potentially equivalent legal approaches raise the fundamental issue of just how far democratic societies should go in recognising differences.

Participation rights under the Framework Convention for the Protection of National Minorities (FCNM): towards a legal framework against social and economic discrimination

Lidija R. Basta Fleiner[1]

1. The context and emerging issues: contested fields of trans-cultural communication

Identity politics represents a major challenge for the liberal constitutional democracy of today. Cultural themes dominate political debate on an equal footing with economic issues, to say the least. This is the case not only in societies with ethnic cleavages, let alone the countries coming out of ethnic wars worldwide. The same is true of Western democracies since 11 September 2001.[2] The debate irrevocably leads to re-visiting the question of national identity in terms of the commonly accepted values underlying a democratic consensus in the societies of Western Europe. The reforms to citizenship became a highly politicised issue in France and Germany in the 1990s, and nationality law was reformed four times in the two countries. Political debate on concepts of nationality, belonging and integration shifted in both countries to a more focused sphere of migration. Contrary to Brubaker's prediction made in 1992[3] – that basic

---

1. Permanent guest professor, Faculty of Political Sciences, University of Belgrade, Serbia; former professor, University of Fribourg, Switzerland; and former First Vice-President of the Advisory Committee on the Framework Convention for the Protection of National Minorities.

2. In one of his recent articles on "Identity, Immigration, and Liberal Democracy", F. Fukuyama argues that a more serious longer term challenge than terrorism faces liberal democracies, namely their integration of migrant minorities – particularly those from Muslim countries. "Europe has become and will continue to be a critical breeding ground and battle front in the struggle between radical Islamism and liberal democracy", since "radical Islamism itself is a manifestation of modern identity politics, a by-product of the modernization process itself". F. Fukuyama, 2006, Vol. 17, Number 2, pp. 5-20, available at: www.journalofdemocracy.org/articles/gratis/Fukuyama-17-2.pdf.

3. R. Brubaker, *Citizenship and Nationhood in France and Germany*, Harvard University Press, Cambridge, MA.

structural differences between French civic and assimilationist, and German cultural and exclusionist idioms of nationhood would continue to affect nationality policy – it was Germany that in 1993 adopted for the first time a law granting entitlement to citizenship on the basis of birth and residence. Again it was France that, in the same year, pursued a restrictive citizenship policy and adopted for the first time a law ending the automatic acquisition of citizenship, at the age of 18, by aliens born in the country. As Nathan Glaser put it, we are all multiculturalists now.[4]

A shift towards migration aspects in citizenship policy in both France and Germany in the 1990s can indeed be interpreted as a sign that citizenship discourse has become principally an issue of strongly politicised debates on nationality policies instead of an academic approach to nationhood. However, rather than pointing to a narrowing of the policy debate, the four nationality law reforms in France and Germany demonstrate the depth of the issue behind the confrontation over nationality policy – namely, the issue of nationhood itself. It is the foundational principles of both nation states, personified in respective concepts of nation as *pouvoir constituant*, that call for reconsideration and revision.[5]

Migration policy is rightly analysed within the relationship between migration, the state and the society. Citizenship models, modes of migrant incorporation, membership of the welfare state, sociocultural exclusion, discrimination and ethnic minority formation, as well as ethnic mobilisation, become major cross-cutting issues to address mature and emergent

---

4. Randall Hansen and Jobst Koehhler, "Issue Definition, Political Discourse and the Politics of Nationality Reform in France and Germany", *European Journal of Political Research*, 44, 2005, pp. 623-644.

5. Even the Swiss concept of composed nation, which builds on minority rights as group rights in order to guarantee collective liberty and identity, remains "hermetically" closed for "immigrated diversity". Differential exclusion of migrants is immanent to Swiss migration policy, even more so than, say, in the French culturally blind concept of nationhood. Swiss "Willensnation"(nation by will) is defined as much by those whom it includes (traditional linguistic and religious communities) as by whom it excludes. The territorial basis for minority rights goes against the individual socio-economic mobility of migrants. Federal design minimises the capacity of powerless migrant groups to act out the full extent of their interests and direct democracy has proved instrumental in fomenting anti-migration sentiments, including racism and discriminatory perception of some migrant groups in the population.

problems in migration policies.[6] As regards the normative elements in future EU policy aiming at "complex equality" and "reasonable accommodation" of cultural diversity among migrants (interculturalism as equal access of migrants to social services in terms of identity-driven equal rights and equal results), these are the issues to be seriously taken into account. The link between inter-ethnic relations, changes in personal and group identity even without a further phase of incorporating migrants into citizenship must take into account this inherent relationship between migration, nation state and society. A further significant step forward would be to focus on the empirical aspects in the relationship between social disintegration, globalisation and intercultural and inter-ethnic conflicts at a micro level.[7]

Reacting to these emerging problems and debates, the Council of Europe called back in 1994 for political and cultural democracy as essential for maintaining social cohesion in Europe. What makes in this regard the international legal standards for the protection of national minorities, particularly the Framework Convention for the Protection of National Minorities of the Council of Europe (FCNM), relevant to the context and emerging issues described so far?

Firstly, the discourse on "reasonable accommodation of cultural diversity" and "equal access of migrants to social services as identity-driven equal rights" draws attention to a new aspect in their protection. It targets their quality as ethnic minorities. For migrant ethnic minorities, unlike national minorities, a rupture has occurred between territory and cultural identity. More importantly, in most cases a rupture between cultural identity and citizenship has also taken place. Nevertheless, the new policy debate for the first time crosses the Rubicon and understands their minority cultural identity as also a part of their human rights' accommodation. Secondly, the preamble to the Framework Convention for the Protection of National Minorities (FCNM) makes it obvious the importance the Council

---

6. "Intercultural Relations, Identity and Citizenship: A Comparative Study of Australia, France and Germany", in M. Craanen (ed.), *Berichte aus Forschungsvorhaben im Rahmen der Förderungsinitiativen "Das Fremde und das Eigene" – 1999-2006*, Transcript Verlag, Bielefeld, and VolkswagenStiftung, Hannover, 2006, pp. 324-325.

7. How low-key political conflicts with ethnic origins can be de-escalated demonstrates a political anthropology at the micro-level that examines how members of different groups live together on an everyday basis and are possibly constrained by networks involving cross-group ties. See: *Das "Fremde" und das "Eigene" Interkulturelle Konflikte in Spanien, Grossbritanien und Deutschland,* in: M. Craanen (ed.), op. cit., pp. 334-335.

of Europe gives to the rights of national minorities: their comprehensive and effective protection by states parties is a key element to promote stability, democratic security and peace in Europe; only advanced pluralist societies, being genuinely democratic, can create a climate of tolerance and dialogue inside each society.

Therefore, it was no accident that the Council of Europe was the first international body to argue in favour of multicultural citizenship as a precondition for inclusive and participatory democracy. This oldest European organisation promoting democracy and the rule of law rightly understood that the European traditional liberal democratic *acquis* faces a major challenge: How to constitute a state that will be inclusive for all major communities in its society? In this sense, Parliamentary Assembly Resolution 1735 (2006) on the concept of "nation" made a far-reaching statement on citizenship and nationhood within a multilateral setting: "The general trend of the nation state's evolution is towards its transformation, depending on the case, from a purely ethnic or ethnocentric state into a civic state and from a purely civic state into multicultural state".

Put differently, effective protection of the rights of persons belonging to national minorities has become the standard for democratic governance and the *sine qua non* for social cohesion within nation states. Without this condition being fulfilled by nation states, Europe will not be able to design a sustainable strategic response to multiple identities of societies and individuals within its border. Especially, given that the European Union has no common minority policy, and will probably not have one in the near future.[8]

This paper maps the FCNM's key legal standards for the protection of minorities and the democratic management of diversity as critical stepping-stones in designing a comprehensive European legal framework against social and economic discrimination. In doing so, it focuses on the participation rights of those belonging to national minorities since the underlying concept of full and effective equality of people belonging to minorities inherently embraces these rights in all areas of economic, social, cultural and political life. Given the different concepts of reasonable accommodation (RA) in Canadian and EU law, this paper also touches upon certain similarities and the considerable conceptual differences

---

8. The number of EU member states who have ratified Protocol No. 12 as of 8 July 2009 is more than telling. Among the 20 ratifications, six are from EU member states (Cyprus, Finland, Luxemburg, Netherlands, Spain and Romania).

between the FCNM's understanding of the protection against discrimination and the general approach underlying "rational accommodation of intercultural identities of migrants" in Europe.

Major importance will be given to the pronouncements of the Advisory Committee on the Framework Convention (ACFC), the convention's monitoring body,[9] as regards the normative content of Article 15, which governs participation of minorities in cultural, social and economic life and in public affairs (political participation). The underlying argument is that the opinions of the ACFC on the implementation of the FCNM by states parties during more than a decade of its jurisprudence have underscored and developed the foundational nature of the participation rights, in terms of both their content and connection to other rights that the states parties are obliged to guarantee to national minorities, under this convention.[10] As already stated, the aim is to demonstrate the relevance of the FCNM but also the principal differences to the concept of RA as embedded in Canadian and EU law respectively. Finally, the paper argues that only an inclusive approach to participation rights for those belonging to minorities, bringing together social and economic rights with the rights in public sphere, can be taken as an important step towards providing a European legal framework against social and economic discrimination, and in favour of both political and cultural democracy in Europe.

---

9. "In evaluating the adequacy of the measures taken by the parties to give effect to the principles set out in the framework Convention the Committee of Ministers shall be assisted by an advisory committee, the members of which shall be recognised experts in the filed of the protection of national minorities" (Article 26, paragraph 1). The composition of the ACFC and its procedure were established in the Rules of Procedure (1998) and further decisions of the Committee of Ministers relevant to the monitoring procedure.

10. Cf. "Commentary on Participation Rights", prepared by the ACFC and FCNM Secretariat, Strasbourg, 2008. Also see M. Weller, "Article 15: Effective Participation", in M. Weller (ed.), *The Rights of Minorities, a Commentary on the Framework Convention for the Protection of National Minorities*, Oxford University Press, Oxford, 2005, pp. 429-461.

2. FCNM participation rights – An important step towards a European legal framework against social and economic discrimination

2.1. Legal nature and the importance of the FCNM[11]

The FCNM marks a milestone in raising international standards on minority protection. Such a statement is by no means an exaggeration, although most of the provisions of the Framework Convention contain rather general principles and – except for the right to freely choose to be treated or not as belonging to a national minority (Article 3) – establish duties for states parties, not individual rights to be directly claimed. Nevertheless, the FCNM is the first multilateral treaty which in a form of hard law obliges the parties to treat the rights of persons belonging to minorities as fundamental rights. Minority rights thus become an integral part of the international protection of human rights, and do not fall within the reserved domain of states. Furthermore, by declaring full and effective equality a key standard for minority protection, the convention introduces a second level of anti-discrimination standards that will in many cases imply additional rights for those belonging to minorities. Last but not least, Article 15 of the convention, which lays down the obligations of states parties in effectuating the participation rights of those belonging to national minorities, goes much further than Article 27 of the UN Covenant on Civil and Political Rights. Moreover, Article 4, paragraph 2, makes clear that participation in social, economic, cultural and political life is a measure of full and effective equality.

This is how the FCNM recognises, for the first time, a political dimension in minority aspirations while "avoiding dangerous and radical" aspirations of self-determination.[12] In the same context, the importance of the participation of national minorities as part of democratic cohesion and political pluralism has been stressed in Parliamentary Assembly Recommendation 1492 (2001). It states, *inter alia*, that "the minority has the responsibility to participate in political and public life of the country in which it lives and

---

11. The Framework Convention for the Protection of National Minorities of the Council of Europe entered into force on 1 February 1998. As of April 2009, it has been signed by 43 states and ratified by 39, out of 47 member states. Belgium, Greece, Ireland and Luxembourg have not ratified, and Andorra, France, Turkey and Monaco have not yet signed the convention.

12. Cf. also W. Kymlicka, "Cultural Rights and Minority Rights: A European Experiment" (manuscript).

to contribute, along with the majority, to the democratic cohesion and pluralism of the states to which it has offered its allegiance".

2.2. Participation is inclusive and covers cultural, economic, social, and public life

Article 15 of the FCNM provides that "the parties shall create the conditions necessary for the effective participation of persons belonging to national minorities in cultural, social and economic life and in public affairs, in particular those affecting them". Undoubtedly, the importance of Article 15 lies in its scope. It stipulates the necessity for the state parties to create the conditions needed for the effective participation of national minorities by imposing on states negative as well as positive obligations. On the one hand, it implies obligations not to interfere in the cultural and other practices on which minority identity is based and not to hamper their participation in public affairs, in particular those affecting them. On the other hand, it obliges states to take measures to support the development of national minorities' identities and to create conditions for their effective participation.

2.2.1. Foundational nature and contextualised approach: Articles 3, 4 and 6

It is not possible to talk about effective participation without taking into account the other rights that states parties have to guarantee under the Framework Convention. The right of persons belonging to national minorities to be involved in affairs affecting them directly or indirectly touches profoundly upon their identity, traditions and cultural heritage, as well as their active participation in political life, and in consequence presupposes that they can enjoy these rights in a non-discriminatory manner. Ensuring full and effective participation of the those belonging to national minorities is the most successful instrument for the effective protection of other rights covered by in the Framework Convention. Put differently: effective participation is a condition *sine qua non* and a measure of the level of protection of all the other principles guiding minority rights in the convention.

The legal nature and the broad normative content of Article 15 are best reflected in the inclusive concept of participation that the convention lays down, and the ACFC persistently embraces this in its opinions. In order to act as a facilitator in a constructive dialogue between state authorities and members of national minorities, the ACFC has endorsed the transversal scope of participation rights and interpreted participation as indeed a critical standard for democratic governance. It may well be that in this sense the ACFC could have been even more persistent. For example, it is notable that in its early pronouncements,[13] the ACFC did not often make an explicit link between education (Articles 6 and 12-14) and participation, although it often requested the authorities to decide "in consultation with concerned minorities". On the other hand, as early as the later opinions of the first monitoring cycle, the ACFC went further in targeting state's non-compliance with its duties under Article 15, when it concluded that these reflected a deliberate state policy and saw them as an element of non-democratic governance. Especially in the post-conflict cases of state reconstruction, the ACFC also used the participation argument in order to warn against "reinforcing ethnic lines as the main pillar of state action".

As regards our theme, a consolidated review of ACFC jurisprudence on participation rights shows that the FCNM monitoring body mainly focused on the following issues:

- scope of application (Article 3);

- equal protection of laws and non-discrimination clauses (Article 4);

- a spirit of tolerance and intercultural dialogue, including anti-discrimination measures (Article 6).

To start with, the ACFC particularly underlined the importance of the relationship between Article 15, and Articles 4 and 5 (maintenance and development of culture) in demonstrating that effective participation of those belonging to national minorities is a key to the full enjoyment of other rights protected under the convention. In fact, Articles 4, 5 and 15 can be seen "as the three corners of a triangle which together form the main foundations of the Framework Convention".[14]

In a similar vein, the ACFC highlighted Article 3 as being critical to the fulfilment of the aim of the convention. It is clear that the effectiveness of participation directly depends on the number of those in any country who are protected under the FCNM. In this context, the comments of the ACFC as regards Article 3 and the personal scope of application of the Framework Convention are particularly revealing. Differences regarding

---

13. The 1st monitoring cycle (1998-2003)

14. "Commentary on Participation Rights", op. cit., p. 6.

the definition of national minorities during the drafting phase – reflecting in fact a more fundamental, political disagreement on their nature as individual or group rights[15] – was the key reason why the convention remained intentionally vague on its personal scope of application. Nevertheless, the ACFC always examined the scope of application applied by each state party, in order to verify whether this margin of appreciation had not been used in a given case for arbitrary and unjustified restrictions in implementing the FCNM.

In fact, the ACFC always maintained the standard concept of "unjustified and arbitrary distinctions" in international law. For instance, the committee used the "scope of application" argument also to reiterate the importance of advisory and consultative mechanisms, saying that certain persons belonging to ethnic minorities should not be excluded a priori from the dialogue because they are not recognised as national minorities under the Framework Convention. This is in line with Parliamentary Assembly Recommendation 1623 (2003), which states: "The Assembly considers that the states parties do not have an unconditional right to decide which groups within their territories qualify as national minorities in the sense of the framework convention. Any decision of the kind must respect the principle of non-discrimination and comply with the letter and spirit of the framework convention."

Citizenship is indeed a decisive element in influencing the FCNM's scope of application in general and minority participation in public affairs, in particular. The absence of a formal definition of minority in the FCNM left a broad margin of appreciation for the ACFC, and it did its best to capitalise on this fact for new migrant minorities, despite encountering resistance from certain states and discontent from the Committee of Ministers. As already said, the ACFC built its arguments in compliance with the general principles of international law. Of indirect influence may have been the EU principle of constitutional tolerance and the human rights foundations of European citizenship. Referring to the concept of

---

15. Notwithstanding the Explanatory Report, according to which the convention "does not imply the recognition of collective rights", the ambivalence between the individual and the collective in minority rights remains. It played a significant role in the work of the ACFC, notably in its conceptual discussions. The "founding fathers" of the FCNM left this ambivalence to one side, since no consensus within the international setting seemed feasible in the near future. As a consequence, the Explanatory Report draws a clear line, almost in a manner of antinomy, between individual and collective rights.

"arbitrary or unjustified distinctions", the ACFC considered as a part of its duty the need to examine the personal scope of application given to the implementation of the Framework Convention in each case. This allowed the committee to go beyond the states' definitions and examine the situation of other minority groups, most notably migrants.[16] The ACFC took the position that, "while it is legitimate to impose certain restrictions on non-citizens concerning their right to vote and be elected, they should not be implied more widely than necessary". As a rule, the committee encouraged the states parties to provide non-citizens with active and passive voting rights in local elections. It consistently recommended flexibility and inclusiveness in the approach taken by states parties. Moreover, the ACFC always emphasised the fact that the application of the Framework Convention to non-citizens belonging to minorities could enhance the spirit of tolerance, intercultural dialogue and co-operation,[17] as provided for in Article 6 of the convention.

It is the normative content of Article 6 that considerably helped the ACFC, through its article-by-article approach, to assess the FCNM's implementation also as regards the inclusion of non-citizens belonging to ethnic minorities who were not guaranteed minority protection in certain cases. This article applies to everyone within the state with respect to threats and discrimination based on ethnicity, language or religion. The committee used the inclusive scope and mandatory character of the obligations on states parties under Article 6 in matters regarding media stereotyping, policy failures and citizenship laws.[18] The principles of tolerance, dialogue and mutual respect, enshrined in Article 6, are intrinsically linked to full and effective equality and non-discrimination. Thanks to a creative teleological interpretation by the ACFC, the positive effects of Article 6 went far beyond providing a framework for balancing the needs of those belonging to a national minority to preserve their own culture and yet be integrated into the society. By systematically targeting migrants' policy

---

16. In its opinion on Germany of March 2002, the committee did not hesitate in referring to the large number of groups of non-citizens living in Germany, the government itself having indicated 7.49 million foreigners living in Germany (paragraph 17). In particular, the committee quotes the official statistics at the end of 1999, it referred to the presence of 1 856 000 citizens from EU states, more then 2 053 000 Turkish citizens, 737 000 Yugoslav citizens, 214 000 Croats and 291 000 Polish citizens. (More in: I. Tanase, "Defining National Minorities: Old Criteria and New Minorities", St Antony's College, University of Oxford, online publication, 2003.)

17. "Commentary on Participation Rights", op. cit., pp. 8 and 27.

18. More in G. Gilbert, "Article 6: Tolerance", M. Weller (ed.), op. cit., pp. 177-191.

failures, the committee in fact "stubbornly" reiterated that economic and social cohesion are not viable in societies where those belonging to large ethnic or religious migrant groups remain at the same time "differentially" included (labour and social welfare) and systemically excluded as regards their cultural identity. This is an important lesson learnt when considering the feasibility and principles of rational accommodation of cultural diversity within a European legal framework.

In its "Report on Non-Citizens and Minority Rights" (2006), the Venice Commission points to the above developments as an indication "that a significantly more flexible and nuanced approach has gained ground in the implementation and monitoring practice under the FCNM, even in those cases where the Government's formal position on the issue has remained intact". Moreover, "a move towards a more nuanced approach to the definition issue can be detected not only in the work of the ACFC, but also in the work of the CM and, although to a lesser extent, in governmental practice". Finally, the Venice Commission also leaves no doubt as to the key standard for arbitrary or unjustified, that is discriminatory, distinctions in granting minority rights:

> 132. Each State shall secure to everyone within its jurisdiction – including non-citizens – the human rights guaranteed by the general human rights treaties binding upon them, mainly by refraining from undue interference in their exercise. A restrictive declaration entered upon ratification of the FCNM and/or a general law on minorities containing a citizenship-based definition can in no way mitigate this international obligation.[19]

Given such developments, the Parliamentary Assembly of the Council of Europe (PACE) re-focused its concerns away from the definition of minority towards the risk of discriminatory exclusion of minority groups by those states that have entered declarations or reservations when ratifying the FCNM. The support backing Recommendation 1623 (2003) stressed in particular that "it would be rather unfortunate if the European standards of minority protection appear to be more restrictive in nature than the universal standards". Namely, Article 27 of the ICCPR is not limited to citizens; at the same time, it remains binding for all states parties to the FCNM regardless of the citizenship criterion in the implementation policy of a considerable number of them. This warning of the PACE against undue restrictions based on the citizenship criterion in states' policies on

---

19. CDL-AD(2007)001.

human rights was also, *mutatis mutandis*, echoed in Resolution 1509 (2006) on the human rights of irregular migrants.

2.2.2. Full and effective equality means positive measures and the obligation of a result

From the very beginning of the monitoring process, the ACFC under-stood the principles of full and effective equality and of a second level of protection against discrimination (Article 4) as cornerstones for the foun-dational nature and inclusive scope of participation under the FCNM. The ACFC particularly built upon paragraph 2 of Article 4 of the Framework Convention, which explicitly demands states parties to engage in a "non-exclusion policy" prohibiting discrimination. It also called on states parties to adopt, where necessary, adequate measures in order to promote, in all areas of economic, social, political and cultural life, "full and effec-tive equality between persons belonging to a national minority and those belonging to the majority". Compared to respect and protection, promo-tion is the third highest level of accommodation. Throughout its opinions, the ACFC has repeatedly related the broad scope of application of these measures of positive discrimination to participation. More importantly, the ACFC has always underlined that it did not consider positive measures as discriminatory. For example, the ACFC saw that some discriminatory situ-ations may be remedied by adopting special measures, such as quotas, to ensure full and effective participation of persons belonging to national minorities in terms of a more significant presence of these minorities in state administrative structures. In particular, the ACFC often made, in its opinions, cross-references among the effective participation, equality and non-discrimination principles, in order to address the problem of differ-ences in social and economic situations between certain minorities and the majority. The ACFC has also concluded that unemployment appears to affect disproportionately persons belonging to national minorities, especially young women, stressing the need to eliminate both direct and indirect discrimination in the labour market, and enhance the recruitment of qualified persons belonging to national minorities in public service. As regards the dispute over minority land rights, the ACFC has often pointed out that both socio-economic and cultural aspects of the problem are directly interrelated with the participation rights of the minority in ques-tion. In a nutshell: it becomes obvious that the ACFC has applied the indirect-discrimination concept,[20] taking fully into account that indirect discrimination as such points to a collective dimension of minority rights, including also migrant minorities.

2.2.3. Participation in public affairs – Not a goal in itself, but an instrument to effectively prevent social and economic discrimination on the basis of cultural identity

In its 10-year work, the ACFC has had to address three key aspects of participation rights in public affairs: constitutional state design (decentralisation and territorial autonomy) and governance of state as a whole, in order to evaluate the inclusiveness of a given constitutional framework for the effective decision-making capacities of minority communities; the entitlement of minorities to decide autonomously on the issues that are of particular relevance to them; and the question of internal democracy within minority communities.[21] The truth of the matter is that the ACFC has varied its attention to these three issues.[22] One can say that throughout all its opinions, the ACFC has never given up stressing the importance of a dialogue between the state and minority organisations. As with representation, the ACFC has always understood consultation of minorities as a stepping stone, but definitely not already as a form of full participation. In many cases, the ACFC encouraged the authorities to make this step forward and give appropriate effect to the opinion and proposals of the minority representatives. In fact, the ACFC looked upon consultative mechanisms and their relevance in the political decision-making process as a very important term of reference to measure both the scope and the effectiveness of the participation rights in a given country.

The opinions addressed a whole set of questions pertinent not only to minorities' auto-determination entitlements and their genuine representation through the organisations and institutions of their choice – the ACFC also ruled, for example, on the various solutions related to elected bodies, in order to monitor the participation of minorities in the legislative process – parties, design of the electoral system at each level, boundaries,

---

20. Indirect discrimination is generally understood as a rule, policy, practice, or procedure that is the same for everyone and thus may look fair, but the side effect of which disadvantages members of a specified group relative to others.

21. M. Weller (ed.), op. cit., pp. 430-431.

22. In 2005, Marc Weller rightly warned that "little or no attention has been devoted to the internal democracy of minorities thus far" (ibid., p. 431).

reserved seat systems, parliamentary practice and veto-type rights, and participation through specialised governmental bodies.

The message of the ACFC was clear in terms of the high level of standards for effective participation in public life: minority representation and minority consultative mechanisms as such are inherent in the political participation of those belonging to a minority. Nevertheless, their mere existence does not mean participation is in reality achieved. Representation is not an aim in itself. Consultative mechanisms are to operate instead as forceful institutional avenues that will actively promote effective participation of minorities, in cultural, social and economic life and in public affairs, in particular those affecting them.

3. Outlook

In fulfilling its task as a treaty body, the Advisory Committee has addressed the implementation of the FCNM as "an unfinished story of human rights" and understood its role as that of discovering and developing normative meanings in the human rights canon in terms of minority protection. Has the ACFC thereby confirmed the foundational nature of participation rights, and has it sufficiently built upon and developed the inclusiveness that lies behind the concept of participation rights?

Here, it is worth remembering that the inclusiveness of participation rights of those belonging to national minorities can be understood in two ways: (a) in terms of the scope of the rights, and (b) in terms of a constitutive nature of a given state construction that should accommodate and further improve inclusiveness as a major principle of effective, legitimate multicultural societies (multicultural nationhood). The latter is still waiting to be more explicitly communicated by the ACFC in its future monitoring work. Nevertheless, the jurisprudence to date represents a good basis for the ACFC to engage in further interpretative possibilities of the "effectiveness" of political participation. As the commentary on participation shows, the interpretative basis has been already provided:

> "Effectiveness" of participation cannot be defined and measured in abstract terms. When considering whether participation of persons belonging to national minorities is effective, the Advisory Committee has not only examined the means which promote full and effective equality for persons belonging to national minorities: it has also taken into account their impact on the situation of the persons concerned and on the society as a whole.

Hence it is not sufficient to formally provide for the participation of persons belonging to national minorities. The measures should also ensure that their participation has a substantial influence on decisions which are taken, and that there is, as far as possible, a shared ownership of the decisions taken.

Similarly, measures taken by the State Parties to improve participation of persons belonging to national minorities in socio-economic life should have an impact on their access to labour market as individual economic actors, their access to social protection and, ultimately, their quality of life. *Full and effective equality may, in this context, be seen as a result of effective participation.*[23]

It remains to be seen whether the ACFC will continue its 10-year proactive interpretation of the FCNM, and whether it will take a bold path in developing the normative content of Article 15 in terms of multicultural citizenship, as suggested in PACE Recommendation 1735 (2006). Whatever the result may be, it will certainly not be dependent on the level of expertise and goodwill of the members of the ACFC. I would fully agree with those who argue that today, "we are facing perhaps an even more difficult stage of FCNM implementation". The challenges for the full and effective compliance by states parties with their obligations under the present convention are far-reaching and systemic: although an integral part of universal human rights, minority rights are often handled as a sort of "special" rights, different and completely isolated from the "general" human rights.[24]

Even with such important tasks still pending for the ACFC, there is no doubt that the most important lessons learnt also affect migrants' accommodation. The ACFC has demonstrated in its jurisprudence that the hitherto traditional differentiation between immigration and "other" countries is now obsolete. There is no viable future for state constitutional politics which ignore both the new reality and states' international legal obligations to guarantee to all those living within its territory – regardless

---

23. "Commentary on Participation Rights", op. cit., p. 13 (author's emphasis).

24. Besides the problem of failed mainstreaming, B. Cilevics, member of the Parliamentary Assembly of the Council of Europe, warns of states' reluctance to guarantee full and effective equality to the national minorities, and criticises the lack of synergy between the EU and the Council of Europe in this field, which additionally undermines the principle of the universality of minority rights (Conference on Ten Years of Protecting National Minorities and Regional and Minority Languages, Strasbourg, March 2008).

of their citizenship status – non-discriminatory protection of their fundamental rights. From a different perspective and in a different approach, the ACFC has thus contributed to the ongoing debate that contextualises migrants' rights and nationality state policies into a broader spectrum of state and society. Such a linkage should be translated not only in social and cultural, but also in constitutional politics. The committee has always encouraged states to give electoral rights to minorities at local levels, where their social, economic and cultural rights come into contact with the day-to-day policies directly affecting them, including protection of their cultural identity and social security against indirect discrimination. A more convincing argument could not be provided to show that social cohesion is viable only (a) with a critical mass of politically cohesive elements in migrant policies and (b) provided that there is legal basis guaranteeing a critical level of political accommodation of minority groups, including large migrant groups.

4. Concluding observations

The FCNM represents the first response to the need for hard-law obligations for states parties within the international legal system of minority rights. Even at first glance, it is clear that this Council of Europe document has embraced the principle of reasonable accommodation of those belonging to national minorities as such, without stating the legal concept per se, in the sense that it has been developed in Canadian law.[25] Some articles are indeed paradigmatic in this regard.[26] A commonality with the Canadian concept is in the discrimination prohibited: namely, as regards religion, language, ethnic or national origin. However, the similarities stop there. The teleology of the FCNM goes much further and is fundamentally different: although positive measures in promoting effective and full equality of those belonging to national minorities also take place at an individual level (obligation of an action), the aim behind this second level of anti-discrimination standards goes beyond a given case, and implies

---

25. Given its reduced, basically "labour market driven", nature, neither can the rational accommodation concept, as introduced in the EU in 2000, be a point of reference here.

26. "In areas inhabited by substantial numbers of people belonging to a national minority traditionally or in a substantial numbers, if there is sufficient demand, the Parties shall endeavour to ensure, as far as possible and within the framework of their education system, that persons belonging to those minorities have adequate opportunities for being taught the minority language or for receiving instructions in this language" (Article 14, paragraph 2).

that such measures should have an additional positive impact on the situation of the persons concerned/given community and on a society as a whole (obligation of results).

Finally, regarding the practical implications of the ACFC jurisprudence outlined above for the institutional and social policy reforms necessary to sustain social and economic integration of migrants by also taking into account their cultural identity, a conclusive question has to be raised: Do legal responses effectively lead to policy implementation? The answer that underlines this paper is straightforwardly positive. The rule of law characteristically demands legally-set standards for policy implementation in the sense that they make policy implementation more or less comprehensive. More notably and more pragmatically, it is again legal settings that are testament to measuring the effectiveness of policies in terms of breaches of international legal obligations as regards a result. Some 43 signatures and 39 ratifications prove that the FCNM has indeed became the European standard in implementing international legal obligations as regards the rights of minorities, including, to a considerable extent, also those groups not recognised as national minorities.

European legal frameworks responding to diversity and the need for institutional change

Indirect discrimination as a means of protecting pluralism: challenges and limits

Frédérique Ast[1]

In the famous case of *Griggs v. Duke Power*,[2] Chief Justice Burger borrowed an image from a La Fontaine fable to illustrate the fact that the right to equality should not be an inaccessible present like the meal which the fox offers the stork.[3] This right must be of practical benefit to all. In this connection, it is not enough merely to prohibit direct, open and obvious discrimination relating to treatment which is deliberately differentiated on suspicious grounds. Treating all individuals identically ignores the diversity of situations and individuals. Refusal to take account of this diversity is liable to perpetuate deep-seated inequalities.

As Aristotle noted, "disputes arise when equal persons do not receive equal shares, or when unequal persons receive equal treatment". So how are we to apprehend requirements relating to the passing of specific tests in order to secure employment or accede to normal schooling where such tests de facto eliminate a large majority of black or Roma people? How should we assess the validity of certain institutional dress codes prohibiting the wearing of any religious symbol? And what of regulations requiring applicants to hold certain diplomas or have specific language knowledge

---

1. Lawyer with the HALDE (High Authority for Action against Discrimination and for Equality). This article reflects only the opinion of its author, not those of the institution for which he works. I would like to extend my special thinks to Ms Sophie Latraverse, Deputy Legal Director of the HALDE, for her invaluable advice, highly relevant suggestions and unstinting support.

2. 401 US 424 (1971). This judgment developed the doctrine of "disparate impact" in connection with a recruitment policy requiring the applicant to hold a high school diploma and sit intelligence tests, which had the effect of excluding a majority of black Americans, such prerequisites having no link with the person's professional performance.

3. In this fable the fox offers a stork some milk on a plate, while the stork offers the fox a meal in an earthenware jar with a long narrow neck, so that neither can actually eat the meal served up.

in order to obtain employment or accede to a service which have the effect of placing immigrant groups at a severe disadvantage?

In the 1970s, English-speaking and European courts began to respond to this kind of question with the concept of indirect discrimination. This concept, which had already been present in the public international law of the League of Nations,[4] and then in the United Nations conventions prohibiting discrimination[5] was further expanded and fleshed out by legislation in the English-speaking countries and then EU law. It recently entered the legal system established under the European Convention on Human Rights and the revised European Social Charter.

The indirect discrimination concept facilitates the detection and prohibition of measures which, on the face of it, would seem acceptable and neutral but which in fact prove highly detrimental to specific groups, without any objective, reasonable justification. It also involves introducing differentiated treatment for certain individuals or groups of individuals. Technically, therefore, indirect discrimination can be a powerful legal means of protecting and guaranteeing pluralism, which is "built on the genuine recognition of, and respect for, diversity and the dynamics of cultural traditions, ethnic and cultural identities, religious beliefs".[6] However, when courts have recourse to this concept, they are implicitly recognising another right, namely that to difference, which European courts are in fact rather tentative about granting.

1. Prohibition of indirect discrimination: a powerful legal means of achieving an "inclusive" society

We might begin by reminding the reader that while the prohibition of indirect discrimination is guaranteed under European law, it is protected

---

4. Article 5 of the 1929 Declaration of International Rights of Man provides as follows: "equality ... precludes any direct or indirect discrimination". Cf. also PCIJ, 10 September 1923, on the situation of German landowners in Poland, (1923) PCIJ 3.

5. See Article 1 of the UN Convention on the Elimination of All Forms of Racial Discrimination (1965) and Article 1 of the UN Convention on the Elimination of All Forms of Discrimination against Women (1979). Cf. also CERD Communication No. 31/2003, *L.R. and Others v. Slovakia* (regarding the removal of a municipality from a funding programme for social housing for Roma people), as well as CEDAW General Recommendation No. 25.

6. ECtHR, *Gorzelik and Others v. Poland* [GC], 17 February 2004, Application No. 44158/98.

within the limits of EU and Council of Europe law, which, unlike the individual states, have no general jurisdiction.

The EU, which under the Amsterdam Treaty has jurisdiction to combat discrimination, has codified a set of innovative Court of Justice case law in the field of discrimination on grounds of nationality and sex. It also extended this case law to a number of further criteria in 2000. For instance, Directive 2000/43/EC[7] prohibits racial and ethnic discrimination in the employment and social fields, covering goods and services as well as social welfare, housing and social benefits. On the other hand, Directive 2000/78/EC[8] prohibits discrimination on the grounds of religion and convictions in the employment field only.[9] With the entry into force of the Lisbon Treaty, conferring binding legal effect on the Charter of Fundamental Rights, all types of indirect discrimination will be prohibited in the field of application of the treaty, that is to say fields in which the EU legislature holds jurisdiction and has actually intervened.[10]

Furthermore, for most Council of Europe states parties which have not ratified Protocol No. 12 to the ECHR, the scope of the ECHR prohibition of discrimination is currently confined to the field defined by the rights and freedoms secured under the Convention, which more or less correspond to the so-called "first-generation" human rights. However, refusals to grant specific social benefits have been condemned under the Strasbourg Court's constructive case law from the discrimination angle.[11] Indirect discrimination is also guaranteed under the revised European Social Charter, which deals mainly with the so-called "second-generation" rights. Despite the promising case law being developed by the European Committee of Social Rights, the legal force of this treaty still

---

7. Council Directive 2000/43/EC of 29 June 2000 implementing the principle of equal treatment between persons irrespective of racial or ethnic origin, OJ L 180/22 of 17 July 2000.

8. Council Directive 2000/78/EC of 29 June 2000 establishing a general framework for equal treatment in employment and occupation, OJ L 303/16 of 2 December 2000.

9. The proposed Council directive on implementing the principle of equal treatment between persons irrespective of religion or belief, disability, age or sexual orientation suggests extending EU practice in matters of discrimination beyond the employment sector: COM(2008)426 final, 2 July 2008.

10. Regarding this interpretation, see CJEC, 23 November 2008, Bartsch, Case C-427/06.

11. For example, ECtHR, *Gaygusuz v. Austria*, 16 September 1996 (relating to emergency unemployment assistance).

falls far short of ECHR and EU law. We have accordingly decided not to go into this case law here.

The very mechanics of indirect discrimination means that it takes account of and protects diversity in our societies. First of all, it highlights the fact that the commonly accepted standards or practices, depending on their object or effect, disadvantage those who do not belong to the group for which they were devised. Secondly, it shows that these discriminating structures must be rectified.

1.1. A tool for protecting diversity

Seeking genuine equality beyond the appearances

Like positive action, indirect discrimination is a legal technique geared to guaranteeing substantive equality.[12] It is a case of overcoming legal formalisms and the appearances of equality in order to achieve a social reality, namely a negative effect on an identified group.

Whereas direct discrimination generally stems from a culpable intention, indirect discrimination arises solely from a concern to comply with structural requirements. These phenomena are intended to home in on standards and practices which are so deeply rooted in our social structures that the economic and social partners no longer even have to consciously choose to act in a discriminatory manner. It is enough for them to comply with their organisations' operational standards, which discriminate for them. The indirect discrimination mechanism, precisely, prevents individuals from taking advantage of the existence of discriminatory structures created by others.

This being the case, indirect discrimination cases involve no-fault objective liability. It is immaterial, in establishing the existence of discrimination, whether withholding certain advantages from part-time workers was solely aimed at making full-time working more attractive if in practical terms this action was detrimental to a large proportion of women.[13] The argument that individual security measures were not specifically aimed or

---

12. In some cases, direct discrimination is also a means of achieving substantive equality. This applies to discrimination against pregnant women, which is apprehended as direct discrimination on grounds of sex.

13. Cf. CJEC, Bilka-Kaufhaus, 13 May 1986, Case 170/84, paragraphs 33 ff.

directed at young Catholic men is also ineffective if in practice the measures have disproportionately prejudicial effects on this particular group.[14]

From this angle, while the primary reason for prohibiting direct discrimination is to correct individual deviant behaviour and punish the perpetrators, the purpose of prohibiting indirect discrimination fits in with a "redistributive justice" rationale, endeavouring to compensate victims of a social structure.[15] Indirect discrimination identifies the existence of differences in the situations facing specific individuals or groups of individuals and takes account of their specific needs. This differentiation overturns the formally egalitarian social constructs in order to achieve genuine equality of treatment, by adjusting the rules.

The right to reasonable accommodation as a corollary of indirect discrimination

Since its *O'Malley v. Simpsons-Sears* judgment,[16] the Canadian Supreme Court has enshrined "a legal obligation applicable in a situation of discrimination, consisting in adapting a standard or practice of universal scope within reasonable limits by granting differential treatment to an individual who would otherwise be penalised by such standard or practice".[17] The limit of this obligation is "undue hardship". The Canadian court conceives the right to reasonable accommodation as a corollary of the right to equality. Even if this right can now also be invoked on the basis of a finding of direct discrimination,[18] it requires all persons claiming the right to prove that they have been victims of discrimination. Since 1998 this reasonable accommodation obligation has been enshrined in the Canadian Human Rights Act on the basis of the non-discrimination principle.

---

14. ECtHR, *Hugh Jordan v. the United Kingdom*, 4 May 2001, Application No. 24746/94, paragraph 154.

15. On the fine distinction between corrective and distributive justice, see J. Garner, "Discrimination as Injustice", *Oxford Journal of Legal Studies*, No. 16, 1996, pp. 367 ff.

16. Canadian Supreme Court, *Ontario Commission of Human Rights and Theresa O'Malley (Vincent) v. Simpsons-Sears Ltd.*, [1985] 2 S.C.R. 536, 17 December 1985.

17. P. Bosset, "Les fondements juridiques et l'évolution de l'obligation d'accommodement raisonnable", in M. Jezequel (ed.), *Les accommodements raisonnables: quoi, comment, jusqu'où?*, Yvon Blais, Cowansville (Quebec), 2007, pp. 3-28, especially p. 10.

18. Supreme Court, *British Columbia (Public Service Employee Relations Commission) v. BCGSEU*, [1999] 3 S.C.R. 3, 22 February 1999.

Whether under EU or ECHR law, the obligation of differentiated treatment deriving from the prohibition of any kind of indirect discrimination more or less corresponds to the Canadian legal obligation for reasonable accommodation. The lack of recognition by EU legislation of any right to reasonable accommodation for ethnic, cultural and religious groups does not alter this fact. In French, despite the terminological resemblance, the legal concepts of "*aménagement raisonnable*" and "*accommodement raisonnable*" cannot be treated as equivalent (both are rendered as "reasonable accommodation" in English).

By guaranteeing a right to *aménagement raisonnable*, the EU legislature intended to raise protection against specified forms of discrimination to the rank of substantive protection. This formulation of protection no longer comes under the category of the right to non-discrimination but is governed by a different set of legal rules. The victims no longer have to prove that they have been discriminated against in order to secure special treatment. They enjoy an individual right provided for by law, whose application they can simply demand, leaving it to the party challenged to demonstrate, if it can, that it cannot legitimately accede to the demand. Some groups which are traditionally considered vulnerable have been granted this kind of protection. This applies, for instance, to people with disabilities, for whom employers must provide "reasonable accommodation" by taking "appropriate measures, where needed in a particular case", unless such measures would impose a "disproportionate burden" on them.[19] It can also apply to pregnant women, whose employers must "take the necessary measures to ensure that, by temporarily adjusting the working conditions and/or the working hours", the workers in question are not exposed to certain risks during their pregnancy.[20] These cases concern a positive obligation established by legislation. In some cases such "short-circuiting" of the right of non-discrimination can even necessitate an accommodation which is no longer merely reasonable. This applies to the fundamental right of an accused person who does not understand or speak the language used by the court, set out in Article 6, paragraph 3.e,

---

19. Article 5 of Directive 2000/78.

20. Article 5 of Council Directive 92/85/EEC of 19 October 1992 on the introduction of measures to encourage improvements in the safety and health at work of pregnant workers and workers who have recently given birth or are breastfeeding, OJ L 348/1 of 28 November 1992.

of the ECHR, to the free assistance of an interpreter.[21] These constitutional and legislative measures are therefore available in addition to the right to reasonable accommodation arising from the principle of non-discrimination, which also comprises a collective dimension.

Protecting groups and minorities

Indirect discrimination is a "hybrid concept"[22] capable of entitling individuals to equality while acknowledging that the discrimination affecting them derives from a form of stigmatisation or ostracism against their particular community. In principle, it only provides protection for individuals who are at a disadvantage because they belong to a specific group. Thus the victims cannot normally be exempted from producing evidence of being affected by a contested measure.

This situation should not, however, obscure the fact that indirect discrimination is a vital mainstay of the system for protecting the rights of minorities, defined as population groups with a specific collective identity, usually enshrined in a specific language, culture or religion.[23] Furthermore, suspect measures are sometimes detected using a "collective rights" rationale. The Plenary of the European Court of Human Rights has ruled that since it was established "that the relevant legislation as applied in practice at the material time had a disproportionately prejudicial effect on the Roma community, the Court considers that the applicants as members of that community necessarily suffered the same discriminatory treatment". It therefore decided not to analyse the individual situation of each of the applicants, while the Chamber had even refused to "assess the overall

---

21. However, this provision "does not go so far as to require a written translation of all items of written evidence or official documents in the procedure. The interpretation assistance provided should be such as to enable the defendant to have knowledge of the case against him and to defend himself, notably by being able to put before the court his version of the events" (ECtHR, *Kamasinski v. Austria,* 19 December 1989, Application No. 9783/82; cf. also ECtHR, *Lagerblom v. Sweden*, 14 January 2003, Application No. 26891/95). The Court has held that this right "is to be regarded as a particular rule in relation to the general rule" of the right to non-discrimination (ECtHR, *Luedicke, Belkacem and Koç v. Germany*, 28 November 1978, Applications Nos. 6210/73, 6877/75 and 7132/75).

22. D. Schiek, "Indirect Discrimination", in D. Schiek, L. Waddington and M. Bell, *Non-Discrimination Law*, Art Publishing, Oxford, 2007, pp. 323-475, esp. p. 332.

23. Cf. in this connection k. Henrard, "Equal Rights versus Special Rights? Minority Protection and the Prohibition of Discrimination", Office for Official Publications of the European Communities, Luxembourg, 2008.

social context" because the applicants had failed to back up their allegations with concrete evidence.[24] The Canadian Supreme Court adopts a
fairly similar stance on cases of systemic discrimination.[25]

Protecting against systemic and institutional discrimination

Systemic discrimination is a discriminatory process which amounts to a
system: it derives from a concatenation of actions, often unintentional,
which involve several individuals but also operational rules and practical
facilities. The Canadian Supreme Court defines it as discrimination arising
merely from the application of methods which were not designed to
promote discrimination, reinforced by the actual exclusion of the disadvantaged group. Exclusion fosters the conviction, both inside and outside
the group, that discrimination is the result of natural forces.[26] Institutional
discrimination, on the other hand, derives from institutional racism. It is
basically "the collective failure of an organisation to provide an appropriate and professional service to people because of their colour, culture,
or ethnic origin. It can be seen or detected in processes, attitudes and
behaviour which amount to discrimination …. Without recognition and
action to eliminate such racism it can prevail as part of the ethos or culture
of the organisation."[27] However, in its capacity as a critique of social imbal-
ance inherited from a given history or culture, indirect discrimination can
be used to combat these forms of discrimination,[28] although in order to
do so it must first of all unveil the covert differences of treatment.

1.2. A means of detecting concealed exclusory phenomena

The attempt to establish de facto equality necessitates a prior diagnosis.
Where this aim is part of an indirect discriminatory process, it requires

---

24. ECtHR (chamber), *D.H. and Others v. the Czech Republic*, 7 February 2006, Application
No. 57325/00.

25. Supreme Court, 16 December 1993, *Symes v. Canada*, [1993] 4 S.C.R. 685.

26. Supreme Court, *Action travail des femmes v. Canadian National Railway*, [1987] 1
S.C.R. 1134.

27. This definition was presented in a report submitted in 1999 at the request of the
British Home Secretary, concerning the inability of British police and judicial insti-
tutions to deal with racist crime: W. Macpherson, *The Stephen Lawrence Inquiry:
Report of an Inquiry by Sir William Macpherson of Cluny*, Stationery Office, 1999.

28. C. McCrudden, "Institutional Discrimination", *Oxford Journal of Legal Studies*, No. 2,
1982, p. 303.

prior detection of seemingly neutral standards which in fact hamper the achievement of genuine equality.

The Luxembourg and Strasbourg judges have recognised and applied two different methods of determining how an apparently neutral measure can be discriminatory. Drawing on the American "disparate impact" doctrine, the so-called "disproportionate impact" approach is geared to verifying whether a given measure "has disproportionately prejudicial effects on a particular group"[29] or if it affects "a substantially higher proportion" (of the group in question).[30] The second approach, namely unfavourable treatment, consists in pinpointing which measure "by nature, or intrinsically, is liable to disadvantage persons belonging to a category protected against discrimination".[31]

EU law seems so far to have more or less disregarded the disproportionate impact method, whereas the European Court of Human Rights would seem now to be prioritising it. Even though the European Court has agreed that "a discrimination potentially contrary to the Convention may result ... from a de facto situation",[32] there are very few cases where it has adopted the unfavourable treatment criterion.[33]

The disproportionate impact method has many disadvantages.

Firstly, it forces victims to produce statistical evidence of quantified disparities[34] demonstrating that they are predominantly disadvantaged. Furthermore, these data can be accepted by the courts only if they meet certain standards. In addition to reliability, the EU Court demands that they "cover enough individuals, [do not] illustrate purely fortuitous or

---

29. ECtHR, *Jordan v. the United Kingdom,* 4 May 2001, Application No. 24746/94; ECtHR, *Hoogendijk v. the Netherlands,* 6 January 2005, Application No. 58461/00.

30. Council Directive 97/80 of 15 December on the burden of proof in cases of discrimination based on sex, OJ L 14 of 20 January 1998; this directive was repealed on 15 August 2009.

31. O. De Schutter, *Discrimination et marché du travail – liberté et égalité dans les rapports d'emploi,* PIE-Peter Lang, 2001, especially p. 95.

32. ECtHR, *Zarb Adami v. Malta,* 20 June 2006, Application No. 17209/02.

33. See below, Thlimmenos judgment.

34. ECtHR, 6 January 2005, aforementioned Hoogendijk judgment on the matter of payment of disability allowance depending on the beneficiary's and her spouse's income, which means that very many married women are ineligible. For the opposite stance, cf. ECtHR, *Thlimmenos v. Greece,* 6 April 2000, Application No. 34369/97.

short-term phenomena, and ..., in general, ... appear to be significant".[35] As to the European Court of Human Rights, even though it has already contented itself with "sufficiently reliable"[36] data, it calls for "incontrovertible official statistics".[37] However, there is a real burden of statistical proof to the extent that most European states prohibit public statistics on ethnic, religious or linguistic differences. In the light of such obstacles, which are usually constitutional, the European Committee of Social Rights has held that "it is for the State authorities to gather data to gauge the extent of the problem and the progress made in remedying the problem and providing for other remedies not subject to such constitutional restrictions".[38] The European Court has not, however, taken up this interpretation, and to my knowledge it has had no practical impact to date.

Secondly, the disproportionate impact method presupposes demonstrating that a measure genuinely affects a considerably larger proportion of the members of one target group than any other. The discrepancy must therefore be not only noticed but also noticeable.

Conversely, the unfavourable treatment approach is highly conducive to detecting potentially suspect measures. In fact, it accepts mere prima facie suppositions, which have not been demonstrated or even documented, to the effect that the measure in question is inherently liable to be detrimental to a given target group. No reference is made to specific proportions of the population or the fact of a disadvantage actually having been noted. Therefore, it is less concerned with the practical effects of a provision than with its object in the strict sense of the term. EU legislation has prioritised this approach,[39] which was initially used by the European

---

35. CJEC, *Enderby*, 27 October 1993, Case C-127/92.

36. ECtHR, *D.H. and Others v. the Czech Republic* [GC], 13 November 2007, Application No. 57325/00, where, in the absence of official information on the pupils' ethnic origin, the Court used statistics from questionnaires which had not been challenged by the state but might have reflected a slightly subjective approach.

37. Cf. aforementioned Zarb Adami and Hoogendijk cases.

38. ECSR Decision of 8 December 2004, Complaint No. 15/2003, *European Roma Rights Centre v. Greece*; ECSR Decision of 7 December 2005, Complaint No. 27/2004, *European Roma Rights Centre v. Italy.*

39. Although statistical data can nevertheless be used (recital 15 of Directives 2000/43/EC and 2000/78/EC and recital 37 of Directive 2006/54).

Court of Justice in respect of migrants,[40] over the disproportionate impact approach, which the court had implemented in order to detect cases of sexist discrimination.[41] Directives 2000/43/EC and 2000/78/EC only require the victim to be able to pinpoint an apparently neutral measure "liable to cause a particular disadvantage" affecting them, forcing the instigator of the measure to justify its relevance. Implementing this method, the independent anti-discrimination agency in France, the HALDE, held, in the specific case of a Moroccan complainant, that the fact that foreign diploma-holders were not exempted from examinations was liable per se to cause a particular disadvantage for foreigners.[42]

Where no objective, reasonable grounds are given for this finding, it necessitates an amendment to the measure in question.

1.3. A means of ensuring social change

There are various ways of establishing differentiated treatment arising from the prohibition of indirect discrimination against a person or group of persons. Sometimes it is merely a case of abolishing a measure or practice detrimental to the minority group, possibly by granting it the same rights as the majority. In other cases, the social and economic partners must introduce different adjustment measures. This situation has the effect of transforming the rule so that it complies with the requirements of an "inclusive" society vis-à-vis minority population groups.[43] The Court of Justice has never issued any judgments relating to indirect discrimination within the meaning of Directives 2000/43/EC and 2000/787EC, but its case law on indirect discrimination on the grounds of sex provides some initial pointers. On the other hand, the courts and independent bodies responsible for equality in some member states, as well as the European Court of Human Rights, have already developed interesting case law on ethnic and religious discrimination.

---

40. CJEC, Sotgiu, 12 February 1974, Case 152/73; CJEC, O'Flynn, 23 May 1996, Case C-237/94, where the court considered indirectly discriminatory the fact of refunding funeral expenses solely for funerals taking place in the national territory.

41. Regarding the slight incompatibility of this definition in Directive 2002/73 prohibiting discrimination on the grounds of sex in matters of goods and services, see D. Martin, *Egalité et non-discrimination dans la jurisprudence communautaire*, Brussels, 2006, especially pp. 209-210.

42. HALDE Decision No. 2007/113 of 14 May 2007.

43. Cf. the conclusions of the Advocate General, Mr Poiares Maduro, as presented on 31 January 2008 in the Coleman case (Case C-303/06), paragraph 19.

Abolishing the rule detrimental to a specific target group

The Dutch Equality Commission and a Swedish industrial tribunal have ruled that the requirement not to have a foreign accent in order to work as a telephone operator constituted indirect discrimination based on race and/or ethnic origin, whereby the employers were unable to demonstrate the need for and appropriateness of this requirement.[44] Similarly, the Cypriot independent body responsible for equality has held that the obligation to be a Greek-speaker to manage a travel agency represented indirect discrimination on the grounds of race and/or ethnic origin.[45] Even though our sources do not indicate whether the judge and the independent body responsible for equality so ordered, the pure and simple abolition of these measures is the logical consequence of the discrimination finding. Abolishing negative measures can sometimes also lead to extending the rule applicable to the "majority group".

General application of the majority rule

In its Ruzius-Wibrink, Kowalska and Nimz judgments,[46] the Court of Justice of the European Communities dealt with the consequences of a finding of indirect discrimination. The cases concerned a mechanism which excluded part-time workers from certain salary benefits and which, in practice, negatively affected a large proportion of female workers. The court held that "where there is indirect discrimination in a clause in a collective wage agreement, the class of persons placed at a disadvantage ... must be treated in the same way and made subject to the same scheme as other workers, such scheme remaining ... the only valid system of reference". By the same token, the HALDE, dealing with a case of a refusal to exempt foreigners from examinations, recommended introducing equivalence measures for foreign diploma-holders vis-à-vis technical education, on the model of the equivalence already existing in

44. Opinion No. 2004-143 of the Commissie Gelijke Behandling and Arbetdomstolen, 4 December 2002, AD 128/2002, *Ombudsman ethnic discrimination (DO) v. Tjänsföretagens Arbetsgivarförbund* and GfK Sv. Aktiebolag cases quoted by D. Schiek, op. cit., p. 431.

45. This 2006 Cypriot case (Ref. A.K.I. 12/06, report of 1 August 2006) is quoted in C. Tobler, *Limits and Potential of the Concept of Indirect Discrimination*, Office for Official Publications of the European Communities, Luxembourg, September 2008, especially p. 59.

46. CJEC, Ruziuz-Wilbrink, 13 December 1989, Case C-102/88; CJEC, Kowalska, 27 June 1990, Case C-33/89; and CJEC, Nimz, 7 February 1991, Case C-184/89.

the field of higher education.[47] However, it is not always so easy to put an end to indirect discrimination, which sometimes necessitates special adjustment measures.

Establishing a differentiated rule tailored to the target group

In its *Thlimmenos v. Greece* judgment,[48] the European Court of Human Rights addressed a case in which a Jehovah's Witness complained of being excluded from the profession of chartered accountant because of a criminal conviction. The applicant had been sentenced for refusing to effect his military service on the grounds of his religious convictions. The Strasbourg Court, sitting in Grand Chamber, ruled that the applicant was in a clearly different situation from other individuals found guilty of serious crimes because "a conviction for refusing on religious or philosophical grounds to wear the military uniform cannot imply any dishonesty or moral turpitude likely to undermine the offender's ability to exercise this profession". The Court made a finding of religious discrimination because the legislation complained of had failed to introduce "appropriate exceptions to the rule barring persons convicted of a serious crime from the profession of chartered accountants". This case law therefore requires the state to define the types of criminal conviction which do not prevent those concerned from exercising the profession of chartered accountant.

In the more recent case of *D.H. and Others v. the Czech Republic*,[49] the applicants claimed to have suffered indirect discrimination to the extent that in their town, Roma children were 27 times more likely than other children to be placed in specialised schools for mentally disabled children. The Czech authorities actually admitted that these schools provided a low level of education for Roma children "with average or above-average intellect". In fact, this situation resulted from the fact that the choice of school was based on the children's performance in tests which were actually designed for the majority population. No measures had been considered to tailor the tests to Roma children having regard to the specific cultural and linguistic obstacles which they face. Nor had any corrective measure been adopted to interpret the results of these tests, which were in fact biased. The European Court concluded that this policy was indirectly discriminatory, recalling that "as a result of their turbulent history and constant uprooting the Roma [are] a specific type of disadvantaged and

---

47. HALDE Decision No. 2007/113 of 14 May 2007.

48. ECtHR, aforementioned *Thlimmenos v. Greece* judgment, 6 April 2000.

49. Aforementioned judgment, see above.

vulnerable minority ...; they therefore require special protection ...; this protection also extends to the sphere of education". This judgment therefore has the direct result of requiring the Czech authorities to review the tests and the corresponding methodology to prevent them being wrongfully used to the detriment of Roma children.

The European Court of Human Rights had never before established a positive obligation to implement reasonable accommodation, as the Canadian Supreme Court did in its above-mentioned O'Malley judgment. It took the plunge with the *Glor v. Switzerland* judgment of 30 April 2009[50] relating to discrimination on the ground of disability. In this case, the applicant, who suffers from diabetes, complained of having to pay the military-service exemption tax even though he had been declared unfit for military service and had not been permitted to conduct alternative civilian service. This tax, provided for by law, was payable by all men, apart from those with severe disabilities, who had not effected their military service. The alternative civilian service was only available for conscientious objectors. The applicant considered that he had suffered dual discrimination because he had been neither authorised to conduct alternative civilian service nor declared non-liable to the exemption tax.

The Court meticulously considered whether "the existence of a measure less seriously infringing the fundamental right in question [the right to respect for private life] and achieving the same end should be excluded". In particular, it asked "what would prevent introducing special forms of service for persons in similar situations to that of the applicant". Drawing on certain practices observed in Europe, it noted that alternatives to military service did exist in the armed forces in the form of "posts tailored" to the person's degree of disability and occupational skills. The Court also said that it was "convinced that special forms of civilian service tailored to the needs of individuals in the applicant's situation are perfectly feasible". It unanimously concluded that the case involved discrimination.

This approach on the part of the European Court is similar to that adopted in Canada on the subject of the right to reasonable accommodation. This right, defined as "a natural corollary" to the right to equality, necessitates "act[ing] within reason to protect it".[51] This doctrinal development, which

---

50. ECtHR, *Glor v. Switzerland*, 30 April 2009, Application No. 13444/04.

51. Aforementioned Canadian Supreme Court judgment, *Ontario Commission of Human Rights and Theresa O'Malley (Vincent) v. Simpsons-Sears Ltd.*, [1985] 2 S.C.R. 536, 17 December 1985.

is also having an impact in Strasbourg, indicates that the indirect discrimination concept may be creating a new balance between the interests of the community and respect for religious, ethnic and cultural pluralism. Nevertheless, we must be careful about any *mutatis mutandis* transposition of the Glor solution to these issues, because there is not necessarily any "European and universal consensus" here equivalent to that of "shielding persons with disabilities from discriminatory treatment". The fact is that it is probably this consensus which provided the Court with the requisite impetus to make a finding of discrimination in that particular case.

At the national level, the Dutch Equality Commission has held that a restaurant dress code prohibiting any kind of headgear is discriminatory against Muslim women. It considered that the restaurant owner in question could have attracted a high-quality clientele with less coercive measures than requiring "appropriate clothing" or prohibiting caps or sports clothing.[52] Setting out these alternatives therefore provides the restaurant owner with useful information on how to put an end to a discriminatory practice.[53]

In the Kumari Singh case,[54] the British High Court granted a Sikh girl the right to wear a kara (a 5 mm-wide steel bracelet, one of the symbols of the Sikh religion) even though her school's rules prohibited the wearing of jewellery for safety reasons. The British Court ruled that exempting this pupil from the school rules was an appropriate measure. The High Court thus implicitly condemned the school's makeshift solution of authorising

---

52. Opinion 2004-112 of the Commissie Gelijke Behandling of 4 September 2004, quoted in Tobler, op. cit., especially p. 58, and in Schiek, op. cit., pp. 429-430.

53. In a 2005 opinion the same commission considered that earmarking social housing exclusively for those with incomes corresponding to 120% of the minimum wage constituted indirect discrimination on the grounds of ethnic origin. It proposed a number of specific adjustments to the City of Rotterdam, which implemented this kind of policy; Henrard, op. cit., especially p. 66.

54. High Court of Justice, Administrative Court, 29 July 2008, *The Queen on the application of Sarika Watkins-Singh (a child acting by Sanita Kumari Singh, her mother and litigation friend) v. The Governing Body of Aberdare girls' High School and Rhondda Cynon Taf Unitary Authority*, [2008] EWHC 1865 (Admin).

the pupil to wear the kara provided she remained isolated from the other pupils in the school premises.[55]

These examples illustrate the idea that prohibiting indirect discrimination can help "preserve a cultural diversity of value to the whole community",[56] taking account of the "special needs of minorities"[57] or of certain groups of individuals. Such developments should not, however, obscure the limits of the application of this principle in its implementation and interpretation by the European courts. If the differentiated treatment of specific population categories is geared to guaranteeing genuine equality of treatment, it does present a challenge to our social constructs, which the court may consider nonetheless justified.

2. The limits of social transformation: reasons for exclusion measures

"Equality is no mere idealistic aim, but an extremely fierce ideological battlefield. Equality jeopardises advantages. The salient points are freedom of choice, the burden borne by individuals who are not responsible for the inequalities, or more prosaically the costs, identified."[58] Although there is a consensus on the equality principle in our "right-thinking" societies, it is nothing less than a political instrument for social refoundation. Indirect discrimination, which is one facet of equality, is geared to critiquing and reviewing our social structures. It is therefore potentially troublesome, some might say downright dangerous. Just as formal equality has abolished privileges, indirect discrimination can overturn our social equilibriums and overhaul our conceptions of social cohesion.

---

55. This solution is similar to that adopted by the South African Constitutional Court, which condemned a refusal to grant a school dress code exemption to a Tamil girl who wished to wear a ring in her nose as a symbol of her cultural and religious identity; *MEC for Kwazulu-Natal, School Liaison Officer and Others v. Pillay*, CCT 51/06 (2007) ZACC 21

56. ECtHR, *Chapman v. the United Kingdom*, 18 January 2001, Application No. 27238/95.

57. Ibid.

58. M. Garon and P. Bosset, "Le droit à l'égalité: des progrès indéniables, des inégalités persistantes", in *La Charte québécoise des droits et libertés après 25 ans*, Vol. 2, Commission des droits de la personne et des droits de la jeunesse, Montreal, 2003, p. 64.

Moreover, a concept which is largely based on Anglo-Saxon law is not so easy to incorporate into some European legal systems. It should be remembered that a civil law judge does not have the same legitimacy as a common law judge. The former usually prefers to use alternative means, where they exist, to protect specific persons who are deemed vulnerable.[59] Furthermore, the fear of encouraging communitarianism and challenging the law as a general standard are also curbing this process of transposition into continental Europe.

This being the case, is it really any wonder that European legislators and judges have been experiencing some difficulty in fully implementing the concept of indirect discrimination? The concept causes genuine problems of implementation in most European Union countries. Apart from the United Kingdom, Ireland and the Netherlands, many European states have seen no practical application of the concept,[60] or if they have it has been extremely marginal.[61] Even though the HALDE has adopted several decisions highlighting cases of indirect discrimination,[62] France has to date seen only one Court of Cassation judgment making proper use of this concept.[63]

Where the right not to suffer indirect discrimination is concerned, it is always possible to justify an apparently neutral measure which places specific classes of persons at a disadvantage. Merely noting the phenomenon of exclusion of a class of persons resulting from implementation of an ostensibly neutral rule is insufficient to demonstrate the existence of discrimination. It is true that in the light of such an appearance of discrimination, the burden of proof no longer lies with the victim. It is for the person instigating the suspect measure to justify it. However, it is ultimately for the court to assess the merits and proportionality of

---

59. Regarding this finding cf. P. Martin, "Droit social et discriminations sexuelles: à propos des discriminations générées par la loi", Droit social, 1996, pp. 562 ff.

60. To our knowledge, the Czech Republic has no case law on this matter.

61. See M. Bell, I. Chopin and F. Palmer, "Developing Anti-discrimination Law in Europe. The 25 Member States Compared", The European Network of Legal Experts in the Non-discrimination Field, Office for Official Publications of the European Communities, Luxembourg, 2007.

62. For example, Délibération, No. 2008-281 of 15 December 2008 on the refusal, constituting indirect discrimination on grounds of origin, to grant equivalence in France to a nursing auxiliary's diploma obtained by a person of Cameroonian nationality in Belgium, even though such equivalence is granted for EU nationals.

63. Cass. Soc., 9 January 2007, No. 05-43. 962.

the measure in question in the light of its main purpose. Such a legal assessment provides the basis for deciding whether or not the negative measures can be deemed legitimate. Depending on a number of contingencies, such reassessment can have a wide variety of outcomes.

2.1. Flexible assessment of the proportionality of exclusion measures

The supervisory procedure implemented by the EU Court is, a priori, strictly regulated. Secondary Community legislation authorises a suspect measure if it is "objectively justified by a legitimate aim and the means of achieving that aim are appropriate and necessary".[64] This supervision therefore requires the instigator of the discrimination to prove that the negative measure pursues a legitimate aim and that it goes no further than what is needed to that end. (S)he must also demonstrate that there are no alternative measures with a lesser impact on the equality principle.

This proportionality test would appear more restrictive than that of the ECHR, which, we should nevertheless remember, represents a protective guarantee subsidiary to that of the states parties. According to its established case law, the Strasbourg Court verifies whether the measure at issue "pursued a legitimate aim" and "whether there was a reasonable relationship of proportionality between the means employed and the aim sought to be realised".[65] Furthermore, apart from the fact that the "meta-juridical" criterion of reasonableness "may degenerate into a non-legal policy consideration",[66] the European Court grants states a margin of appreciation whose "scope ... will vary according to the circumstances, the subject-matter and its background".[67] As a result, the reasons given for ostensibly discriminatory measures are generally assessed flexibly, or indeed contingently.[68]

---

64. See Article 2(2) of Directives 2000/43/EC, 2000/78/EC, 2004/113/EC and 2006/54/EC.

65. ECtHR, the aforementioned *Thlimmenos v. Greece* judgment, 6 April 2000.

66. See the dissenting opinion of Judge Zupančič in ECtHR judgment, *Chassagnou v. France*, 29 April 1999,.

67. ECtHR, *Rasmussen v. Denmark*, 28 November 1984, Series A No. 87; ECtHR, *Inze v. Austria*, 28 October 1987, Series A No. 126.

68. H. Surrel, "L'appréciation contingente des justifications", in F. Sudre and H. Surrel (eds), *Le droit à la non-discrimination au sens de la Convention européenne des droits de l'homme*, Bruylant, Brussels, pp. 119-158.

The practical applications of the supervision carried out by the EU and European courts show that these divergences may, or may not, lead to different solutions.

In the case of *Asnar v. France*[69] the applicant complained of the discriminatory nature of the rule imposing an effective 15-year period of service in order, under specific conditions, to be able to retire. His career had been interrupted by a period of military service which was compulsory for men, placing him at a disadvantage vis-à-vis female colleagues. The European Court of Human Rights ruled that "the difference in treatment is grounded in the application of the same principle, namely calculating the time effectively spent in the civil service. The Court considers that this principle represents per se an objective and reasonable justification for the difference in treatment". Conversely, in its Nimz judgment of 1993,[70] the European Court of Justice held that the requirement for part-time workers, mostly women, to have double the period of service required of full-time workers to secure a higher salary grade amounted to indirect discrimination because no objective relationship could be shown between the nature of the duties performed and the experience afforded by the performance of those duties after a certain number of working hours had been completed. Even though the proportionality test has never been modified, this approach was relaxed in 2006. In its Cadman judgment, the court considered that "recourse to the criterion of length of service is appropriate to attain the legitimate objective of rewarding experience acquired which enables the worker to perform his duties better, the employer does not have to establish specifically that recourse to that criterion is appropriate to attain that objective as regards a particular job, unless the worker provides evidence capable of raising serious doubts in that regard".[71]

Supervision of proportionality is therefore subject to case-by-case appraisal, the outcome of which would be extremely difficult to predict. However, EU case law is apparently increasingly receptive to certain arguments tending to justify exclusion measures. The economic argument is a case in point.

---

69. ECtHR, *Asnar v. France*, 17 June 2003, Application No. 57030/00.

70. CJEC, Nimz, 7 February 1991, Case C-184/89.

71. CJEC, Cadman, 3 October 2006, Case C-17/05, regarding a salary system taking account of length of service for pay rises.

2.2. The economic cost of abolishing exclusion measures

In the 1980s, the Luxembourg Court built up case law favourable to female workers, prohibiting the withholding of a whole range of benefits from part-time workers, including supplementary retirement pensions, allowances in the event of termination of contract, entitlement to continued payment of salary in the event of illness, etc.[72]

On the other hand, the court's case law has proved more permissive vis-à-vis a series of measures introduced by the public authorities in the 1990s, even though they were detrimental to women. By granting member states a certain "margin of appreciation in the social policy field",[73] the court recognised the justification and/or proportionality of unfavourable measures resulting from such economic factors as the configuration of the employment market,[74] lightening of burdens on SMEs,[75] preservation of balance in the social security system,[76] or the need to ensure proper management of public expenditure.[77] Even if the court says otherwise, this means that "budgetary considerations" underlying social policies may justify exclusion measures in the EU context.[78]

The proportionality test used in the field of indirect discrimination on the grounds of sex suggests that the public authorities are perhaps only marginally required to bear the cost of discrimination.[79] In our view, it is not impossible that this case law should be retained in respect of other types of discrimination on grounds of race, ethnic origin or religion, particularly in the current economic context. However, other factors must be considered in assessing the situation.

---

72. CJEC, Bilka-Kaufhaus, 13 May 1986, Case 170/84; CJEC, Kowalska, 27 June 1990, Case C-33/89; CJEC, Rinner-Kühn, 13 July 1989, Case 171/88. For more recent examples: CJEC, Schröder, 10 February 2000, Case C-50/96; CJEC, Ursula Voß, 6 December 2007, Case C-300/06.

73. CJEC, Seymour Smith and Perez, 9 February 1999, Case C-167/97; CJEC, Kachelmann, 26 September 2000, Case C-322/98.

74. CJEC, Enderby, 27 October 1993, Case C-127/92.

75. CJEC, Kirsammer-Hack, 30 November 1993, Case C-189/91.

76. CJEC, Thomas, 30 March 1993, Case C-329/91; CJEC, Graham, 11 August 1995, Case C-92/94.

77. CJEC, Jorgensen, 6 April 2000, Case C-226/98.

78. CJEC, Nikoloudi, 10 March 2005, Case C-196/02.

79. Regarding the question who bears the cost of discrimination, cf. C. Tobler, "Indirect Discrimination", Intersentia, Antwerp, Oxford, 2005, especially p. 250.

2.3. Contingent appraisal of social cohesion

The relevance and legitimacy of a rule which applies to all and has the effect of excluding certain groups of people are not appraised with the same care depending on the characteristics of each group. The European Court of Human Rights exercises stricter supervision of distinctions vis-à-vis race, nationality and sex because "only very strong considerations" can justify such distinctions.

For instance, in its *Zarb Adami v. Malta* judgment,[80] the Court adjudicated on the conditions for the selection of jurors in the Maltese criminal courts. Having been fined for his fourth refusal to serve as a juror, the applicant challenged the penalty on the grounds that it subjected him to obligations and duties which women did not have to bear. Following a legislative reform, however, women had to serve on juries as frequently as men, at least in theory: male and female jurors were selected from among the working population, in the economic sector and the professions. They enjoyed exemptions in respect of family dependents and could be challenged by lawyers, irrespective of their sex. However, the simple fact is that the juries are still principally made up of men. Asked to explain this statistical finding, the Maltese Government pointed out that for "cultural reasons" lawyers tended to challenge female jurors, and "for social-cultural reasons" women found it easier to be exempted because of their family responsibilities. These explanations did not convince the Court, which made a finding of indirect discrimination.

Where racial discrimination is concerned, the Court also firmly condemned the school segregation of Roma children in the above-mentioned *D.H. and Others v. the Czech Republic* judgment: it is "shameful that such a situation should exist in Europe in the 21st century".[81] However, this case law favourable to the Roma people is still an isolated case. Despite their tradition of living and travelling in caravans, the Court has never recognised their right to be treated differently under the general rules on urban and rural planning and development.[82] Similarly, even though it was adjudicating after the D.H. judgment, the 5th Section of the Court refused to

---

80. ECtHR, aforementioned *Zarb Adami v. Malta* judgment, 20 June 2006.

81. In the words of Judge Jungwiert in his dissenting opinion in the case of *D.H. v. the Czech Republic*.

82. ECtHR, aforementioned *Chapman v. the United Kingdom* judgment, 18 January 2001.

consider that language tests leading mainly Roma children to be placed in special classes might point to indirect racial discrimination.[83]

Nor is its case law very promising vis-à-vis other groups which are ultimately linguistic or religious minorities,[84] although a careful reading of a number of scattered judgments seems to offer a number of openings.[85] At all events, the European Court recognises that this kind of situation represents a separate category in disputes relating to religious freedom in which it must pronounce on "the compatibility with the Convention of the interpretation of a law which is, on the face of it, neutral as regards the exercise of freedom of worship".[86] The fact remains that the above-mentioned *Thlimmenos v. Greece* judgment constitutes an exception. The European Court of Human Rights has shown little inclination to recognise a difference of situation requiring differentiated treatment of religious minorities, even in its most recent case law.[87] In general terms, therefore, since it is impossible to "discern throughout Europe a uniform conception of the significance of religion in society",[88] the Court respects national conceptions relating to "the meaning or impact of acts corresponding to the public expression of a religious conviction".[89]

Accordingly, the Court has systematically refused to consider that persons wearing religious symbols can be exempted from general health and

---

83. ECtHR, *Oršuš and Others v. Croatia*, 17 July 2008, Application No. 15766/03. The case has now been brought before the Grand Chamber.

84. Cf. ECtHR, Belgian Linguistic Case, 23 July 1968, Series A No. 6; ECtHR, *Mathieu-Mohin and Clerfayt v. Belgium*, 2 March 1987, Series A No. 133; and ECtHR, *Podkolzina v. Latvia*, 9 April 2002. Regarding these judgments, cf. J. Ringelheim, *Diversité culturelle et droits de l'homme. La protection des minorités par la Convention européenne des droits de l'homme*, Bruylant, Brussels, 2006, esp. pp. 278 ff, 298 ff and 184 ff.

85. For example, European Commission of Human Rights, *S.H. and H.V. v. Austria*, 13 January 1993, which suggests that under certain circumstances persons of the Jewish faith should be able to secure postponement of judicial hearings set for the date of a major Jewish festival. E. Bribosia, J. Ringelheim and I. Rorive, "Aménager la diversité: le droit à l'égalité face à la pluralité religieuse", *Revue trimestrielle des Droits de l'Homme*, April 2009, pp. 319-373.

86. ECtHR, *Vergos v. Greece*, 24 June 2004, Application No. 65501/01, paragraph 40.

87. ECtHR, *Shingara Mann Singh v. France*, 13 November 2008, Application No. 24479/07.

88. ECtHR, *Otto-Preminger-Institut v. Austria*, 20 September 1994, Application No. 13470/87.

89. Cf., for example, ECtHR, *Dahlab v. Switzerland*, 15 February 2001, Application No. 42393/98.

safety rules. It holds that "pluralism and democracy must … be based on dialogue and a spirit of compromise necessarily entailing various concessions on the part of individuals which are justified in order to maintain and promote the ideals and values of a democratic society".[90] Moreover, although this case law is now fairly old and has been greatly criticised, the European Commission of Human Rights saw no religious discrimination against Muslim and Seventh Day Adventist employees who, because of certain religious prescripts, could not work at specific times and had therefore been dismissed.[91] In its recent *Kervanci* and *Dogru v. France* judgments,[92] the European Court of Human Rights accepted the expulsion of two lower secondary schoolgirls for absenteeism from physical education classes. The reason for their failure to attend was that they had been prohibited from wearing the Islamic headscarf during these lessons. In these cases the Strasbourg Court had ignored the applicants' proposal to replace their headscarves with hats, and had seemed content with the fact that the applicants had been able to continue their education by correspondence. Nor did it draw any legal consequence from the fact that at the time of the incidents, "*des traitements circonstanciés*" (various types of alternative approaches) had been observed in some schools.

The Strasbourg Court has thus adopted a similar stance to that of the individual states, which generally do not recognise minorities or which attach vital importance to the observance of secularism. In two recent judgments, issued on 17 March 2009,[93] the Belgian Conseil d'Etat deemed inadmissible an anti-discrimination association which challenged the prohibition of headgear as stipulated in the rules of a specific secondary school. It stated that "the rule complained of, far from infringing the applicant's

---

90. ECtHR, *Dogru v. France*, 4 December 2008, Application No. 27058/05, and ECtHR, *Kervanci v. France*, 4 December 2008, Application No. 31645/04.

91. European Commission of Human Rights: *X. v. the United Kingdom*, 12 March 1981, DR 22, p. 39; *Stedman v. the United Kingdom*, 9 April 1997, DR 89-B, p. 104. Regarding these cases and the subsequent Konttinen and Kostesk cases, see Bribosia, Ringelheim and Rorive, op. cit., and J. Ringelheim, "Le multiculturalisme aux miroirs de la jurisprudence de la Convention européenne des droits de l'homme", *Revue de l'Association française pour les Nations Unies*, Section Aix-en-Provence, 2007, Vol. 23, No. 2, pp. 1-33.

92. ECtHR, aforementioned *Dogru v. France* and *Kervanci v. France* judgments, 4 December 2008.

93. CE, *MRAX v. the French Community and Vauban Royal Secondary School*, 17 March 2009, No. 191.532; CE, *MRAX v. Gilly Royal Secondary School*, 17 March 2009, No. 191.533.

social purpose [wearing her headscarf], had the effect of confirming and consolidating it". Concurrently, on 31 March 2009, the Paris Administrative Court ruled that the discharge of a female official from the postal service "was motivated not by her belonging to the Seventh Day Adventist Church or the Post Office administration's desire to discourage her religious practice, but by the person's persistent and culpable decision not to work on Saturday in breach of the new organisation of the service", even though she had had Saturdays off for the previous 19 years of her career.[94]

This position contrasts radically with the tradition in English-speaking countries, where religious freedom is one of the founding values of all public freedoms. For instance, in its famous Multani judgment,[95] the Canadian Supreme Court recognised that the symbolic value of the kirpan (a small steel dagger with a curved blade, which is one of the symbols of the Sikh religion) was such that it could not be equated with a weapon and that consequently students could not be prohibited from wearing it to school. Judge Danielle Grenier of the Quebec Superior Court had ordered such specific measures of adjustment as the obligation to wear the kirpan sealed inside a wooden sheath sewn safely inside solid material, covered up by the student's clothing.

As for the EU court, it has not yet had occasion to pronounce on situations of religious discrimination, apart from its old Viven Prais case law.[96] In this case, nonetheless, it had held that the administration was required to hold competitive examinations on dates not coinciding with religious festivals, where possible. If this first tentative case law were followed up, the position of religion, at least in the employment field, might undergo some change in a number of member states. In any case, with the entry into force of the Lisbon Treaty, it would have an additional legal grounding to move certain areas forwards. For the first time in EU construction, the treaty recognises minorities. Article 1.a reads as follows: "The Union is founded on the values of respect for … the rights of persons belonging to minorities", which "values are common to the Member States in a society in which pluralism … prevail[s]".

---

94. CAA Paris, *Marie Henriette X v. La Poste*, 31 March 2009, No. 08PA01648.

95. Supreme Court, *Multani v. Commission scolaire Margerite-Bourgeoys*, [2006] 1 S.C.R. 256, 2 March 2006.

96. CJEC, Viven Prais, 27 October 1976, Case C-130-75.

As the European Court of Human Rights put it in its famous Gorzelick judgment, "the harmonious interaction of persons and groups with varied identities is essential for achieving social cohesion".[97] The right not to suffer indirect discrimination is a suitable legal instrument for guaranteeing respect for ethnic, religious and cultural diversity in our Western societies. It forces our social structures to go beyond appearances, to take a fresh look at themselves and if necessary to adapt in order to meet the needs of new groups of citizens.

Nevertheless, the use of indirect discrimination is subject to appraisals which can vary, or indeed diverge. Depending on the legal, social and societal cultures, an identical situation may be reassessed to give rise to reasonable accommodation or, on the contrary, be preserved as its stands despite its exclusory effect. It is therefore the harnessing of the indirect discrimination concept rather than the concept itself which can help pinpoint different shades of responses to the question of respect for diversity. The courts must provide stimuli to this end, calling for the requisite reforms or even revolutions, drawing on the example of the American Supreme Court in its famous Brown judgment.[98] But should we leave the courts the entire responsibility for deciding whether the collective rule should be imposed on all or whether some individuals or groups should enjoy special regulations? In our view, this calls for a full-scale democratic debate.

---

97. ECtHR, *Gorzelik v. Poland* [GC], 17 February 2004, Application No. 44158/98.

98. Supreme Court, *Brown et al. v. Board of Education of Topeka et al.*, 347 US 483, 17 May 1957, declaring school segregation of white and black students unconstitutional.

Emerging standards of reasonable accommodation towards minorities in Europe?

Jennifer Jackson Preece[1]

1. Introduction

The concept of reasonable accommodation creates a positive obligation incumbent upon public service providers and employers to ensure substantive equality of opportunity for their clients and employees. Reasonable accommodations may include modifications or adjustments to the work or public environment or to the manner or circumstances under which the job is performed or the service provided. Crucially, however, any such accommodation must be proportionate; an accommodation that would impose an undue hardship upon the institution or employer or that fundamentally alters the nature of the service or business is generally not considered reasonable.

Reasonable accommodation regimes of varying scope and content may be found in several jurisdictions. In the United States, for example, a concept of reasonable accommodation is included in the Americans with Disabilities Act (1990),[2] where it protects the rights of disabled employees, and in Title VII of the Civil Rights Act (1964),[3] where it prohibits employers from discriminating against employees because of their religion. In Canada, following on from the 1999 Canadian Supreme Court decision in Meiorin,[4] all positive obligations arising from the Canadian Charter of Rights and Freedoms' Article 15 – equality provisions (including race, national or ethnic origin, colour, religion, sex, age or mental or physical disability) – are subject to a duty to accommodate to the point of undue hardship. The Council Directive establishing a general framework

1.   Senior Lecturer, European Institute and International Relations Department, London School of Economics, London (United Kingdom).

2.   United States, Americans With Disabilities Act (1990), available at www.ada.gov/pubs/ada.htm, accessed 15 May 2009.

3.   United States, Civil Rights Act (1964), available at http://uspolitics.about.com/od/civilrightsact/Civil_Rights_Act.htm, accessed 15 May 2009.

4.   *British Columbia (Public Service Employee Relations Commission) v. British Columbia Government and Service Employees' Union (BCGSEU)*, [1999] 3 S.C.R. 3, referred to as the Meiorin case.

for equal treatment in employment and occupation (2000)[5] introduces a EU-wide obligation to provide reasonable accommodation to persons with disabilities. This article will examine whether, and to what extent, already existing European standards in the area of equality support the emergence of a broader norm in favour of reasonable accommodation towards minorities.

2. The "European equality duty"

The core idea implicit within reasonable accommodation is that equality should extend beyond procedural requirements that ensure similar cases should be treated similarly to include substantive guarantees which recognise the need to treat different cases differently. This assumption in turn gives rise to an "equality duty" that public institutions and employers are expected to satisfy through positive measures. In assessing the emergence of reasonable accommodation within European law, it is thus necessary to elaborate the core content of the existing "European equality duty". Once this has been established, it will then become possible to examine the possibilities and limitations of extending this duty to include the reasonable accommodation of persons belonging to minorities.

What I have termed the "European equality duty" does not exist as a single, comprehensive statement. Instead, European norms of equal rights and protection against discrimination may be found across a wide array of European Union (EU) and European human rights law. While there is much inconsistency in this growing corpus of codification and associated case law, one can nevertheless discern a common pattern of development from early attempts that were mostly focused on procedural issues towards a more substantive view of equality.

2.1. EU law

Problems of equality and discrimination initially entered into EU law as procedural requirements of the Common Market project. It was immediately apparent that the Common Market between member states required procedural equality in employment rights for all nationals. For this reason, discrimination on grounds of nationality was prohibited in Article 12 of the EC Treaty (1957) which stipulates that: "Within the scope of the application of this Treaty, and without prejudice to any special provisions

---

5. Directive 2000/78/EC; OJ L 303, 2 December 2000, p. 16.

contained therein, any discrimination on grounds of nationality shall be prohibited."

This basic guarantee was augmented by a variety of other procedural provisions including, *inter alia*, EC Treaty Article 39(2), which defines the principle of free movement to include the prohibition of nationality discrimination in employment, remuneration, and other conditions of work and employment and the subsequent Regulation (EEC) 1612/68 on free movement for workers within the Community, which ensures equality of social and tax advantages. At the outset, these guarantees were understood to protect against direct discrimination. But soon the European Court of Justice came to recognise that the prohibition on nationality discrimination included indirect as well as direct forms of discrimination.[6]

A similar progression may be observed with regard to gender equality, the only other equality provision included in the original EC Treaty. Here too, the original intention was to prevent procedural asymmetries between member states with respect to gender equality from distorting competition within the Common Market. It was feared those jurisdictions in which gender equality pay provisions had been implemented would lose business to other jurisdictions with cheaper female labour. Accordingly, Article 119 of the EEC Treaty (now Article 141 of the EC Treaty) guaranteed equal pay for men and women. But it was only in the 1970s that the European Court of Justice began to put this guarantee into direct effect, allowing individuals to rely on this provision as the basis for enforcing equal pay from member states.[7] There followed a number of directives which reinforced the principle of gender equality in the workplace including, *inter alia*, the Directive on the implementation of the principle of equal treatment for men and women as regards access to employment, vocational training and promotion, and working conditions (1976) (Directive 76/207/EEC), the Directive on the progressive implementation of the principle of equal treatment for men and women in matters of social security (1979) (Directive 7/79/EEC), the Directive on implementation of the principle of equal treatment for men and women in occupational social security schemes (1986) (86/378/EEC), the Directive on the application of the principle of equal treatment of men and women engaged in an activity, including

---

6. Case 15/69, *Wurttembergische Milchverwertung-Sudmilch-AG v. Salvatore Ugliola* [1969] ECR 363.
7. Case 80/70, *Defrenne v. Belgian State* (I) [1971] ECR 445.

agriculture, in a self-employed capacity (86/613/EEC), and the Directive on the burden of proof in cases of discrimination based on sex (1997) (97/80/EC). In 2006, the Directive on the implementation of the principle of equal opportunities and equal treatment of men and women in matters of employment and occupation (recast) (2006/54/EC) was adopted which brought together these various gender equality provisions along with some principles established under the European Court of Justice's case law to provide a comprehensive statement of gender equality. This Recast Directive recognised both direct and indirect discrimination and positive measures intended to promote equal treatment between the sexes.

In 1999, with the coming into effect of the Treaty of Amsterdam, the EU acquired a broader mandate in the area of equality and protection from discrimination. Article 13(1) of the EC Treaty gave the Community competency to take appropriate action to combat discrimination based on sex, racial or ethnic origin, religion or belief, disability, and age or sexual orientation.[8] This article provided a legal basis for broadening the scope of EU equality provisions, and thus resulted in two further directives – the Council Directive implementing the principle of equal treatment between persons irrespective of racial or ethnic origin (2000/43/EC) and the Council Directive establishing a general framework for equal treatment in employment and occupation (2000/78/EC). These two new directives not only extend the scope of equality protection to new categories of persons but also strengthen the substantive content of that protection by recognising new forms of discrimination (for example, harassment and failure to make a reasonable accommodation – see below) and by paying far greater attention to effective enforcement than was hitherto the case.[9] Finally, the Charter of Fundamental Rights of the European Union, although currently a declaratory statement, identifies both procedural and substantive equality as core values of the EU and its member states.[10] The charter will become binding once the Lisbon Treaty (2007) enters into force.

---

8. The Treaty of Amsterdam (2007), available at www.eurotreaties.com/amsterdam treaty.pdf, accessed 15 May 2009.

9. Waddington and Bell, "More Equal than Others: Distinguishing European Equality Directives", *Common Market Law Review*, 38, 2001, pp. 587-611.

10. The Charter of Fundamental Rights of the European Union, available at http://ec.europa.eu/justice_home/unit/charte/index_en.html, accessed 15 May 2009.

2.2. European human rights law

European human rights law also discloses an understanding of equality that was initially largely confined to procedural matters but, over time, has grown to include a more substantive dimension. Article 14 of the European Convention on Human Rights (ECHR) (1950) stipulates that the "enjoyment of the rights and freedoms set forth in this convention shall be secured without discrimination on any ground such as sex, race, colour, language, religion, political or other opinion, national or social origin, association with a national minority, property, birth or status".[11] Initially, the European Court of Human Rights largely limited itself to cases of direct discrimination. But, more recently, its decisions have acknowledged the difficulties created by indirect discrimination and the substantive view of equality this entails. In *Thlimmenos v. Greece*, for example, the Court found that Article 14 also applies to situations where states fail to treat differently persons whose circumstances are significantly different.[12] Following on from this, in *D.H. and Others v. the Czech Republic*, the Court established that Article 14 applies not only to individual acts of discrimination but also to systemic practices directed at racial or ethnic groups. Even more importantly, the judgment in D.H. ruled that "a difference in treatment may take the form of disproportionately prejudicial effects of a general policy or measure which, though couched in neutral terms, discriminates against a racial or ethnic group" and, for the first time, the Court specifically acknowledged that such a situation may amount to "indirect discrimination" in breach of the ECHR. The Court also established that intent was not a requirement in cases of indirect discrimination, that an allegation of indirect discrimination shifts the burden of proof to the state, and that statistics are not a prerequisite for finding indirect discrimination. Thus the landmark decision in D.H. effectively brought the Court's Article 14 jurisprudence into line with the principles of anti-discrimination law that prevail within the EU.

---

11. European Convention on Human Rights (1950), available at www.hri.org/docs/ ECHR50.html, accessed 15 May 2009.

12. *Thlimmenos v. Greece*, ECtHR, judgment of 6 April 2000, paragraph 44. See also Jenny E. Goldschmidt, "Reasonable Accommodation in EU Equality Law in a Broader Perspective", *ERA Forum*, 8, 2007, pp. 39-48.

2.3. A broader context of equality and non-discrimination law

EU law and European human rights law do not exist in isolation. They are themselves embedded in a larger body of practice having to do with equality and non-discrimination. Member states of the European Union and the Council of Europe are also signatories to a variety of international treaties which further specify such obligations, including among others the International Covenant on Civil and Political Rights (ICCPR) (1966), the International Covenant on Economic, Social and Cultural Rights (ICESCR) (1966), the International Convention on the Elimination of All Forms of Racial Discrimination and the UNESCO Convention against Discrimination in Education (1960). Here, too, the approach taken combines procedural and substantive understandings of equality and allows for positive measures intended to combat the latter. The generally accepted view is that equality does not entail identity of treatment and that there are circumstances in which the law is justified in making distinctions between individuals or groups. Indeed, in its first general comment, the Committee on Economic, Social and Cultural Rights states that "an initial step towards the realization of the Covenant rights is to identify the disadvantaged sectors of the population, which should be the focus of positive State action aimed at securing the full realization of their rights".[13] Moreover, the prohibition of discrimination is not held to preclude positive measures being taken in favour of disadvantaged groups. For example, in its general comment on Article 26 of the ICCPR (a general non-discrimination clause), the Human Rights Committee notes that:

> the principle of equality sometimes requires States parties to take affirmative action in order to diminish or eliminate conditions which cause or help to perpetuate discrimination prohibited by the Covenant. For example, in a State where the general conditions of a certain part of the population prevent or impair their enjoyment of human rights, the State should take specific action to correct those conditions. Such action may involve granting for a time to the part of the population concerned certain preferential treatment in specific matters as compared with the rest of the population. However, as long as such action is needed to correct discrimination in fact, it is a case of legitimate differentiation under the Covenant.[14]

---

13. United Nations Committee on Economic, Social and Cultural Rights, General Comment No. 1, paragraph 3 in HRI/GEN/Rev.4 (2000).

14. United Nations Human Rights Committee, General Comment No. 18, paragraph 10 in HRI/GEN/1/Rev.4 (2000).

In sum, the workings of the various UN treaty bodies are consistent with the rationale that such prohibition is only directed at distinctions which lack an objective or reasonable basis.

2.4. Basic obligations arising under the "European equality duty"

The basic obligations arising under the "European equality duty" extrapolated from European Union and European human rights law and reinforced by a broader context of international law and practice in the area of equality and non-discrimination may be summarised as follows:

- equality is understood in both procedural and substantive terms;

- there is an obligation to treat similar cases the same, and dissimilar cases differently;

- "direct discrimination" shall be taken to occur where one person is treated less favourably than another is, has been or would be treated in a comparable situation;

- "indirect discrimination" may take the form of disproportionately prejudicial effects of a general policy or measure which, though couched in neutral terms, discriminates against a particular group – this holds true even absent discriminatory intent;

- when it comes to assessing the impact of an allegedly discriminatory measure or practice on an individual or group, statistics may be relevant but are not a requirement;

- allegations of indirect discrimination shift the burden of proof to the respondent who must show that the difference in treatment is not discriminatory;

- positive measures may be required to diminish or eliminate conditions which cause or help to perpetuate discrimination against particular disadvantaged groups within society;

- the general prohibition of discrimination determines the outer limits of legitimate positive measures – it is widely held that such measures are justifiable only in so far as they are specific, proportionate and do not constitute undue hardship.

3. Scope for reasonable accommodation towards minorities?

3.1. Positive measures

Having outlined the basic content of the "European equality duty", it is now possible to evaluate the potential scope for extending positive measures of reasonable accommodation to persons belonging to minorities. "Positive measures" is an umbrella term used to describe a variety of practices aimed at addressing historical or structural disadvantages of particular groups and thus facilitating a higher degree of substantive equality for the members of such disadvantaged groups. Such practices may include measures aimed at identifying and removing discriminatory practices; target policies intended to increase the proportion of an under-represented group by using criteria such as geographic location that do not overly discriminate; outreach programmes (information, training, education, etc.) intended to improve the social inclusion of disadvantaged groups; and accommodation programmes intended to reduce barriers to participation by offering personal accommodation based on a combination of merit and disadvantaged group membership.[15] The "European equality duty" is consistent with positive measures of this kind.

Both the Race Equality Directive and the Framework Directive on Equal Treatment in Employment and Occupation contain positive measure provisions. Article 5 of the Race Equality Directive emphasises that:

> With a view to ensuring full equality in practice, the principle of equal treatment shall not prevent any Member State from maintaining or adopting specific measures to prevent or compensate for disadvantages linked to racial or ethnic origin.

Article 7(1) of the more general Framework Directive on Equal Treatment in Employment and Occupation is similarly worded:

> With a view to ensuring full equality in practice, the principle of equal treatment shall not prevent any Member State from maintaining or adopting specific measures to prevent or compensate for disadvantages linked to any of the grounds referred to in Article 1.

---

15. Marc de Vos, *Beyond Formal Equality: Positive Action Under Directives 2000/43/EC and 2000/78/EC,* European Commission, 2007, pp. 13-14.

Both directives thus recognise the desirability of positive measures in certain circumstances but they do not make such measures compulsory. This is in keeping with the European Court of Justice's case law which regards positive measures as an exception that must be specific to its justification (*Bilka, Commission v. France, Abrahamsson, Briheche*).[16] While this may at first glance appear to be a rather narrow interpretation of positive measures, it nevertheless also recognises the overriding importance of circumstance in delineating the scope for legitimate action. The obvious implication here is that the different circumstances confronting different groups may legitimately justify different standards of treatment, which adds an important element of adaptability, and potentially even elasticity, to the concept of positive measures.

3.2. Reasonable accommodation

Reasonable accommodation is a type of positive measure. Its purpose is to remove barriers to access or participation for members of certain disadvantaged groups in those circumstances where it is equitable to do so. Disadvantage is herein understood to extend beyond economic indicators of relative poverty or deprivation to include social indicators of dignity and respect. Dignity and respect are intrinsic to an individual's self-worth and happiness. Crucially, however, these intrinsic social goods do not originate within the individual but are conferred by majority public opinion. History demonstrates that in a pluralist society comprised of a variety of ethnic, cultural, racial and other identities, majority public opinion tends to disadvantage minority groups in the marketplace for social goods.[17] Because minority ways of life frequently differ, often visibly, from majority expectations there is a propensity for majority public opinion to regard minority life choices with misunderstanding, suspicion and sometimes even hostility. Majority attitudes of this kind often have the net effect of disparaging those individuals who choose to exercise minority life choices – a dynamic that state neutrality towards the manifestation of identity is powerless to prevent. The reasonable accommodation of minority

---

16. Case 170/84, *Bilka-Kaufhaus GmbH v. Weber von Hartz* [1986] IRLR 317; Case 35/97, *Commission v. France* [1998] ECR I-5325; Case 407/98, *Abrahamsson and Anderson v. Fogelqvist* [2000] ECR I-5539; Case 319/03, *Briheche v. Ministre de L'Intérieur, Ministre de l'Éducation Nationale and Ministre de la Justice* [2004] ECR I-8807.

17. Jennifer Jackson Preece, *Minority Rights: Between Diversity and Community*, Polity Press, 2005.

identities is intended to constrain and aspires to reverse that tyranny of public opinion which is habitually biased against minority lifestyles.

Reasonable accommodation should not be confused with positive or affirmative action (yet another variant under the rubric of positive measures). Accordingly, employers are free to specify necessary job qualifications and to insist that all appointed persons possess such qualifications. Indeed, the core idea of a reasonable accommodation assumes that an individual member of a disadvantaged group is otherwise competent but requires some necessary adjustments, for example in work environment or work schedule, to ensure their equal and effective participation. For this reason, reasonable accommodations are not block exemptions. They are directed at the individual member of the group and not the group per se, prescribed only where necessary, and are tailored to the specific characteristics of each and every case.

The "European equality duty" incorporates criteria for reasonable accommodation. For example, Article 5 of the Framework Directive on Equal Treatment in Employment and Occupation creates a duty of reasonable accommodation for disabled workers:

> In order to guarantee compliance with the principle of equal treatment in relation to persons with disabilities, reasonable accommodation shall be provided. This means that employers shall take appropriate measures, where needed in a particular case, to enable a person with a disability to have access to, participate in or advance in employment, or to undergo training, unless such measures would impose a disproportionate burden on the employer.

Similar accommodation duties, although rare, are also imposed with respect to pregnant workers and workers who have recently given birth (EC Directive 92/85) and young workers (EC Directive 94/33).

While the language of accommodation as such is not typical of other areas of European discrimination law and practice, such differences may be more a matter of form than of content:

> To the extent that a difference exists between disability and other prohibited grounds [of discrimination], it is in the level of recognition that is currently afforded as to when certain forms of disability discrimination take place. For the most part, anti-discrimination laws in respect of the other prohibited grounds are concerned with the removal of considerations that are (or have become via the operation

of law) quite obviously irrelevant. Whereas in the context of disability, the prohibition is typically seeking to remove considerations that, for many in today's society, would at first glance appear to be relevant and it is here that the duty to accommodate operates to correctly steer the legal analysis and provide the necessary clarification.[18]

There is no obvious reason why a similar logic should not be applied to other contexts where analogous societal assumptions are also impeding full equality for the members of certain disadvantaged groups, most notably persons belonging to minorities.

3.3. Religion or belief

Equal rights and anti-discrimination law pertaining to religion or belief is an interesting case in point. Here, as with respect to disability, widespread societal assumptions frequently complicate efforts to ensure full equality for persons belonging to religious minorities. Indeed, a Eurobarometer survey conducted in January 2007 found that 44% of Europeans considered discrimination based on religion or belief to be widespread.[19] Similar findings have been cited by the European Network Against Racism[20] and the United Nations Special Rapporteur on Freedom of Religion or Belief and the United Nations Special Rapporteur on Contemporary Forms of Racism, Racial Discrimination, Xenophobia and Related Forms of Intolerance.[21]

The "European equality duty" currently provides protection against discrimination on grounds of religion or belief through prohibitions of both direct and indirect discrimination, harassment and victimisation. Provisions of relevance to this protection may be found in the EU Equality Directive, the ECHR, the European Social Charter, and the Charter of Fundamental Rights of the European Union, among others. Thus far, these provisions have not been interpreted to impose a duty of reasonable accommodation per se on grounds of religion or belief. But one could easily foresee circumstances in which a request for reasonable accommodation could

---

18. R. White, "EU Disability Policy and the Equal Opportunity Principle", Sheffield Hallam University Law Research Group Papers (Sheffield, 2005), pp. 7-8.

19. European Commission, "Discrimination in the European Union", *Eurobarometer*, 263, 2007, p. 14.

20. See various reports available at www.enar-eu.org, accessed 21 May 2009.

21. See various reports available at www2.ohchr.org/english/issues/racism/rapporteur/index.htm, accessed 21 May 2009.

be formulated, and justified, in terms analogous to those currently used under the disability rights rubric. Does the requirement to work on a day which conflicts with the obligations of religious observance put members of particular religions at a disadvantage compared with members of other religions or those with secular beliefs? If so, should work schedule adjustments intended to facilitate religious observance be required so long as they do not entail undue hardship? Similarly, do uniform requirements which conflict with religious dress observances constitute a barrier to equal participation? If so, is it reasonable to expect uniform exemptions with respect to religious dress? Just as in the context of disability, the requirements of substantive equality may compel the removal of regulations like those noted above which, for many in society, appear to be legitimate and yet, on further consideration, are seen to constitute an illegitimate barrier to equal access or participation.

The EU Network of Independent Experts on Fundamental Rights in their "Thematic Comment No. 3: The Protection of Minorities in the European Union" (2005), argues that freedom of religion in Europe should be viewed as:

> imposing on both public and private parties an obligation to provide reasonable accommodation to all religious faiths, where the application of generally applicable and neutral [policies] might otherwise result in indirect discrimination on the grounds of religious belief.[22]

Already, as early as 1976, the European Court of Justice ruled in *Vivien Prais v. Council* that employers are "obliged to take reasonable steps to avoid fixing for a test a date which would make it impossible for a person of a particular religious persuasion to undergo the test".[23] Similarly, in *Thlimmenos v. Greece*, as has already been recalled, the European Court of Human Rights found that the refusal to take into account the religious beliefs of a job applicant in certain circumstances can constitute indirect discrimination.[24] In addition to this body of case law, positive state duties with respect to religion and especially religious minorities may be derived from Article 5, paragraph 1, of the Framework Convention for the

---

22. EU Network of Independent Experts on Fundamental Rights, "Thematic Comment No. 3: Protection of Minorities in the EU", 2005, p. 34, available online at http://ec.europa.eu/justice_home/cfr_cdf/doc/thematic_comments_2005_en.pdf, accessed 15 May 2009.

23. Case 130/74, *Vivien Prais v. Council* [1976], ECR I – 01589.

24. See *supra* footnote 12.

Protection of National Minorities (1995), which requires state signatories to "promote the conditions necessary for persons belonging to national minorities to practice their religion".[25] The EU Network of Independent Experts on Fundamental Rights notes a growing corpus of practice amongst EU member states that allows for certain accommodations towards religious minorities, most notably with respect to religious dietary requirements, the observance of religious holidays, and, albeit controversially, in some cases also religious dress.[26]

Perhaps even more significantly, there has been some speculation that the EU Equality Directive creates an indirect duty to make reasonable accommodations on the basis of religion or belief.[27] In the absence of specific agreements for accommodation, the refusal to accommodate religious beliefs or practices may be construed as indirect discrimination, which is prohibited under the directive. Take, for example, the issue of rescheduling work hours to accommodate religious observance. If a request to attend a religious observance on Saturday contrary to usual working hours is denied, then this puts the religiously observant employee at a disadvantage as compared with other employees, and would, therefore, need to be justified. If justification in the area of religion is subject to the same burden of proof currently used with respect to gender equality in employment, then the employer will be expected to show that the refusal has a legitimate aim and that this aim is appropriate and necessary.

Interestingly, the requirement for reasonable accommodation of religion entered into US jurisprudence in just such a manner. In 1972, Title VII of the United States Civil Rights Act (1964) was amended to incorporate a duty on the employer to accommodate the religious practices of employees so long as this did not impose undue hardship on the employer. However, whereas under the Americans with Disabilities Act undue hardship is interpreted to constitute significant difficulty or expense, under Title VII (religion provisions) undue hardship includes anything that imposes more than a minimal cost on an employer. Common accommodations arising under the Title VII provisions include the rescheduling of work for religious

25. Council of Europe, Framework Convention for the Protection of National Minorities (1995), available at http://conventions.coe.int/Treaty/Commun/QueVoulezVous.asp?NT=157&CL=ENG, accessed 16 May 2009.

26. EU Network of Independent Experts on Fundamental Rights, op. cit., pp. 35-40.

27. Lucy Vickers, *Religion and Belief Discrimination in Employment – The EU Law*, European Commission, 2006.

observance and amendments to or derogations from uniform requirements to allow for religious dress.

Similar requirements with respect to indirect discrimination and religion
or belief in the workplace are already apparent in the national implementation strategies of EU member states regarding their Equality Directive
obligations. Thus, it appears that reasonable accommodation practices,
although not directly stipulated, are emerging within European Union
member states as a consequence of EU prohibitions against indirect
discrimination. These practices include flexible work arrangements to
enable religious observance and religious dress exemptions to uniform
requirements. Even more importantly, the failure to provide such accommodation is being subject to objective justification tests that require
employers to prove indirect discrimination is not taking place.

For example, although the term reasonable accommodation is not used,
the Employment Equality (Religion or Belief) Regulations (2003)[28] which
transpose the Equality Directive undertakings with respect to religion
into UK law effectively place a comparable duty upon employers. Indirect
discrimination on the basis of religion or belief is prohibited by the
Employment Equality (Religion or Belief) Regulations. Indirect discrimination is herein understood to mean that an organisation must not have
selection criteria, policies, employment rules or any other practices which,
although they are applied to all employees, have the effect of disadvantaging persons of a particular religion or belief unless the practice can
be justified. This definition of indirect discrimination extends coverage to
include practices of religious observance and dress.[29] To justify any alleged
act of indirect discrimination, an employer must demonstrate that the
practice in question has a legitimate aim, and that the practice is proportionate to that aim (namely, necessary and there are no alternative means
available).[30]

---

28. United Kingdom, Employment Equality (Religion or Belief) Regulations (2003), avail-
    able at www.opsi.gov.uk/si/si2003/20031660.htm, accessed 16 May 2009.

29. United Kingdom Equality and Human Rights Commission, "Religion or Belief and
    the Workplace, Putting the Employment Equality (Religion or Belief) Regulations
    2003 into Practice", available at www.acas.org.uk/media/pdf/f/l/religion_1.pdf, p. 7,
    accessed 15 May 2009.

30. Ibid., p. 8.

The Netherlands Equal Treatment Commission "Advisory Opinion on Employment, Religion, and Equal Treatment" adopts a similar perspective:

> The prohibition of discrimination based on religion implies more than respect for the religious persuasions of the employees. To a certain extent the employer will have to enable employees to conduct themselves in accordance with the rules of their religious persuasions. This means that an employee must be able to arrange his life in accordance with religious duties and rules. So the [Netherlands] Equal Treatment Act [1994] also protects conduct which is a direct manifestation of a religious persuasion, considering the significance of religious duties and rules.

Here too, it is indirect discrimination which gives rise to obligations comparable to a reasonable accommodation duty. The advisory opinion cites uniform regulations that forbid head coverings as an illustrative example of indirect discrimination.[31] Section 2 of the Netherlands Equal Treatment Act (1994) imposes stringent requirements needed to make otherwise indirect discrimination measures justifiable: once again, there is an objective justification test which must be satisfied – the aim of the rule or policy must be legitimate (namely, sufficiently important or corresponding to a real need of the organisation), the rule or policy must be proportionate to that aim, and it must be impossible to achieve the aim by other means that are not problematic or less problematic for the group affected.

3.4. Race and ethnicity

The positive measures specifically incorporated within the Race Equality Directive are commonly interpreted as positive or affirmative action and not as reasonable accommodation. More importantly, the wording of Article 5 suggests that the positive measures arising in this respect are permitted but not required. Nevertheless, there is no prima facie reason to assume that the Article 5 provisions of the Race Equality Directive should not give rise to an interpretation which mandates reasonable accommodation type measures. Again, Opinion No. 3 of the EU Network of Independent Experts on Fundamental Rights is instructive. It suggests that otherwise optional positive or affirmative action measures "may in certain circumstances be required as a form of accommodation of the specific

---

31. Ibid., p. 6.

situation of minorities. This is the case where, in the absence of such accommodation, minority groups would be suffering a form of indirect discrimination ...."[32]

Thus, the Race Equality Directive may also provide an opening towards the reasonable accommodation of persons belonging to minorities in Europe.

4. Conclusion

The current "European equality duty" does not specifically require but is nevertheless compatible with a broader view of reasonable accommodation that could extend to include persons belonging to minorities. There is scope under the umbrella concept of positive measures for European states to adopt accommodative practices of this kind as part of their equal rights and anti-discrimination strategies. In this regard, the indirect discrimination framework provided by the EU Equality Directive with respect to religion or belief and the EU Race Equality Directive with respect to race and ethnicity is particularly significant. The main focal point for normative change in this policy area should therefore be directed at educating European states on the advantages of adopting a broad view of indirect discrimination and reasonable accommodation.

---

32. EU Network of Independent Experts on Fundamental Rights, op. cit., p. 24.

Reasonable accommodation: going beyond the European Convention on Human Rights to reflect the plurality in national institutional settings

Eduardo J. Ruiz Vieytez[1]

1. Democracy and diversity: the need of a democratic pluralisation

In contemporary European societies, cultural uniformity has ceased to be the natural or desirable state of coexistence. Today, as a result of globalisation, increasing population movements, and a growing tide of assertion of identities, multiculturality is the ultimate substratum on which public policies must be drafted and implemented.

This multicultural substratum composed of diverse identities is actually not a new phenomenon. In any European society we can find historical elements of religious, linguistic or cultural plurality. The new development is the increasing visibility of that plurality and a higher awareness of it among the majority of people. Certain migratory processes have no doubt added greatly to this by increasing and complicating the traditional interplay of diversities.

However, despite the economic and social changes brought about by globalisation, politically we remain anchored in national state reference frameworks. Some international reference frameworks do exist, but they are actually structured around the national entities of which they are composed. Although states are faced with a gradual erosion of their operational capacity in the economic and social spheres, in terms of management of identities the state can be said to be still the strongest player. The planet is structured politically around states, and it is on this basis that people situate themselves in identity terms. Other possible traditional affiliations have lost ground to a legal reference framework for conferring identity. Europe is no exception to this trend. In the minds of most Europeans, each state continues to be seen as one society, one natural or unquestionable space. State borders continue to justify differences in

---

1. Director, Pedro Arupe Institute of Human Rights, University of Deusto (Spain).

the management of rights, and when we talk about integration or social cohesion, we are actually referring to societies understood in the sense of states, unless otherwise specified.

However, management of religious, linguistic or cultural diversity within political spaces is unavoidable today in pluralist democracy. It is becoming necessary to explore ways of harmonising differences in a more changing and uncertain context characteristic of post-modernity. Now, this management of plurality is normally accompanied by other values such as that of social cohesion, which seem to promote the existence of values or elements of identity shared by all those who live in a given society. Thus, while diversity is celebrated within today's politically correct discourses, social cohesion is also the guiding principle such discourses refer to. However, the two ideas can pave the way to diverging consequences or give rise to different policies in terms of recognition of rights. Therefore, the tension between diversity and cohesion must be reconsidered from a pluralistic and open idea of democracy.

2. Legal instruments for democratic pluralisation

The organisation of Europe into national political communities has resulted in a process of nationalisation of human rights, which strictly speaking should be universal. Rights have been severely affected by the arrangement in national domestic compartments. The consequence of this is that both entitlement of the rights and, above all, their content have been filtered through the dominant identities in each society. Rights are enjoyed and interpreted depending on the dominant cultural or identity paradigms, of each national society. This has led to exclusions from the perspective of entitlement and exercise of several fundamental rights.

The deepening of democracy in multicultural societies demands as a matter of urgency a pluralised approach to universal human rights. In the face of what I call the "identitarian state" (or state of identity), it is necessary to open up new channels of belonging and identity through a redefinition of the idea of inclusive and plural citizenship. It is not a case of de-identifying the public sphere, but of pluralising it, so that people can enjoy/exercise their human rights through their identity, and not in spite of it. This process is what I call democratic pluralisation.

Several political and legal avenues may be explored for the technical development of this pluralisation process. A first possibility, as already mentioned, consists in reinterpreting the idea of citizenship on the basis of a more normative approach.[2] But other possibilities exist in the stricter legal sphere. First, there is what we might call the "minority approach", based on promoting so-called minority rights, now systematised in important legal texts such as the Framework Convention for the Protection of National Minorities (1995), the European Charter for Regional or Minority Languages (1992) or Article 27 of the International Covenant on Civil and Political Rights (1996), among others. Pluralisation could perhaps be achieved through the legal concept of minority and the setting out of specific rights and parameters entailed by that concept.

Another possible avenue would be the inclusion of a "multicultural clause" in declarations of rights, on the model of Section 27 of the Canadian Charter of Rights and Freedoms.[3] This clause requires rights and freedoms to be interpreted with due regard to the multicultural heritage of the Canadian society. Thanks to this, the internal interplay of rights can be renewed from a pluralising perspective. Another approach would be to build on the legal principle of equality, working towards the idea of complex equality, and on that of non-discrimination, already present in all human rights instruments. In particular, it is important to mention here the idea of indirect discrimination and so-called "discrimination through non-differentiation" (or "discrimination by equalisation"). Lastly, there is the technique of reasonable accommodation, widely used in the Canadian context to manage certain types of diversity, mainly in the cultural and religious spheres.

Clearly, there is nothing to prevent a combination of several of the techniques mentioned in order to achieve the sought-after pluralisation. The links between some of them are obvious. However that may be, our starting point is to explore the law in its current state of development so that substantial changes in its positive content can be ruled out from the start. It is a question of tailoring the potential of these approaches, particularly reasonable accommodation, to the model prevailing in Europe.

Reasonable accommodation is a legal instrument or concept which originates from the labour relations field in the United States, where the concept began to be used following the promulgation of the 1964

2. This possibility is discussed at greater length in the chapter "The evolution of institutional cultures: migrants' access to services and rights", in this same volume.

3. This article reads as follows: "This Charter shall be interpreted in a manner consistent with the preservation and enhancement of the multicultural heritage of Canadians."

Civil Rights Act. In the mid-1980s, the idea was taken up in Canada as a significant qualitative extension of the notion of non-discrimination. Reasonable accommodation is derived not so much from the wording of legislation as from a conception of the right to equality that gradually took shape through case law. The concept first came to the fore in the case known as Simpsons-Sears, in which the Supreme Court recognised for the first time that an apparently neutral rule (in this instance, a work schedule) can have a discriminatory effect on an employee because it is incompatible with his or her religious observances.[4]

This instrument of reasonable accommodation has generously developed in the French-speaking province of Quebec, whose Charter of Human Rights and Freedoms[5] includes, in Article 43, the right of minorities to maintain their culture. Thus, the courts use reasonable accommodation to put an end to or avert discrimination affecting the exercise of any of the rights recognised in the Canadian or Quebec charters of rights and freedoms. It is, therefore, a legal concept originating in case law which is founded on the right to non-discrimination. Recognising it means accepting exceptions to the uniform application of the law or, to put it another way, accepting plurality in the application of law. Reasonable accommodation seeks an inclusive form of equality through differential treatment of persons who would otherwise be penalised or discriminated against in some of their elementary rights through the application of a certain legal rule. It also means prohibiting all indirect or systematic discrimination, whether caused intentionally or involuntarily.

3. Importing reasonable accommodation

Reasonable accommodation is therefore a legal technique which may be of the utmost interest in terms of its possible extension to European systems. Canadian experience may become an important point of reference from which to inject European political systems with larger doses of plurality in the recognition and protection of the basic rights of all types of minorities. The underlying assumption is that all citizens enjoy rights and freedoms recognised as basic by international and constitutional instruments, independently of whether or not they belong to a minority group of the society. This obviously also includes the right to equality in

---

4. *Ontario Commission of Human Rights and Theresa O'Malley (Vincent) v. Simpsons-Sears Ltd.*, [1985] 2 S.C.R. 536. Judgment of 17 December 1985.
5. Charte des droits et libertés de la personne, adopted on 27 June 1975.

respect of those same rights. The principle of equality does not mean uniform treatment in all cases. It can be implemented through differences of treatment or accommodations which serve to protect citizens from the unintended discriminatory practices caused by neutral laws which may have prejudicial effects for some groups.

We should therefore consider whether reasonable accommodation or, possibly, any other of the previously mentioned concepts can be used in European systems. This means asking ourselves about the legal bases of our own systems and considering whether we have the means of receiving those concepts in the framework of international or European law.

At first sight, the idea of reasonable accommodation does not seem to exist as such in international human rights law, although it is not explicitly proscribed either. It is arguable, in this connection, that the interpretation of the concept of proportionality, which is one of the criteria to be met by any restriction of rights, might take us closer to the technique of reasonable accommodation. It might be thought that a law or practice could be branded as disproportional in relation to the legitimate aim pursued by the restriction if it does not permit or require a form of reasonable accommodation. In analysing this question, we will look mainly at the two main spheres of international human rights protection which concern us: the universal sphere, with particular reference to the positions of the United Nations Human Rights Committee, and the European regional system, in which the European Court of Human Rights plays the leading role.

If we focus on the area of accommodations with regard to religious differences, it may be said that the Human Rights Committee generally appears receptive to the idea of reasonable accommodation, unlike the European Court of Human Rights. Indeed, the International Covenant on Civil and Political Rights and the Human Rights Committee are not so much interested in the relations between Church and State as in ensuring that the rights recognised in Articles 18 and 27 of the covenant are guaranteed. On the basis of non-discrimination and respect for fundamental rights, the United Nations gives states a free hand to organise their relations with religions. The universal system would seem to take a more holistic view, being unreceptive to national particularities and adopting a more universalist approach in the interpretation of rights. So, although in the *Bhinder v. Canada* case[6] the committee held that it was inappropriate to apply

---

6. United Nations Human Rights Committee, *Bhinder v. Canada* case, Document CCPR/ C/37/D/208/1986 (1989), decision of 28 November 1989.

the concept of accommodation as it was not justified by a legitimate aim compatible with the purposes of the covenant, this case does not mean rejection of the idea of reasonable accommodation. On the contrary, it could be inferred from the case that if the aim pursued had been different, the committee might have reached the opposite decision.

In the European system of human rights protection, the interpretation of "measures necessary in a democratic society" plays a key role. Limitations of freedom of religion must be necessary in a democratic society in order to be permitted. The so-called "national margin of appreciation" takes on great importance in this context. Each state can decide on the framework of regulations governing religion, a choice which depends on the particular national context.[7] Europe thus has a more receptive approach to intense secularism and shows greater distrust of accommodation. It is generally considered that accommodation belongs to the private sphere, but does not constitute an obligation for the state, which supposedly guarantees its neutrality in this way. Europe accepts intense secularism as a limit to freedom of religion and manages to establish a strong equation between the idea of secularism and that of democracy, particularly in some national contexts.[8]

For all these reasons, Strasbourg case law shows a reluctance to accept reasonable accommodation in the field of religious diversity,[9] and the same applies to linguistic diversity, which is also ultimately defined by the national margin of appreciation, in this case reflected in the adoption of a certain language as the official language. It is possible that in religious matters European case law is conditioned to an excessive degree by an idea of exclusive secularism present in such countries as France or Turkey, the weight of which in the most important cases brought hitherto is obvious. At any rate, the Strasbourg Court accepts a very broad view of

---

7. Among others, ECtHR, *Leyla Sahin v. Turkey* case, judgment of 10 November 2005, paragraph 109.

8. Ibid., paragraph 114; *Dahlab v. Switzerland*, judgment of 15 February 2001; *Refah Partisi v. Turkey*, judgment of 13 February 2003.

9. Besides the aforementioned *Leyla Sahin v. Turkey* and *Dahlab v. Switzerland* cases, two additional cases can be cited: *Kervanci v. France*, judgment of 4 December 2008, and *Kosteki v. Macedonia*, judgment of 13 April 2006.

the national margin of appreciation, occasionally echoing certain prejudices with regard to particular religious expressions.[10]

For the purposes of our analysis, a more positive line of enquiry would be to focus on a less extensive and less concrete line of decisions revolving essentially around the *Thlimmenos v. Greece* case of 2000. This judgment states that the right to enjoy the rights of the European Convention without discrimination is violated when, without objective and reasonable justification, states fail to apply a different treatment to persons whose situations are substantially different.[11] This is the embodiment in case law of so-called "discrimination through non-differentiation", acceptance of which would in practice be the preliminary to the introduction of reasonable accommodation. It seems, however, that subsequent decisions have not further pursued this line of approach opened up on the basis of Article 14 of the Convention, although the Thlimmenos doctrine has not been forgotten.[12] And although the latest judgments on freedom of religion seem to reduce the scope of the national margin of appreciation,[13] it continues to play a decisive role in the contextualised interpretation of rights.

The thought-provoking Thlimmenos doctrine has not been applied again with the same result, and so an assessment of the Strasbourg Court's case law in this field cannot be very positive. Nevertheless, in some of the cases in which this doctrine was referred to, there were cultural differences which could have served to justify differentiated treatment, although this was not the Court's assessment in the specific circumstances. In particular,

---

10. This may be seen, for example, in the *Sahin v. Turkey* case, where the wearing of headscarves is associated with an alleged alienation of women, and in a number of assessments of Islamic law contained in the *Refah Partisi v. Turkey* judgment.

11. *Thlimmenos v. Greece* case, judgment of 6 April 2000, paragraph 44.

12. Indeed, there are a good many later judgments which, despite a finding of non-discrimination, refer explicitly to the doctrine contained in the Thlimmenos case. The following can be mentioned: *Chapman v. the United Kingdom*, *Beard v. the United Kingdom*, *Jane Smith v. the United Kingdom*, *Coster v. the United Kingdom* and *Lee v. the United Kingdom*, judgments of 18 January 2001; *Fretté v. France*, judgment of 26 February 2002; *Pretty v. the United Kingdom*, judgment of 29 April 2002; *Posti and Rakho v. Finland*, judgment of 24 September 2002; *Natchova and Others v. Bulgaria*, judgment of 6 July 2005; *Stec and Others v. the United Kingdom*, judgment of 12 April 2006; *Zeman v. Austria*, judgment of 29 June 2006; *Snegon v. Slovakia*, judgment of 12 December 2006; *Dobal v. Slovakia*, judgment of 12 December 2006.

13. *Folgero and Others v. Norway* case, judgment of 29 June 2007; *Hasan and Eylem Zengin v. Turkey*, judgment of 9 October 2007.

the Chapman, Beard, Jane Smith, Coster and Lee cases, all against the United Kingdom,[14] referred to the particular living conditions of certain Roma communities, which can be clearly identified as cultural differences which might justify reasonable accommodation. Furthermore, the Court itself points out that the fact of being a member of a minority with a traditional lifestyle different from that of the majority of a society does not confer an immunity from general laws intended to safeguard assets common to the whole society, but it recognises that it may have an incidence on the manner in which such laws are to be implemented.[15] In practice, this means recognising the legality of reasonable accommodation in the field of cultural diversity.

The Court has also recognised that the fact of establishing exceptions to certain provisions of general application on the basis of a religious difference may constitute a measure adopted by the state to ensure effective respect for freedom of religion.[16] To some extent this places reasonable accommodation within the obligations which states must discharge in guaranteeing certain rights provided for in the Convention. Similarly, the Strasbourg Court considered it incompatible with Article 9 of the Convention to be obliged to swear an oath on the Gospels, which could open the way to a concrete accommodation which would avoid discrimination for persons not belonging to the majority religion.[17] However, in a similar case relating to differences that were more ideological than religious, the response was the opposite.[18]

The European Court of Human Rights seems more favourable to the idea of indirect discrimination. Indeed, the Court does not rule out the possibility that a rule or practice might be discriminatory when it clearly has a greater negative effect on a certain group than on the rest of the population. Although this type of discrimination has been worked on more from the perspective of gender equality, it would also be applicable to the case

---

14. Cited in footnote 12 above.

15. *Beard v. the United Kingdom* case, judgment of 18 January 2001, paragraph 107.

16. *Cha'are Shalom Ve Tsedek v. France* case, judgment of 27 June 2000, paragraph 76.

17. *Buscarini and Others v. San Marino* case, judgment of 18 February 1999, paragraph 39.

18. *McGuinness v. the United Kingdom* case, decision of 8 June 1999, paragraph 4.

of groups defined by cultural criteria.[19] The concept of indirect discrimination can therefore also be predicated on Article 14 of the European Convention on Human Rights (and Protocol No. 12 to the Convention), and therefore can be invoked by the European Court of Human Rights. The most significant judgment here is possibly that in the *D.H. and Others v. the Czech Republic* case,[20] where the Court finds indirect discrimination on ethnic or racial grounds, which opens the way to the protection of different minorities and to a requirement for concrete accommodations due to their vulnerable position.

Furthermore, Europe has incorporated into its shared legal *acquis* the notion of indirect discrimination, mainly through the so-called anti-discrimination directives,[21] in the European Union framework. Although indirect discrimination does not coincide exactly with the legal obligation to accommodate, it no doubt brings the interpretation of the application of rights significantly closer to that possibility.[22]

Lastly, outside the sphere of protection of the European Convention on Human Rights, it should be pointed out that there are other legal developments in Europe pointing in the direction of reasonable accommodation. In addition to the previously mentioned directives, it should be noted that nearly all national legal systems accept the need for certain adjustments or accommodations in rules according to variables such as physical disability or gender. The technique employed in these cases is similar to that of reasonable accommodation, whether in legislation or through case law. The difference lies in the reason justifying the obligation to accommodate or adjust. From a certain standpoint it might be considered that the reasons in question are neither sought nor desired by individuals. But given a proper understanding of culture, identities are also mostly forged

---

19. *Hugh Jordan v. the United Kingdom* case, judgment of 4 May 2001, paragraph 154; *Kelly and Others v. the United Kingdom*, judgment of 4 May 2001, paragraph 148; *McKerr v. the United Kingdom*, judgment of 4 May 2001, paragraph 165; *Shanaghan v. the United Kingdom*, judgment of 4 May 2001, paragraph 129.

20. *D.H. and Others v. the Czech Republic* case, judgment of 13 November 2007.

21. Council Directive 2000/43/EC of 29 June 2000 implementing the principle of equal treatment between persons irrespective of racial or ethnic origin and Council Directive 2000/78/EC of 27 November 2000 establishing a general framework for equal treatment in employment and occupation.

22. Article 5 of Directive 2000/78/EC refers explicitly to the obligation to provide "reasonable accommodation" for disabled persons.

on the basis of contexts, being individual choices in this domain heavily influenced by external conditions.

Consequently, reasonable accommodation can be seen as a right of minorities to preserve their differences vis-à-vis the majority by being entitled to accommodations and adaptations with regard to neutral rules which are applicable to all but which have prejudicial effects for them in respect of any basic right. This same technique seems to be accepted without any major difficulties in the case of other groups defined by non-cultural factors, as in the case of disabled persons. The path to take would therefore be to extend its scope to the cultural sphere in order to complete the operation of the principle of equality. This could be achieved in Europe either through the concept of indirect discrimination or by focusing on so-called "discrimination through non-differentiation", which already has a basis in the case law of the European Court of Human Rights.

4. Challenges for reasonable accommodation: linguistic diversity

We may conclude from the foregoing that reasonable accommodation can be a sound and effective instrument for pushing forward the democratic pluralisation demanded by present-day multicultural societies. This is the case with the Canadian model, which could be exported to European systems. However, after recognising the potentiality of such a legal concept for pluralist societies, some criticism can also be levelled against the use of this technique. In particular, I will refer here to two different issues still to be resolved in this process. The first of these concerns the application of reasonable accommodation to the remaining main cultural element, this is to say language and linguistic varieties. The second concern refers to the delicate question of the balance between traditional and recent diversities.

As we have seen, there are sufficient arguments in favour of applying the technique of reasonable accommodation to the field of religious and cultural diversity, following the Canadian example in this matter and the incipient European case law. However, when we look at the diversity brought about by language, the complications of pluralisation seem to increase significantly.

On the one hand, the European Court of Human Rights is very reluctant to recognise accommodations in the linguistic sphere beyond those expressly provided for in the Convention itself as guarantees of a fair hearing (Articles 5, paragraph 2, and 6, paragraph 3.a). The Court itself says that linguistic freedom per se does not exist in the Convention[23] and there is no instance of a position favourable to accommodation other than the specific case of *Cyprus v. Turkey*, where it was established that it was necessary to provide education in Greek to persons of that linguistic group in the north of the island, under certain circumstances.[24] The United Nations Human Rights Committee is also reluctant to recognise accommodation or indirect discrimination on grounds of language, if we exclude the highly atypical case of *Diergaardt v. Namibia*.[25] Similarly, the proportion of requests for linguistic accommodation is conspicuously low in the Canadian context (Bouchard and Taylor, abridged report 2008: 28).[26]

Nevertheless, the concepts analysed above (reasonable accommodation, indirect discrimination and discrimination through non-differentiation) can in theory be applied to situations of linguistic diversity. The different outcome that seems to apply to reasonable accommodation in the linguistic field may be due to the explicit different legal treatment given to languages and religions, the two main components of collective identity. While in the field of religion democratic states tend to observe a principle of secularism which implies public neutrality towards religion, in the linguistic sphere states opt explicitly for one (or several) of the existing languages, which is considered (explicitly or implicitly) as official language. Now, this does not rule out the possibility of extending the technique of reasonable accommodation to linguistic diversity and seeking new interpretations of the principle of equality when we are faced with increasing linguistic plurality. What we wish to consider here is whether we should not in fact follow the same pattern in linguistic as in religious matters and gradually apply reasonable accommodation as a legal instrument

---

23. *Fryske Nasjonale Partij and Others v. the Netherlands*, decision of 12 December 1985, paragraph 3; *Inhabitants of Leeuw-St. Pierre v. Belgium*, decision of 15 July 1965; *X and Others v. Belgium*, decision of 26 July 1963; *Georges Clerfayt, Pierre Legros et al. v. Belgium*, decision of 17 May 1985.

24. *Cyprus v. Turkey*, judgment of 10 May 2001, paragraphs 277-278.

25. *J.G.A. Diergaardt (late Captain of the Rehoboth Baster Community) et al. v Namibia*, Document CCPR/C/69/DF/760/1997, decision of 25 July 2000.

26. It may be observed that the Quebec Government's official web page on "intercultural Quebec" defines as the first common value "the need to speak French in Quebec", ahead of the second ("Quebec is a free and democratic society") and third ("Quebec is a secular society") values. See www.quebecinterculturel.gouv.qc.ca/fr/valeurs-fondements/index.html.

bringing us closer to more democratic management of a pluralist society in the linguistic field too.

The use of reasonable accommodation presupposes the existence of a neutral legal instrument which has adverse or discriminatory effects on a certain group because of the group's identity. It is obvious that this identity can be determined by language in the same way as by religion. It is also clear that certain legal rules may entail a disadvantage for the members of a certain linguistic group when its usual or preferred language of communication is in a relegated position. And it is not difficult to show that there can be neutral legal rules which lead to differences of treatment based on linguistic criteria, either because these differences were deliberately sought (for example, by designating a language as the official or working language of a certain institution) or because sociolinguistic reality comes to the fore, with some languages enjoying a higher status than others. This second possibility may be reminiscent of the situation usually observed in connection with religious diversity.

Therefore, the legal technique of reasonable accommodation theoretically fits in the linguistic sphere as it does for the religious one. The consequent question is why then this extension of the concept has not been proposed yet. Is public treatment of language comparable to that of religion from an analytical point of view? This is not usually considered to be the case, and my stance here will be to argue that this comparability, although not complete, can and must be greater than it is assumed at present. It is generally acknowledged that there is a need for an explicit definition of the languages to be used preferentially by the public authorities. These decisions tend to be justified by numerical majorities, history or the potential of the different languages. But in any case, language is a component of identity which is as strong as, if not stronger than, religion. At the same time, in developed societies it is less and less clear that common official or working languages have to be predetermined, given the complex social relations of any society and the evolution of translation technologies. Given increasing social plurality and the state's neutrality with regard to religion, it is not unthinkable to transpose the schema to cultural or linguistic plurality and demand a certain degree of neutrality to public authorities. The explicit support given to dominant or majority languages continues, in most circumstances, to be an instrument for strengthening a certain single national conception of society, which is increasingly incompatible with the egalitarian enjoyment of human rights.

To some extent, certain general linguistic accommodations already operate in all democratic societies, when, for example, the possibility of being informed of a criminal charge in one's own language or of conducting one's defence in that language is incorporated into the rights of the defence, independently of whether that language has official or majority status in the particular legal context. This exception to strict application of the official language constitutes in my view an example of generic reasonable accommodation (thus, incorporated in the positive law), and not part of the substance of the right to a fair trial itself (or habeas corpus). If this were the case, the linguistic element would make up part of the substance of the right, but in fact it only applies when the involved person needs an exemption from the general linguistic rule in order to properly enjoy his right to defence or to a fair trial. It is again a legally recognised exemption in the applicability of a legal instrument (the one designating the official language) which in theory is supposed to be neutral.

Therefore, the designation of an official language can be seen as a neutral instrument which, nevertheless, creates in certain groups (notably those who do not know the language in question or do not consider it their own) a real difference of treatment which was not intended but which may affect their enjoyment of several basic rights. In such circumstances it would be appropriate to apply reasonable accommodations consisting in granting exemptions from the use of the official language and allowing the use of other languages (normally minority languages) via the technical means necessary in each case. Here again, the test for reasonableness will be the proportionality of the necessary adjustment and the importance or substantial character of the right affected. This has always been considered essential in the case of defence rights in criminal proceedings, and that is the reason why such an accommodation enjoys a permanent basis in positive law. As for other fundamental rights, the same technique could also be applied, along with the proportionality and reasonableness tests that must guide any cultural accommodation.

However that may be, the field of reasonable accommodation in linguistic matters remains unexplored. The reason for this is possibly the high sensitivity of the linguistic issues in contemporary societies. In fact, in today's Europe language is by far the most relevant element of defining collective (national) identities, and language is seen as much more attached to the territory than religion. This explains that still many resistances arise when proposing any pluralisation in the field of working languages, since the symbolic value of official languages remains extremely high and sensitive for the national identity of many Europeans, as it can also be in the case of Canada. The resolute transposition of reasonable accommodation to the linguistic field would make it necessary to redefine a sensitive area of the management of public affairs in multicultural societies. In any case the plurality of our societies will also be reflected in linguistic phenomena, and contemporary law must also give responses to such realities. This does not necessarily mean that it would not be possible to pursue active linguistic policies in support of the languages traditionally spoken in a given society, although such policies would have to be reshaped and rendered compatible with greater linguistic openness of the entire public apparatus.

5. Reasonable accommodation and traditional diversity

Lastly, we must address another, equally important issue when talking about democratic pluralisation, which is that of the conflict between historical and recent diversity. In the specific cases of Quebec and Canada, the model of interculturalism and that of multiculturalism coincide in not assessing or promoting all diversities in the same way. On the contrary, in the Canadian models there is a preference for certain constitutionally protected cultures, such as the indigenous nations, so-called denominational communities, the French and English-speaking minorities in the different provinces, and the national minority of Quebec. The other groups and communities making up Canadian society as a result of different waves of immigration had to resign themselves to making a smaller impact on the constitution, via the aforementioned Section 27 of the charter of rights. Reasonable accommodation may thus be seen as an instrument for avoiding discrimination against recent or non-constitutionalised identities. The Canadian courts are clear in pointing out that the new minorities cannot demand the extension of rights conferred specifically on the groups protected in the constitution, not even in cases where the circumstances of the former might be considered equivalent to those of the latter.[27]

What is at issue here is extension of the legal recognition of diversity and the ability of any society to constitutionalise or "freeze" certain collective situations more than others. There has to be an objective and reasonable justification for this, but when that justification can be questioned, from a pluralistic perspective, the debate on accommodation reappears. The historical, geographical or traditional justifications may no doubt

---

27. *Adler v. Ontario*, [1996] 3 S.C.R. 609; judgment of 21 November 1996.

constitute an objective and reasonable basis depending on the circumstances present (for example, the specific nature of certain traditional lifestyles or languages, despite a smaller number of speakers compared with immigrant languages). Nevertheless, the fact that the difference of treatment is constitutionalised cannot in itself presuppose a sufficient legal basis for confining the accommodation process to minority communities that find themselves in a comparable situation to those recognised in the constitutional framework. This was the position expressed by the United Nations Human Rights Committee in the *Waldman v. Canada* case.[28]

Ultimately, when we are discussing the issue of greater multicultural recognition, a debate must be launched in parallel on the adjustments and arrangements already present in each national system. While those traditional arrangements may serve legitimate purposes and be necessary to ensure respect for certain diversities, they cannot at the same time constitute impassable barriers for other elements of identity currently present in those societies. Accordingly, the principle of non-discrimination must be implemented with due regard to those general accommodations or arrangements which already exist in a given system and which may on the other hand be forerunners of the multicultural openness we are aiming for.

6. Conclusion

Reasonable accommodation is a legal technique set within the framework of policies for the democratic management of diversity. Without exhausting the scope of those policies, it represents an instrument that may prove very effective for present-day societies in underpinning what we refer to as practices of intercultural harmonisation. Although, in the strict sense, reasonable accommodation is the management of exceptions and solutions on a case-by-case basis, its general application would consolidate good practices for managing diversity in increasingly complex societies.

As it stands, international human rights law could serve as a basis for introducing reasonable accommodation into European legal systems. The rules against discrimination found in all the major treaties, including the European Convention on Human Rights, could provide the legal cover

---

28. Human Rights Committee, *Waldman v. Canada*, decision of 3 November 1999, Document CCPR/C/67/D/694/1996, paragraphs 10.4 and 10.7.

for using this concept in Europe. The ideas of complex equality, indirect discrimination and discrimination through non-differentiation, which are already present in our systems, even if only in an incipient or fragmentary manner, serve these purposes without the need for any far-reaching legislative reform. On the contrary, what is needed is case law development and interpretative work that move forward in this direction, helping to adapt the exercise of basic human rights to the existing plurality of identities.

Ultimately, it is a case of assuming that democracy is a not a mere question of majorities, but a necessary incorporation of minorities from an equality perspective, which clearly calls for accommodations that take account of their different situations. Reasonable accommodation does not in any way seek to establish a system of privilege or separation, but, on the contrary, a process of equalisation through differentiated treatment, and of social cohesion. Nowadays, the law can no longer perform with the same rigour its traditional function of providing certainty and security, because existing (and changing) complexity diminishes its effectiveness as an instrument of social forecasting. It is for this reason that we are obliged to interpret rights frequently on a case-by-case basis having regard to the objective and subjective circumstances. This increases the sphere of action of the courts and reduces the power of definition of positive laws. It is perhaps for this reason that the technique of reasonable accommodation comes to us from countries which follow the common law model, with a more casuistic approach to the law. This casuistic methodology is more appropriate in assuming a permanent negotiation between those who make up the social context in each case. In any event, the concept of reasonable accommodation can provide a suitable opportunity to go further in the democratic pluralisation required by present-day societies, without the need for costly legislative changes.

Part B – Reasonable accommodation or mutual accommodation for all to develop our institutional and national cultures?

European legal frameworks that respond to diversity and the need for institutional change: to what extent are the Canadian concept of "reasonable accommodation" and the European approach of "mutual accommodation" reflected in those frameworks?

Which conceptual approach provides the better way forward in the European context?

Jane Wright[1]

1. Preliminary remarks

It is instructive to begin with some preliminary remarks to identify the background to the following discussion. This paper is written in the context of a project to elucidate the means by which intercultural competences in social services may be protected and promoted. As such, the following discussion will examine the legal mechanisms that are arguably most appropriate to manage cultural diversity and foster intercultural competences in access to social services by the members of migrant communities. The debate regarding the suitability of mechanisms is taking place against the broader backdrop of Council of Europe work focusing on how best to build social cohesion in states. It is necessary therefore as a preliminary issue to identify markers of social cohesion. The suitability

---

1.   Professor Law, School of Law and Human Rights Centre, University of Essex, Wivenhoe Park, Colchester CO4 3SQ.

of legal tools can only be assessed by reference to the aims sought to be achieved. Where one legal system, whether national or regional, proposes to borrow from another, it is important also to understand the context in which a particular rule or institution has operated in order to evaluate how suitable it may be for another system. This is an essential principle applied by comparative lawyers the world over: many systems face essentially the same problems, solutions may be suggested by looking to other states but they must be adapted to suit the borrower.

With regard to "social cohesion", its essential meaning is encapsulated by the idea of the glue that binds a society together, but precise definition is elusive. The High-Level Task Force on Social Cohesion has endorsed the definition elaborated in the Revised Strategy for Social Cohesion, namely "Social Cohesion is the capacity of a society to ensure the well-being of all its members, minimising disparities and avoiding marginalisation".[2] Further, the achievement of social cohesion has to centre on "actively managing differences and divisions in the context of democratic citizenship. This is the bridge building element". It is beyond the scope of this paper to review in detail the work of the task force but two key principles are identified in their report which may illuminate the search for the appropriate means to manage diversity and promote intercultural competence: the first principle of the task force approach is "social rights" – a social rights approach is particularly sensitive to the situation of the vulnerable and marginalised; secondly, participation and dialogue must be enhanced, particularly at local level. "Social cohesion especially is something that is generated and manifested at local level and so challenges us to develop new approaches, not least those that are somehow simultaneously local, national and international in scope and focus."[3] Thus, social rights and participation and dialogue are key markers of social cohesion.

Issues of access to social services, both in terms of the goods delivered and the process of delivery, naturally engage social rights; these rights are traditionally framed in terms of undertakings by states, rather than individual rights that are justiciable before courts and supervisory institutions. There is no watertight distinction between civil and political rights on the one hand and social rights on the other. The indivisibility and interdependence of all human rights has been recognised by the international

---

2. "Towards an Active, Fair and Socially Cohesive Europe", Report of the High-Level Task Force on Social Cohesion, TESC(2007)31 E, Strasbourg, 28 January 2008, at p. 14.

3. Ibid., at p. 25.

community.[4] Jurisprudence under the European Convention on Human Rights (ECHR), especially the Article 8 right to respect for private and family life, engages aspects of social rights. However, for the purposes of the present debate, the type of rights we are discussing and the extent to which states may be willing to accept increased levels of justiciability cannot be ignored. It must also be borne in mind when reflecting on the use of the Quebec approach as a template for Europe that, in contrast with the ECHR and many European bills of rights, Chapter IV of the Quebec Charter of Human Rights and Freedoms is devoted to "economic and social rights".

Although clearly a highly contested issue, mechanisms designed to respond to diversity can be seen as vehicles to redress the inherent partiality of the state: contrary to the views expressed by some theorists,[5] a state will not be neutral as to language, calendar and very often not as regards religion. According to Kymlicka, "[With regard to the USA] what Walzer calls the 'neutral state' can be seen, in effect, as a system of 'group rights' that supports the majority's language, history, culture and calendar. Government policy systematically encourages everyone to learn English and to view their life-choices as tied to participation in English-language institutions".[6] The dominance of majority cultures applies equally to European states. Thus, in the absence of special measures to promote recognition of migrant community languages, cultures and religions, the communities are potentially disadvantaged and threatened with assimilation.

The starting premises of international human rights standards are the principles of equality and non-discrimination.[7] The protection of minorities is based upon the twin pillars of the prohibition of discrimination and the necessity for measures to protect and promote their separate identity.[8]

---

4. The Vienna Declaration and Programme of Action of the 2nd United Nations World Conference on Human Rights (1993), at paragraph 5.

5. See Walzer, "Comment", *Multiculturalism and the "Politics of Recognition"*, pp. 100-101, quoted by W. Kymlicka, *The Rights of Minority Cultures*, Oxford University Press, Oxford, 1996 at p. 10.

6. Ibid.

7. Universal Declaration of Human Rights, Articles 1 and 2.

8. A. Eide, "The Council of Europe's Framework Convention for the Protection of National Minorities", in K. Henrard and R. Dunbar (eds), *Synergies in Minority Protection. European and International Law Perspectives*, Cambridge University Press, Cambridge, 2008, at p. 127.

When members of migrant communities seek the right to use their own language in public spaces and public contacts they seek to be placed on the same footing as majority communities. Member states of the Council of Europe are parties to a whole raft of human rights instruments which secure various rights on a non-discriminatory basis. The question at the heart of the debate on reasonable accommodation is whether the right to reasonable accommodation is already explicitly/implicitly protected. If it is not, should it be, and, if so, by what means?

Following the break up of the Soviet Union, European states have in the last two decades focused much effort on seeking to reduce tensions between minority and majority communities through the introduction of both "hard" and "soft" law approaches.[9] However, it is arguable that such efforts have largely been driven by the desire for security[10] and thus have addressed the needs and concerns of what are termed "traditional" minorities (those frequently defined by links to particular states or former states) and their kin-states, rather than the "new" migrant communities. Clearly, this does not mean that existing frameworks cannot be used or adapted to the situation of new minorities, but the political will of states is frequently lacking as can be seen by state responses to the Framework Convention, where most contracting parties explicitly restrict its application to historical minorities, who have been resident on the territory for a considerable length of time. This pattern is not repeated throughout Europe, the United Kingdom is a notable exception for having addressed the position of a wider range of groups under the umbrella of the Framework Convention. While states may be resistant, there is an emerging consensus that "new" minorities should be brought under the umbrella of "minority protection".[11]

---

9. Contrast the treaty-based approach of the Council of Europe in the Framework Convention for the Protection of National Minorities (FCNM) with the politically binding commitments of the Organization for Security and Co-operation in Europe, especially the document of the Copenhagen meeting of the OSCE (then CSCE) and the "silent diplomacy" of the High Commissioner on National Minorities of the OSCE.

10. The preamble to the FCNM recites the "upheavals of European history [that] have shown the protection of national minorities is essential to stability, democracy and peace in this continent".

11. K. Henrard and R. Dunbar, "Introduction", in Henrard and Dunbar, op. cit., at p. 12. See also A. Bloed and R. Letschert, "The OSCE HCNM", in Henrard and Dunbar, op. cit., at p. 112 ff., and J. Packer, "Confronting the Contemporary Challenges of Europe's Minorities", Helsinki Monitor, 16 (3), 2005, pp. 227-231.

The aim of the Council of Europe's project is to elaborate "a proposal for a legal framework that can foster interculturalism and institutional change/transformation in European plural societies". In this context, the Canadian approach of reasonable accommodation of difference will be evaluated and compared with European approaches to the protection and promotion of rights that pertain, essentially, to issues of cultural identity, as well as other frameworks that might provide useful models. It will be revealed that to all intents and purposes the concept of reasonable accommodation is inherent in European jurisprudence, but the means of implementation are not so fully developed. By way of contrast with reasonable accommodation, it is instructive to reflect on the notion of mutual accommodation as described by Austrian political scientist Rainer Bauböck.

2. Mutual accommodation

Mutual accommodation is not a normative concept as such, but it suggests a way of looking at the world and the peoples and groups within it that may yield signposts to greater social cohesion. In his work on social and cultural integration of immigrants in a civil society, Bauböck discusses the forms of adaptation which a society will undergo in order to maintain its cohesion and he distinguishes three modes of adaptation: segregation, assimilation and accommodation. Segregation involves the maintenance of the existing social structure "by confining inserted individuals or groups within clearly-marked segments"; assimilation also preserves the existing social structure, but gradually difference is abolished or eliminated; finally, there is mutual accommodation, which:

> involves the adaptation of [immigrant communities] to existing conditions, as well as a change in the structure of the larger society and a redefinition of its criteria of cohesion. Accommodation involves an internalization of difference. The collective characteristics of inserted groups become accepted as distinctions within common social positions and membership groups.[12]

---

12. R. Bauböck, "Social and Cultural Integration in a Civil Society", in R. Bauböck, A. Héller and A. R. Zolberg (eds), *The Challenge of Diversity Integration and Pluralism in Societies of Immigration*, Ashgate Publishing, Avebury, 1996, at p. 114, quoted by E. Vasta, Integrating Cities II, 5-6 November 2007, Palacio Real, Madrid: www.compas.ox.ac.uk.

Thus, mutual accommodation involves changes in the majority or dominant society itself so that society really does embrace "equality" in the fullest substantive sense.

It is the writer's view that mutual accommodation connotes a situation where majority and minority and migrant communities working together to yield solutions, rather than the idea of a dominant group making concessions from its own baseline for minority cultures, practices and viewpoints. It is pertinent here to recall the task force's view that social cohesion is driven especially at local level[13] and through dialogue and partnership.

3. "Reasonable" accommodation

Deriving from Canadian jurisprudence regarding "adverse impact" or "indirect discrimination", "reasonable accommodation" is the term originally applied to the requirement for an employer to take steps to mitigate the effect of a contract term that is neutral on its face but impacts disproportionately on a section of the workplace.[14] In Canadian law, the workplace duty to accommodate means that employers must eliminate rules, practices and standards that discriminate on prohibited grounds such as disability, sex, religion, race and family status. An employer must show that any discriminatory standard is reasonably necessary by demonstrating that "it is impossible to accommodate individual employees sharing the characteristics of the claimant without imposing undue hardship upon the employer".[15]

The jurisprudence has shifted from drawing artificial and problematic distinctions between direct and adverse impact or indirect discrimination. In a radical break with the bifurcated approach, the Supreme Court in Meiorin[16] proposed that an employer should demonstrate that any prima facie discriminatory standard (that is, direct or indirect) is a "bona fide operational requirement" and can therefore be justified. In order to do this

---

13. High-Level Task Force on Social Cohesion, op. cit.

14. *Ontario Commission of Human Rights and Theresa O'Malley (Vincent) v. Simpsons-Sears Ltd.*, [1985] 2 S.C.R. 536.

15. *British Columbia (Public Service Employee Relations Commission) (BCPSERC) v. The British Columbia Government and Service Employees Union (BCGSEU)*, [1999] ("Meiorin") 35 ChRR D/257 (SCC), quoted in R. Hatfield, *Just Labour*, Vol. 5, winter 2005.

16. Ibid.

the employer must show that: (i) the standard was adopted for a purpose rationally connected to the performance of the job; (ii) the employer honestly believed that the standard was necessary to fulfil the legitimate work-related purpose; and (iii) that the standard is reasonably necessary to achieve that legitimate work-related purpose, so to accommodate the relevant employee would impose undue hardship on the employer.

In determining the point at which accommodation would constitute "undue hardship", some hardship is acceptable; it is only "undue" hardship that is a justification for an impugned difference in treatment. In the workplace context, relevant factors are: the financial cost of the accommodation; the relative interchangeability of the workforce and facilities and the prospect of substantial interference with the rights of other employees.[17]

What is of interest for present discussion is the implicit recognition by Justice McLachlin in Meiorin, giving judgment for a unanimous court, that owing to imbalances of power, it may well be inappropriate to consider any term "neutral" on its face, and moreover, describing a term as neutral means that its legitimacy is never questioned: rather, the focus will then shift to whether the individual claimant can be accommodated. In other words the analysis shifts attention "away from the substantive norms underlying the standard to how individuals can fit into the "mainstream". McLachlin quotes extensively from the work of Day and Brodsky:

> [The distinction between direct and adverse impact/indirect discrimination] allows those who consider themselves "normal" to continue to construct institutions and relations in their image … [A]ccommodation seems to mean that we do not change procedures or services, we simply "accommodate" those who do not quite fit. We make some concessions to those who are "different", rather than abandoning the idea of "normal" and working for genuine inclusiveness. In short, accommodation is assimilationist. Its goal is to try to make "different" people fit into existing systems.[18]

In this analysis, Day and Brodsky are alluding to the inherent limitation in the power of a concept such as reasonable accommodation to transform

---

17. Ibid., at paragraph 63.

18. Shelagh Day and Gwen Brodsky, "The Duty to Accommodate: Who Will Benefit?", *Canadian Bar Review*, 1996, p. 433 at p. 462, per Justice McLachlin, Meiorin, at paragraph 41.

a society into something that is different from what has gone before; it is submitted that the concept of mutual accommodation, of all parties undergoing change, has the greater transforming power.

The case law on reasonable accommodation developed in the context of the application of human rights legislation to private disputes but has now been extended to all persons governed by human rights legislation.[19] The key then to unlocking a request for reasonable accommodation is to establish discrimination in the enjoyment of human rights. Justice McIntyre defined discrimination in the following terms:

> a distinction, whether intentional or not but based on grounds relating to personal characteristics of the individual or group, which has the effect of imposing burdens, obligations, or disadvantages on such individual or group not imposed upon others, or which withholds or limits access to opportunities, benefits and advantages available to other members of society. Distinctions based on personal charac-teristics attributed to an individual solely on the basis of association with a group will rarely escape the charge of discrimination.[20]

In order to consider whether there is a need to import the reasonable accommodation concept we need to examine the situation in Europe in order to determine whether analogues already exist.

4. European analogues for reasonable accommodation?

4.1. Direct and indirect discrimination under the European Convention on Human Rights and the revised European Social Charter

The first hurdle that needs to be established under the Canadian doctrine of reasonable accommodation is that there has been a difference in treat-ment, which the defendant must then justify or accommodate up to the point of undue hardship. In terms of rights, both direct and indirect discrimination are prohibited under both the European Convention on

---

19. *British Columbia (Superintendent of Motor Vehicles) v. British Columbia (Council of Human Rights)*, [1999] 3 S.C.R. 868.
20. *Andrews v. Law Society (British Columbia)*, [1989] 1 S.C.R. 143 (SCC) at pp. 174-175.

Human Rights[21] and the revised European Social Charter.[22] Thus, the first stage of the Canadian approach is mirrored in Europe. In the well-known case of Thlimmenos, the European Court of Human Rights stressed that the principle of equality means treating equals equally and unequals unequally. In a judgment subsequently quoted with approval by the European Committee of Social Rights, the European Court of Human Rights said:

> the right not to be discriminated against in the enjoyment of the rights guaranteed under the Convention is also violated when states without an objective and reasonable justification fail to treat differently persons whose situations are significantly different.

A difference in treatment or failure to treat differently can be justified where there is a legitimate aim and there is a reasonable relationship of proportionality between the means employed and the aim sought to be achieved. The proportionality analysis applied by the supervisory organs in Europe is analogous to the examination of justifications put forward for the limitation of rights by the Canadian Supreme Court. In Eldridge, the Supreme Court stated that the concept of reasonable accommodation is equivalent to the concept of "reasonable limits" as provided for in the Canadian charter which in turn has a direct counterpart in the European concept of proportionality. A recent decision of the Supreme Court of Canada in Multani (decision to ban the wearing of the kirpan was quashed)[23] has direct analogues in Europe[24] and any failure to accommodate sincerely held religious belief could in principle be a violation of Article 14 in conjunction with Article 9 of the ECHR. The European case law stops short though of giving a right to reasonable accommodation.

In *Autism-Europe v. France*, the European Committee of Social Rights found that France had violated Articles 15, paragraph 1, and 17, paragraph 1, of the revised European Social Charter, whether read alone or in

---

21. See Article 14 of the ECHR applied in *Thlimmenos v. Greece* (2000), 31 EHRR 411, and *D.H. v. the Czech Republic* (2008), 47 EHRR 3.

22. Article E of the revised European Social Charter applied in *Autism-Europe v. France*, Collective Complaint No. 13/2002, decision on the merits of 4 November 2003, paragraph 52.

23. *Multani v. Commission scolaire Marguerite-Bourgeoys and Attorney General of Quebec*, [2006] 1 S.C.R. 256.

24. See for example the English High Court decision in *R on the application of Watkins-Singh v. The Governing Body of Aberdare Girls' High School*, [2008] EWHC 1865.

conjunction with Article E in that the proportion of children with autism in either general or specialist schools was much lower than other children, whether or not disabled. The committee stated that: "human difference in a democratic society should not only be viewed positively but should be responded to with discernment in order to ensure real and effective equality".[25] The committee recalled its previous jurisprudence that the Charter requires practical action to make it effective but acknowledged that measures should be taken that allow states to "achieve the objectives of the Charter within a reasonable time, with measurable progress and to an extent consistent with the maximum use of available resources. States parties must be particularly mindful of the impact that their choices will have for groups with heightened vulnerabilities ...". The notion of an obligation that is measured by available resources imports the same principles that are considered in determining the point of "undue hardship" in the Canadian jurisprudence.

A state will violate the European Convention on Human Rights or the revised European Social Charter if it indirectly discriminates against anyone in the enjoyment of the rights set out, but the remedies are different. The scope of protection is different under the two instruments: the ECHR applies to everyone within the jurisdiction;[26] the protection of the undertakings set out in the revised European Social Charter is limited to "foreigners" only in so far as they are nationals of other contracting parties lawfully resident within the state. In both cases, the fact of discrimination will not entitle a citizen to require adjustment or accommodation. Henrard has observed that:

> [*Thlimmenos v. Greece*] constitutes an immensely important opening towards substantive equality considerations, towards establishing positive obligations on states to adopt differential treatment and special measures. On the other hand, the use of the *Thlimmenos* rationale has not yet led to the recognition that states should adopt minority specific measures.[27]

The individual human rights set out in the ECHR provide for individualised justice and possibly the payment of just satisfaction. A violation may lead

---

25. *Autism-Europe v. France,* op. cit., at paragraph 52.

26. But see Article 16 of the ECHR which permits states to restrict the political activity of "aliens".

27. K. Henrard, "A Patchwork of 'Successful' and 'Missed' Synergies", in Henrard and Dunbar, op. cit., at p. 328.

to change in state practice in the relevant forum, but it would seem to be of limited use where what is sought is programmatic change directed at groups and their members. The European Social Charter, on the other hand, provides for a system of collective complaints according to which NGOs with consultative status with the Council of Europe have standing. Where a complaint is upheld, a recommendation is addressed to the relevant contracting party.

4.2. European Union instruments

Following extensive lobbying by civil society groups to extend discrimination law, Article 13 was included in the EC Treaty following the coming into force of the Treaty of Amsterdam. This provision empowered the Community to "take appropriate action to combat discrimination based on sex, racial or ethnic origin, religion or belief, disability, age or sexual orientation". In 2000 two directives were adopted.

Council Directive 2000/78/EC on equal treatment in employment and occupation prohibits both direct and indirect discrimination on grounds of religion or belief, disability, age or sexual orientation and by virtue of Article 5 requires employers to make reasonable accommodation to guarantee compliance with the principle of equal treatment in relation to persons with disabilities. This means that an employer must "take appropriate measures to enable a person with a disability to have access to or advance in employment unless such measures would be disproportionately burdensome for the employer". The directive recites a number of factors to determine reasonableness: financial and other costs which would be incurred by the employer; the scale and financial resources of the employer; and the availability to the employer of financial or other assistance.[28]

Directive 2000/43/EC was adopted to combat direct and indirect discrimination on the grounds of racial or ethnic origin in relation to employment, training, education, social security, health care, housing and access to goods and services. It is permissible for a state to take positive action to prevent or compensate for disadvantages linked to racial or ethnic origin (Article 5), but there is no requirement as such for a state to take such measures.

---

28. See, for example, United Kingdom Disability Discrimination Act 1995, Section 6, which also includes the extent to which a step taken would disrupt any of the employer's activities.

Most recently, the European Commission has proposed a directive that would prohibit discrimination based on age, religion and belief, sexual orientation and disability by all persons in both the public and private sectors, including public bodies, in relation to, *inter alia*, social protection, including social security and health care, social advantages and education. Pertinent to present discussion, in an imaginative step beyond the reactive, rights-based approach to redressing discrimination, Article 4 is proactive and would require measures in favour of persons with disabilities to be "provided by anticipation, including through appropriate modifications or adjustments". Such measures should not impose a "disproportionate burden" which according to Article 4(2) takes account of "the size and resources of the organisation, its nature, the estimated cost, the life cycle of the goods and services, and the possible benefits of increased access for persons with disabilities". Article 11 requires member states to "encourage dialogue with relevant stakeholders, in particular non-governmental organisations".

It will be appreciated that the concept of "indirect" discrimination presupposes that a norm is neutral on its face: by definition such a norm must disfavour a certain section or certain sections of the population and then in line with the views expressed above concessions may be made to the "other" "non-favoured" groups. The limitation inherent in both of the concepts of indirect discrimination and reasonable accommodation is that they are applied within the context of particular relationships; in other words, they require an employer, or other relevant body whether public or private, to react to a request; they are norms that are fleshed out by courts in litigation. In themselves, they do not require, what might be termed as, the dominant party to take proactive steps on their own initiative to realise the right of equality before the law and equal protection of the law. They are remedial in nature and it is arguable that such models are poorly constructed or adapted to achieve a fairer society premised upon equality. This approach seems to be antithetical to achieve structural changes in the democratic management of diversity and difference which would postulate the involvement of all groups within society in determining how we are to live together.

5. An alternative, inclusive approach in order to precipitate mutual accommodation?

An alternative approach is one that involves all parties, majorities and minority groups, both traditional and new minorities, in the development of processes and procedures. While it must be acknowledged that states have refused to bring "new" minorities within the scope of the Framework Convention for the Protection of National Minorities (FCNM), it is a useful model because it moves beyond the idea of minorities as the passive beneficiaries of concessions by the majority. Central to its provisions is the requirement in Article 15 for states to create "conditions" that will secure "effective participation of persons belonging to national minorities in cultural, social and economic life and in public affairs, in particular those affecting them". Further, Article 4 requires states to "adopt, where necessary, adequate measures in order to promote, in all areas of economic, social, political and cultural life, full and effective equality between persons belonging to a national minority and those belonging to the majority".

The Advisory Committee on the FCNM has prepared a commentary setting out its interpretation of the state's obligations under Article 15. The commentary observes that barriers to equal access to economic sectors and social services should be removed and that states should "promote [the participation of minorities] in the delivery of benefits and outcomes".[29] Legislation prohibiting discrimination is necessary, but not a sufficient condition, to assure participation. Training programmes for public service staff should be developed and in the health-care sector "the recruitment of health-care mediators belonging to national minorities should be encouraged".[30]

There is both a vertical and a horizontal dimension to participation: members of minority communities need to be encouraged to engage in dialogue with public authorities and also with members of the majority population. The commentary points out that this can only be achieved if there are effective communication channels between all groups. Mutual accommodation in the sense described above can only occur through these exchanges which must take place between the resident/citizen and the state and between residents inter se. As the commentary points out "intercultural dialogue" should be extended to "all segments of society".[31]

Models of legislation/policy initiatives that are predicated on duties cast upon public authorities coupled with participation by all groups in

---

29. ACFC/31DOC(2008)001, at p. 4.

30. Ibid., at p. 6.

31. Ibid., at p. 13.

the development of policies and practices are likely to pave the way for a more inclusive democratic approach towards the realisation of intercultural competences. Mutual accommodation as described above connotes the transformation of society through internalisation of difference, requiring a process of adaptation by all parties and solutions that are achieved through participation by the citizenry as a whole.

The Advisory Committee on the FCNM has described the approach of the United Kingdom to the promotion of non-discrimination and equality as "particularly advanced",[32] and it may be useful to examine the strategy that has been developed to tackle persistent inequality. In common with its European partners, the United Kingdom has a raft of anti-discrimination legislation that has been produced over the last 40 years. Under the Equality Act 2006, public authorities are required to promote race equality and good race relations and the Advisory Committee has commented that: "These positive duties have helped to increase awareness about racism and discrimination among the general public and to raise expectations about the performance of public institutions among persons belonging to minorities."[33]

However, inequalities persist and the legislation is complex and difficult to navigate. In April 2009, the Labour Government brought forward a new Equality Bill which will replace the various statutes and, significantly for present discussion, will introduce a number of new duties on public bodies, which if properly implemented will secure greater equality and fairness. The purposes of the bill are to harmonise discrimination law and to strengthen the progress on equality. The explanatory notes published with the bill state that "[T]he practical effect is that listed public authorities will have to consider how their policies, programmes and service delivery will affect people with the protected characteristics".[34] The protected characteristics are: age; disability; gender reassignment; marriage and civil partnership; pregnancy and maternity; race; religion or belief; sex; and sexual orientation (Chapter 1, Clause 4). The bill makes a significant change regarding remedies for discrimination in employment by providing that an employer may be required to remedy matters for

32. Advisory Committee on the FCNM, "Second Opinion on the United Kingdom", adopted 6 June 2007, ACFC/OP/II(2007)003.
33. Ibid., at paragraph 11.
34. Equality Bill (Volume I), Explanatory Notes, at paragraph 7.

the benefit of the wider workforce, not just the claimant (who may well have left their job).

The United Kingdom approach as seen in the Equality Act 2006 and the Equality Bill might reasonably be described as a "macro" strategy to tackle inequality. Clause 1 of the bill requires public authorities in their strategic decision making to consider what action can be taken to reduce socio-economic inequality. This is a wide ranging public law duty that cannot give rise to any private law claim by individuals (Clause 3). However, if taken seriously, it could result in support for individuals and families who find themselves marginalised in access to education and heath services. Examples given by the government include a decision by the Department of Health to allocate central government funds to target areas with the worst health outcomes; or providing assistance to parents encountering difficulties navigating the education system to get their child a place at school.[35] Building upon equality duties enshrined in previous legislation, the Equality Bill creates a new single public sector equality duty which will require public bodies to consider the needs of diverse groups with the protected characteristics when designing and delivering public services (Clause 143). The explanatory notes suggest that the duty could lead a local authority "to introduce measures to facilitate understanding and conciliation between Sunni and Shi'a Muslims living in a particular area with the aim of fostering good relations between people of different religious beliefs". Examples given in the government's own literature include ensuring that meals on wheels services provide culturally diverse food to reflect the religion and beliefs of service users.[36] Significantly, a public authority should consider the need to encourage persons who share a protected characteristic to participate in public life or in any other activity in which participation by such persons is disproportionately low. Public procurement of goods and services has also been brought within the remit of the bill (Clause 149) and may be subject to regulations prescribed by secondary legislation.

In strategic terms, it also makes sense to further the management of diversity through encouraging states to give undertakings, rather than creating fresh individual rights. The current project is focused upon social rights and social rights are generally framed as undertakings rather than

---

35. "A Fairer Future. The Equality Bill and Other Action to Make Equality a Reality", published by the Government Equalities Office, April 2009.

36. Ibid.

as the justiciable rights of individuals. Domestic courts are generally less comfortable in addressing the rights of individuals that have the capacity to impact on the public purse. The boundary between the legal domain and the political arena is contested. Creating justiciable social rights is a highly political issue. It seems sensible to further elaborate the rights and obligations in the ECHR and the European Social Charter which already exist, in particular focusing on the further implementation of the prohibition on direct and indirect discrimination, rather than creating new rights. This could be done through a recommendation agreed upon by Council of Europe Ministers; such a recommendation would be addressed to the accommodation of difference in the delivery of public services and would enumerate the means by which this could be delivered. The needs of communities can only be established through dialogue and negotiation at local level and it is at that level that resource priorities and allocation have to be determined. The legal principles are arguably already in place; the next stage in furthering social cohesion and accommodating difference and diversity is to consider in practical terms how those rights should be implemented.

6. Concluding remarks

From the various models described above, we can discern two broad approaches to the prohibition of discrimination and the promotion of equality: a "micro" approach where legislation aims to protect individuals from discrimination and possibly to require the provision of reasonable accommodation; and a "macro" approach that, as well as protecting against discrimination, focuses on the development of policies and practices through the work of equality bodies and other public institutions charged with the duties of working towards greater equality. As described above, a rights-based approach to prohibit discrimination and further equality is necessary but not sufficient to realise equal access in the delivery of public services. Improvements in social cohesion through the fostering of intercultural competences require both approaches, but particularly the targeting of initiatives for communities at a local level in order to secure policies that reflect the communities for whom they are formulated.

It is suggested that public authorities engaged in the delivery of services to communities should be required to take account of the diverse needs of the people they serve. The imposition of legal obligations in this regard would constitute a constructive attempt to fulfil the treaty obligations laid down in Articles 4 and 15 of the FCNM. The assessment of need can only take place at local level and requires the engagement of all parties. In devising appropriate policies and practices, cultural and religious diversity can and must be respected and managed. Although deriving from the field of conflict prevention, there is much good practice that can be drawn upon and readers' attention is drawn to the Initiative on Conflict Prevention and Diplomacy, which has drawn up a series of handbooks to collate advice aimed at resolving inter-communal conflicts.[37] The work has grown from the practice of the OSCE High Commissioner on National Minorities and therefore derives from a security imperative, which is described as a "human rights informed" approach, rather than a "human rights based" approach. However, the practical advice given regarding the need to "map" situations, establish the facts and take account of demographic data is transferable across a range of situations concerning majority and minority actors. It is only through knowing and understanding local communities and their needs that full equality in the delivery of public services can be realised.

---

37. See, for example, Z. Machnyikova, *Managing Linguistic and Religious Diversity*, published by the Folke Bernadotte Academy for the Initiative on Conflict Prevention through Quiet Diplomacy.

Accommodations for minorities or accommodations for all

Bringing about harmonious coexistence in pluralist societies

Tariq Ramadan[1]

1. Introduction

The debate over legislation has become a central issue in all Western countries. Changes in legislation, adjustments, accommodations or simply the applications (and implications) of case law are natural phenomena familiar to all societies and ones which they must develop and maintain in order to preserve the rule of law in keeping with the social realities of their time. So there is nothing new in reflecting on developments in laws in a constitutional framework, nor is there anything new regarding the need to sometimes revise the constitution itself, where one exists. What is clearly new today, however, is the extent of the "Islamic question": new citizens of the Muslim faith have settled in the West for one, two, three, sometimes four generations and they are now – unlike their parents – increasingly more visible. This new visibility (an indication that the new generations have come out of their social ghettos) alongside continuing immigration has brought new questions to the fore: cultural and religious questions of course, but also legal and political ones. Should we be adapting our laws or simply ask the new arrivals (be they citizens or immigrants) to comply with the existing legal framework? How are we to deal with "the Islamic question" (the transnational extent of which is unprecedented) when Islam is so different (or runs counter to) the laws of secular countries? All countries, in one way or another, are faced with these serious and worrying questions.

---

1. Professor of Islamic Studies, Oxford/Erasmus.

Preliminary remarks

Before looking at the legal issues, we need to ascertain the framework and mindset in which such a debate must take place. Western societies are experiencing severe identity crises with the reality of the new cultural and religious pluralism. Who are we now? What are our roots? What will we become? What are the characteristics of our national and/or cultural identity? These are all questions which are evidence of an underlying tension, doubt and crisis driving people to emotional reactions of fear and introspection, or to populist doctrines exploiting these issues for their own ends. One might therefore be tempted to try to address the emotionalism (and the often accompanying unwillingness to listen) by turning to the law. Here, there is a twofold danger: first, of legislating on matters which are not of a legal nature (social policies, urban and cultural isolation, etc.)[2] and, second, of importing the prevailing emotionalism into the legislative sphere which, because of the very nature of the link made between the two, will inevitably produce timorous, restrictive approaches as we have seen in France over religious symbols, in Ontario (Canada) regarding arbitration tribunals and in Switzerland with the initiative to prohibit minarets.

It is therefore essential to begin by specifying a framework and approach for the debate on the relationship between legislation and social developments. Reiterating the letter and the spirit of laws, clearly setting out the list of inalienable principles (equal treatment, dignity, justice and freedom, etc.), and specifying the objectives of the debates on the laws in force are all elementary ground rules which need to be repeated in a situation where there is a climate of tension and fear. Intellectuals, politicians and legal professionals need to adopt a calm, collected and constructively critical approach and not be carried away by general crises, group hysteria and media hype.[3] The form of communication and the vocabulary used are fundamentally important in clarifying the nature of the legal operations undertaken: explaining that the changes are necessary, that the aim is to secure equal treatment or that questions of law need to be approached in a "reasonable" way (to use the very apposite Canadian word paired with accommodation) are not secondary or merely procedural questions. Form, here, is an integral part of the substance.

---

2. "Making the mistake of legislating" as the sociologist Nilüfer Göle so rightly puts it.
3. The overblown media attention so frequently in evidence.

2. Studying legislation

We need then to have an in-depth look at whether the leeway to be found in existing laws enables us to solve problems caused more by what we imagine to be potential incompatibilities rather than by actual facts.[4] Frequently, problems have been envisaged or created because of a biased, restrictive, timorous interpretation of laws. In point of fact, laws often say and permit much more than interpretations suggest.

Our societies have become more multicultural with an ever-growing diversity of religions. The latitude provided by constitutions and national legislation is often much wider than it appears and offers ways of solving numerous problems brought about by the presence of "new" citizens. However, as I have said, we also have to have a positive state of mind vis-à-vis pluralism in our societies: the same text read by a legal professional (a lawyer or judge, or even by a parliament) having a positive and confident view of diversity will tend to be interpreted in a receptive and inclusive way whereas if it is read through the prism of mistrust of the new citizens, their religion and/or their culture, it will be interpreted in a restrictive way as a means of protection, and on occasion exclusion.[5] These phenomena are natural and frequent and, moreover, are not always intentional.

There is a second approach which should not be overlooked. This is studying the rights and case law in respect of the religions (and cultures) which are either in the majority or long established in the country in question. The two fundamental rights (freedom of conscience and freedom of religion) have already been interpreted, revised and applied in a multitude of ways providing precedents of immeasurable value. The important thing here is to draw attention to and maintain equal treatment between all religions: this objective should remain a priority in the application of the law and, accordingly, a significant amount of explanation must be carried out on at least two levels:

- in recent years the presumptions about Islam and its followers have led to the view that Muslims want specific legislation (or even Sharia

---

4. As I explained in my book, *To be a European Muslim*, Islamic Foundation, 1999.

5. The debates in France between the Conseil d'Etat, which held that there was nothing in a particular draft law that ran counter to the secular nature of the state, and the members of the National Assembly and politicians who saw in it a move intrinsically opposed to secularism is a good example. The uncertainty over interpretations remained until March 2004 when a more restrictive law was passed, excluding girls wearing the Islamic headscarf from school.

Law). But in looking at the relevant laws and decisions, it is clear that Muslims were merely being granted either rights guaranteed under ordinary law, or rights already acknowledged to other religions;[6]

- it is essential to bear in mind that the objective of equal treatment must sometimes lead to rebalancing and adjustment policies requiring differential treatment in order to secure equality before the law. The various religious communities do not all have the same history, the same degree of national institutionalisation or the same wealth: in order to be treated equally before the law (as regards recognition, place of worship and general institutions, etc.), it is sometimes necessary for the state to make specific preferential choices in order to achieve equality since it is a case of rectifying a de facto inequality.

These two points are important in clarifying the ins and outs of the legal approach. Our first thoughts should not focus immediately on change, but rather on the possible scope for inclusion. There is often much more scope than one might imagine.

3. "The Islamic question"

We should not hide the fact that the majority of these new debates are a result of the Muslim presence in the West. However, what is lacking at the very heart of the legal approach is consideration of what the real issue is: the Islamic legal tradition is not a monolithic framework with which one can or cannot come to an agreement and which must be included or excluded because of what it is – religious, sacred, static even dogmatic. This image is erroneous and its consequences can be particularly serious.

Just as constitutions and laws have significant room for manoeuvre in their interpretations, the legal tradition in Islam is particularly flexible and allows numerous adaptations and very specific adjustments. It is important for the West to be more familiar with the potential creativity of legal interpretations in Islam (such as those produced today by Islamic legal councils in Europe and the West). Very often there is confusion between

---

6. Conflicts emerged in Canada and the United Kingdom (regarding arbitration tribunals) which caused great alarm because they were called "Sharia courts" even though this was merely an approach to managing private affairs authorised under ordinary law. There is much debate about the issue of Islamic schools and, once again, it would appear that "Islamic schools" themselves are the problem despite the fact that other private religious schools (Catholic, Protestant, Jewish, etc.) are more numerous and are part of the accepted educational landscape.

cultural resistance, the specific interpretations of a school of law or literalist approaches and the monolithic entities that "Islam" and the "Sharia" are thought to be. Things are much more complex and legal experts need to know and acknowledge the different legal opinions, not to focus on just one of them or choose the one which best corresponds to the expectations of the country in question, but to bring matters to the attention of Muslim scholars and citizens in order to create an internal debate and consider the available options vis-à-vis a particular issue.[7]

Contrary to the presumptions about the incompatibility of Islamic references with secularised societies, and in the light of the facts and figures relating to Muslim citizens, it will be seen that the vast majority of the latter have no legal problems and that they have found pragmatic solutions in the Western environment. We must therefore not exaggerate the differences or incompatibilities of legal references. They may exist but between the margin for manoeuvre in the law in democratic societies and the acknowledged flexibility in Islamic legal traditions, it is possible to find satisfactory solutions without amending existing legal frameworks.

4. Problem situations

Nonetheless, it cannot be denied that there are sometimes difficult and complex situations for Muslim citizens living in the West. Certain legal schools have rules which may make the situation delicate and there are also interpretations of law, or legal agreements with the countries of origin, which make solutions much more difficult to find.

Questions relating to practices, festivals, places of worship, dress code (related to function: public servant or user), marriages (more broadly private law), divorce, childcare, social or medical support, cemeteries, etc. are all fields in which conflicts (and occasionally conflicting interpretations) may emerge. Three approaches have developed in recent years – sometimes in the same country: a simple refusal to discuss the matter, claiming that the "new arrivals" must adapt to the society "welcoming" them (this was often, but not exclusively, the majority position in France); specific arrangements enabling Muslims to fulfil what they believed to be religious injunctions (particularly in the United States and the United

---

7. Situations such as swimming classes for prepubescent children, doctors who need to be the same sex as the patient, marriage contracts, witness statements, etc. are all issues of debate between schools and Muslim scholars and which require study within the Muslim community.

Kingdom); and, thirdly, an approach focusing not solely on the minority but taking a fresh look at ordinary law at the request of a section of the population so as to ensure that adapting the law for some did not create an injustice for others (the philosophy of reasonable accommodation in Canada goes some way towards achieving this ideal).

I believe that a number of strict conditions should apply to this "reasonable" approach (which, moreover, should be conceived in and adapted to the country to which it relates):

- a study should be undertaken to verify whether the latitude in the law already makes it possible to find a solution without the need for an accommodation;

- the Muslim partners should be contacted in order to get to know the views of the different schools on these questions and the flexibility that is possible;

- it must be ascertained that the accommodations concern in practice all citizens and that the process of adjustment and accommodation never violates the principle of equality;

- in addition, there should be multidimensional communication: amid the fears and mistrust there is a need to create the conditions for calm debate and then to provide clear and transparent information (to journalists if appropriate, to politicians and of course to the general public).

Mistrust, fears, repeated controversies, the nagging question of immigration all create an atmosphere requiring legal professionals – usually discreet and calm – to take measures, both preventive and ongoing, to clarify and openly explain matters to the political class and journalists. The "Islamic question" is not, and has never been, just a legal matter in the strict sense of the word; a poor presentation of legislative questioning concerning the presence and rights of Muslims (use of vocabulary, already established practice, reminders of the need for equal treatment, etc.) may be counterproductive and lead to avoidable stumbling blocks. The arrangements concerning the question of secularism in France and the debate on arbitration tribunals in Ontario, Canada and in the United Kingdom were influenced and led in a particular direction by the atmosphere of crisis and controversy preceding or surrounding them: it is impossible in such matters to be heard and to take action calmly and reasonably.

5. Societies and laws are changing

One should also remember that societies as well as laws naturally change. There is nothing new in this area and the idea that constitutions and legislation have to be accepted as they are by the "new arrivals" and that there is no question of changing "our fundamental, strict and immutable laws", which "are part of our cultural and legal identity",[8] is fantasy or reflects a mindset which has become dogmatic and often rigid.

The work of legal readjustment is part of a natural and welcome process in democratic societies. The conditions set out above are important and the aims must be repeated and respected. Living together in harmony will be possible only if one remains faithful to the aims of the rule of law, equal treatment of citizens and respect for beliefs within the latitude inherent in ordinary law. This does not mean that one should never consider possible amendments but the latter must be conceived and presented not as privileges offered to new citizens but as a rebalancing from which all citizens of the society in question can benefit.

Two phenomena need to be highlighted in these recurring debates on the question of the "rights of minorities". There are trends in all countries, especially in Europe, towards increasingly more restrictive interpretations of the law with the aim, of course, to protect against desires for specific treatment presumed to be expressed by the new citizens. Political parties (as in France, Switzerland, the Netherlands, etc.) have even asked for changes to the constitution or certain laws to make them more precise or, more specifically, more restrictive with regard to the "rights of minorities" (understood here as "Muslims"). The law on religious symbols in schools in France is clearly one such example. These phenomena, which on the face of it affect "minorities" or "Muslims", have and will have consequences for all citizens. Closed, timorous, protective stances regarding an exclusive and erroneous perception of the legal and cultural identity of the country enclose the debates and questions within reflections which are often dogmatic, rigid and sometimes quite simply racist (and used to their own ends by the populism of certain political parties). There has to be some early groundwork, based on facts and figures, to combat fears and perceptions and to show how the attitude of introspection is now turning against the whole of the population.

---

8. Comments heard during the debates on the question of secularism and religious symbols in France in 2003.

The second phenomenon is relatively interesting and instructive. While there is a considerable outcry about the question of adjusting laws in the social and private sphere (marriage, place of worship, etc.), little or nothing is known about the arrangements being made to authorise the financial and economic activities which are considered by certain Muslim economic operators, bankers and entrepreneurs as the only "legal" (halal) ones. The introduction of procedures complying with Sharia Law and the legal changes which that has presupposed has produced no outcry in Western societies. We know that it is a question of opening markets and attracting financial "manna". The acquiescence and silence accompanying these very real transactions should cause us to think long and hard about the very nature of the controversies and how they are manipulated in the social and political sphere: over and above the (occasionally blatant) hypocrisy of words and practices, it is a question of power relationships and of interests. Muslim populations today are both very vulnerable and seen as offering little contribution to the general interest (unlike the financial investments from rich Muslim contributors already established here in the West, the oil kingdoms or elsewhere). This image absolutely has to change, but it is likely that over time it will naturally evolve. The settlement of Muslims in the West and the phenomena of visibility and institutionalisation will gradually normalise the Muslim presence. The signs are that the present crises will come to an end although this does not mean that the legal question will have been resolved once and for all. There has to be reflection and research at national level so as to stay unstintingly on course in pursuit of the initial objective which is to respect freedom of conscience and ensure the equal treatment of all citizens.

6. Conclusion

The debate is a lively one and sometimes people on all sides are unwilling to listen. There are signs that things are changing – but unfortunately not always in the right direction. We must devote more effort to studying the room for manoeuvre in laws and the flexibility of Islamic rules. There must be closer and more sustained collaboration between Western and Muslim legal experts who are the ones who need to be undertaking this study. New, more innovative and creative initiatives could emerge from such co-operation.

The "Islamic question" has often been approached from the standpoint of "immigration", but what we are discussing today is linked not to immigration but to the question of citizenship and harmonious coexistence in our Western societies. These societies, it must be reiterated, will not survive without renewed immigration. Instead of homing in on the new immigrants (and the anecdotes about them), as certain parties do, in order to question the ability of Muslims to integrate into Western societies, we should be doing precisely the opposite. A fair, reasonable and politically responsible attitude would be to turn to the new citizens of the Muslim faith who live harmoniously in their society so that they can assist with the installation process of the new arrivals. Islam, through these new citizens, is already "integrated"; we now need to think about assisting the integration of those immigrants who will continue to settle in the West. Not only because this is what they want, but also because it is in our economic interests.

As I have said, this cannot be carried out calmly without a considerable amount of explanation and support. The experience of the meetings and debates which took place during the drafting of the report on reasonable accommodation in Canada is of considerable interest. Transparency, a willingness to listen and dialogue must go hand-in-hand with reflection on any legal adaptations when and if such are really necessary. Our societies need this dialogue and we need to provide the opportunity for everyone's views to be discussed in a regulated framework which will limit extremist ideas but nevertheless allow fears and rejectionist tendencies to be expressed.

This is in the interest of all citizens and it is this dimension which must be highlighted. Reflection and approaches at legal level are designed to preserve the freedoms and equality of all citizens before the law. We are not talking about privileges or preferential treatment but processes which are normal and essential in a democratic society that wishes to remain faithful to its ideals. Greater freedom for some should mean greater freedom for everyone. This is the exact opposite of the false equation whereby restricting the freedoms of the "new arrivals" or of the "minorities" will result in the preservation, or indeed the increase, of the freedoms of the majority. It is exactly the opposite: when you violate the freedom of conscience of one section of society, no matter how much in a minority it may be (or be perceived as being), it is everyone's freedom that is violated.

The evolution of institutional cultures: migrants' access to services and rights

Eduardo J. Ruiz Vieytez[1]

1. From migration to diversity

The purpose of this paper is to provoke some reflection on the legal and political access of migrants to services and rights within plural democratic societies. The paper does not adopt a purely legal approach to the topic, since traditional legal methodologies are showing themselves to be insufficient to deal with multicultural realities. Political and moral considerations based on values such as justice and equality will also be incorporated. The final goal is to deconstruct traditional discourses or reinforce new approaches in favour of a more open interpretation of the existing regulations. For pragmatic reasons, the promotion of institutional changes towards multicultural realities will be proposed via reinterpretation of the existing legal framework. Therefore, the starting point of the proposal does not challenge the basis of the legal system itself, but only the way it is implemented in respect to certain sectors of the society, migrants, minorities or aliens (non-nationals).

The very topic of the paper provokes some difficulties in itself, which must be addressed before opening the way to further considerations. In this respect, two different questions may arise. It would be necessary to know what we understand by "institutional cultures" as well as by "migrant". The first concept may not be particularly relevant for this discussion. We can understand "institutional culture" as a combination of political culture and practice at a given institutional level, normally the state. However, in some cases different institutional cultures could coexist within the same state, due to ideological or territorial differences. As for this paper, I will consider institutional culture as the dominant political perception of managing public spaces and resources. Of more importance, however, is the fact that the term migrant is a non-technical word from a legal perspective. Migrations create specific contexts and situations and most of these reflections are conducted by this kind of realities. Sociologically, the migrant does exist, not only for the receiving society, but for the particular

---

1. Director, Pedro Arupe Institute of Human Rights, University of Deusto (Spain).

experience of the migrant him/herself. But when the notion is translated to a legal system, we normally find that migrant is not a technical word. It is true that at the United Nations level, the concept of migrant has been incorporated into some political bodies and even legal documents,[2] but in fact, the legal meaning of the word is not the sociological one. Domestic legal orders do not refer to migrants, since there is normally no formal definition of migration or of a migrant person.

The key issue from a legal perspective is whether the migrant person goes through an international border or not. The hard link between individuals and states is that of nationality (or citizenship). From the point of view of the legal system, we can speak about aliens, foreigners, or non-nationals, but not about migrants. Besides this, we all know that there are different and important legal consequences for anybody that is working or living in a state of which they are not a national. However, the social and cultural consequences of being a migrant are much more uncertain. Obviously, it is possible to be a migrant without being non-national. Internal migrations occur, and in some cases their implications could be more relevant for the people concerned than international migration. At the same time, it is inaccurate to identify many foreigners as migrants, even if they live permanently in the host country. It is clear that the level of social or cultural differences compared to the majority of the host society can differ dramatically from one case to another.

Therefore, when reflecting on institutional cultures, we can only make political and legal proposals from the perspective of relevant legal concepts, such as that of alien. Talking about migrants may not help from a progressive and multicultural perspective. Obviously, the effects of migration or even the migrant identity of many people cannot be denied, but when thinking about public responses to this kind of situation, it may be a better approach to avoid the concept of migrant. In fact, it is impossible to determine when a migrant ceases to be such. It is quite reasonable to use the concept of migrant during the first period of stay of a person who arrived from abroad seeking a better life. But to refer to him/her as a migrant after a period of 10, 20 or 30 years (or even more, to refer to his/her children as second-generation immigrants) is much more doubtful. From a human rights perspective, it may be counterproductive. Thus, it is possible to identify different fields for public intervention around the

---

2. For example, the International Convention on the Protection of the Rights of All Migrant Workers and Members of their Families, adopted in the framework of the United Nations in 1990.

phenomenon of international migrations. Public policies devoted to the regulation of migration flows correspond to migration in its most restrictive meaning. In fact, migration happens to be a process and the word "migrant" can only be used to refer to a person who is within such a process, and not to those who have already finished their movement. If migration is just a process (which can be regulated by law), much of what is called "integration of migrants" is in fact "democratic management of diversity", in particular when thinking about cultural, identity or political elements.

From the core of migration policies, which refer to the regulation of flows, another three different domains for public intervention can be observed. On the one hand, the whole social and economic/labour field. Normally, migration results from a desire to improve one's social condition, but even in other cases, states must regulate, ensure and promote adequate social integration of newcomers. A second field of public intervention is related to cultural or identity elements. As we said before, cultural elements are basic components of human dignity and they must be taken into consideration when regulating the public space. It is mistaken to consider that integration of immigrants is achieved when they get a stable job and the corresponding working permit, as if they had left their identity behind in the migration process. Finally, a third domain of public intervention (and legal regulation) is that of effective political participation of new citizens, which relates to naturalisation and nationality law.

Therefore, the first proposal is to consider migration as a process (which can be regulated by law), but not to speak of immigrants when we refer to concrete people. The approach of this paper will be that it is necessary to move from a discourse on "integration of migrants" to one of "democratic management of diversity". The issue becomes not how to "accommodate" immigrants into our society, but how to rethink the whole of society at every instant (this is to say, how to accommodate diversities), which is a much more inclusive approach. In a nutshell, there is a need to change the perspective from which public policies are designed and implemented in this field. These are policies that should no longer focus on the control of immigration but veer towards the democratic management of pluralist societies, composed in increasing numbers of culturally diverse citizens.

Movements of populations, both old and new, did not create multiculturality in Europe, but rather emphasised the pre-existing plural reality. The construction of nation states was characterised by the exclusion of numerous identities; nation states having been very effective agents in the homogenisation of culture and identity in their respective societies. As an outcome of immigration, multiculturality is neither a problem nor an ideal, but simply a reality to be managed. The need today is to find formulas and proposals for the management of this phenomenon that are at once democratic and compatible with human rights. My reflection starts from the awareness that a real framework of human rights cannot be constructed without incorporating the identities of people and groups, especially if these are minorities in their respective political scopes. We consider the distinctive elements of collective identities (religion, language, culture, etc.) as basic factors in the personal development of all human beings. These constitute real factors of personal integration and symbolic referents of extreme importance. This is why the effective presence of these elements in the public space has extraordinary importance for the individuals that share them (irrespective of how many they share). From here comes the importance of cultural factors in the design of a complete framework of human rights and, consequently, citizenship.[3]

2. A proposal for a new reading of citizenship

Within this complex context of today's developed and pluralist societies, two different but complementary topics must be subject to reflection. On the one hand, the access to social services for people who are not nationals of the state. On the other hand, the definition of criteria to manage the so-called cultural differences in the needs and attitudes in respect of the public space and resources. Both issues are closely linked with what I have called the "identitarian state" (or "state of identity") model, and both should be overcome politically through the idea of citizenship and the equality principle.

The political strategy to lead this fight against the "identitarian state" will focus on the idea of citizenship. In this respect, the two main ways of exclusion that are present in our current legal systems can be identified

---

3. As indicated in the UNESCO Universal Declaration on Cultural Diversity (approved by its General Conference on 3 November 2001): "The defence of cultural diversity is an ethical imperative, inseparable from respect for human dignity. It implies a commitment to human rights and fundamental freedoms, in particular the rights of persons belonging to minorities and those of indigenous peoples. No one may invoke cultural diversity to infringe upon human rights guaranteed by international law, nor to limit their scope" (Article 4 of the declaration).

with two different "filters", both affecting the entitlement to and the exercise of fundamental human rights. The two sources of exclusion are:

- the filter of belonging;

- the filter of identity.

The first one (filter of belonging) corresponds to the instrument of nationality or citizenship. According to it, we once again find a clear and legally relevant distinction between nationals and foreigners. This basic difference legitimises social and cultural policies (including severe differences in access to services and rights) in respect to those persons who are not nationals of the state they live in. The question does not challenge the whole distinction between these two obvious categories, but only to what extent it is relevant and reasonable when it generates differences in entitlement to social fundamental rights.

The second filter (identity) refers to the dominant position of a given culture (including values, languages, religious traditions, attitudes and so forth) within a particular state-based society. There is no possible public neutrality towards cultural elements, since they manifest themselves in a multitude of ways in everyday life, including within the public sector. The point is that dominant cultures create closed spaces (the states and their respective legal orders), where human rights are in fact nationalised, and interpreted through those prevailing cultures. This affects extensively the way in which fundamental rights are implemented or exercised in a particular national context, and the possibilities for adaptation to the increasing plurality in society.

To combat ideologically both fronts, I have proposed a double reconsideration of the idea of citizenship: against a closed system of belonging, an inclusive citizenship must be adopted; and against a closed circuit of identity, a plural (or multicultural) citizenship is necessary. Implementing the fundamental meaning of these two concepts, cultural diversity can be managed in a democratic way, and more open and effective access to the services and rights of those considered to be migrants can be facilitated.[4]

---

4. See E. J. Ruiz Vieytez, *Minorías, inmigración y democracia en Europa. Una lectura multicultural de los derechos humanos*, Tirant lo Blanch, Valencia, 2006, pp. 477-508; R. Dunbar and E. J. Ruiz Vieytez (eds), *Human Rights and Diversity. New Challenges for Plural Societies*, Humanitarian Net, Bilbao, 2008.

Inclusive citizenship is based on the idea of the fair treatment of all residents and the right to participate. Nowadays, the democratic legitimacy of the state demands the participation of all residents in the processes of political decision making, in an equitable manner based on their contribution to the prosperity of the country.[5] The political documents demanding a more open and wide-ranging concept of citizenship for foreign residents are numerous.[6] Political and legal citizenship must be linked to effective or factual residence and not to national assimilation.

Plural citizenship is based on the concept of cultural freedom.[7] It implies that all citizens must enjoy the best possible range of cultural opportunities, in a way in which they can develop their individual or collective potentialities through the cultures they belong to or they identify with. Since elements defining collective identities (religion, language, cultural values and so forth) are crucial factors in the development of any human being, today it is not possible to build a human rights framework without considering the identity issue. The presence of these elements in the public space in an appropriate manner, consistent with the standards of rights and services provided in a given society, has an extraordinary importance for achieving social justice and cohesion. According to this, the public space must be re-negotiated on a permanent and reasonable basis among all the identities that make up a plural society at any given moment.

Therefore, the first stage would be to distinguish between the exclusion determined by the two filters referred to as regards access to services and/or rights: on the one hand, the alienness (the legal exclusion provoked by the nationality filter), and, on the other hand, the minority condition of those who are different in cultural or identity terms from the prevalent majority. Of course, both elements can be present in the same person,

---

5. Recommendation 1500 (2001) of the Parliamentary Assembly of the Council of Europe, of 26 January 2001, paragraph 4.

6. For example, Recommendation 1206 (1993) of the Parliamentary Assembly of the Council of Europe, of 4 February 1993, paragraph 7; Recommendation 1500 (2001) of the Parliamentary Assembly of the Council of Europe, of 26 January 2001, paragraph 11.4.b; Recommendation 1625 (2003) of the Parliamentary Assembly of the Council of Europe, of 30 September 2003, paragraph 5; Recommendation No. 30 of the United Nations Committee on the Elimination of Racial Discrimination, of 1 October 2004, paragraph 13.

7. As used by the UNDP (United Nations Development Programme), *Human Development Report 2004, Cultural Liberty in Today's Diverse World*, available at http://hdr.undp.org/en/reports/global/hdr2004.

but we will also find people affected by only one of the two factors. In fact, these are two elements of diversity, and the real issue we are dealing with is the democratic management of a situation of diversity. The key problem is to understand "otherness" within our own society (which would in turn become a different and pluralist society). It is obvious that migration flows are decisive in initiating the debate, but again the debate itself is not only on managing migration, but on managing diversity with a wider perspective. The difference of approach can be decisive when defending solutions, in particular in times of crisis.

3. Questions on access to rights and services

Any given society creates a set of responses to what it considers are social and cultural needs. The state articulates provisions and undertakes positive obligations in respect of certain situations. In respect of access of migrants and other differentiated people to social resources, two different questions can be formulated:

- Is it possible and/or legitimate to create legal filters (belonging filters) for the enjoyment of rights and services by migrants?

- Who defines the contents of the rights (or services)(identity filters) that the state is obliged to provide, and how are they defined?

When answering the first question, it is necessary to go back to the distinction between the terms "migrant" and "alien". Legally speaking, there is no reason to deny access to any service or right to any person who is a national of the state on the basis of belonging. Therefore, the question can only be formulated in respect of non-nationals. Traditionally, it has been considered that states are free to define the rules for foreign people to access their territory. This, however, does not imply that they are free to regulate their conditions of stay. Even in international law prior to the Universal Declaration of Human Rights, the treatment of foreigners within a given state was not an exclusively internal matter. States are obliged to respect a minimum standard of rights (and consequently services) to all people, regardless of their nationality and legal status. Problems arise when interpreting an extension to this minimum.

However, in today's democratic societies, legitimised on the basis of their respect for human rights, a further step is required. Thus, when dealing with long-term foreign immigrants, the conceptual answer that should be given in democratic states is that of inclusive citizenship. Effective integration in the host society does not derive so much from access to the labour market or administrative legality, but from the incorporation of the individual into the political community as a citizen. Citizenship is not reduced to being a mere legal instrument of belonging, but implies a symbol in itself, a bond of identity with the respective political community. The long-term immigrant is, from this perspective, just a new citizen.

However, even considering foreign migrants as new citizens, it seems reasonable that the legal order can adopt some restrictions on accessing certain rights or services, according to the law itself. As has been said already, according to the principle of inclusive citizenship, any long-term resident must be considered a full citizen as regards social and cultural rights. Nevertheless, when citizens are outside the law, for the sake of the coherence of the system they cannot be allowed to enjoy certain public resources before there has been some adjustment to the legal situation. This is a particularly difficult issue when we have to deal with the situation of permanent resident foreigners being in an illegal (irregular or non-legal) administrative situation. While a universal set of minimum rights is ensured, the access to some additional social and cultural rights or services can be more controversial. The only obvious option is to widen immigration law and to adapt it to the social situation and the existing migratory flows and future labour market possibilities. A long-term unlawful situation of a significant number of people shows a profound weakness in the legal system itself. Permanent instruments to legalise what is de facto a social reality are needed. On the contrary, if the legal system determines a violation of the law, it must have the means to avoid the situation.

In respect to the second question, one of the consequences of the organisation of the world into nation states has in fact been the nationalisation of human rights through domestic constitutional law. Human rights have been incorporated into national legal orders, normally through the constitution, as fundamental or constitutional rights. However, from a pluralist perspective, the interpretation of the content of each of the fundamental rights made by states and their institutions (namely courts and legislators) does not always respect the substantial essence of all human rights. This happens especially in relation to identity differences. Thus, it is commonly understood that particular fundamental rights may be exercised through the official or dominant cultural elements of the respective state (for example, languages, moral values, cultural understandings, and so forth).

Nevertheless, human rights are not only rights within a state, but universal rights which must be respected, independently of the state where they are exercised. The international and universal dimension is co-substantial with the idea of human rights. Therefore, the enjoyment of rights cannot be totally conditioned by identity; on the contrary, universal rights must be able to be exercised through any identity as far as is reasonable and feasible, but always with an open mentality. It is a question of being able to exercise human rights through one's own identity, and not despite it. Thus, for example, freedom of expression will include in its protection not only the content of what is expressed, but also the language used to express it. The same can be said with respect to linguistic, religious or cultural demands with regard to rights such as education, private and family life, political participation, and freedom of association, among others. This all implies the need to adapt the state, in a reasonable and proportional manner, so that it is able to put into effect this multicultural principle through the concrete exercise of each of the rights that are recognised to all persons. In fact, today there is less and less necessity for the state to officially support concrete identity elements, such as religions, languages and so forth. The public institutions must be guided by the idea of serving the different identities present in the public space, promoting them equally and facilitating the solution of conflicts that could arise among them. The state must be at the service of citizens and their identities, and not vice versa.

Moreover, if the national or traditional cultures of a country are worth protecting and incorporating into public policies, why should the culture of recent, and perhaps more vulnerable, immigrants not be given the same importance? The argument of considering that migrants consented when moving to a different country (used, for instance, by Kymlicka) does not seem convincing, since many migrants feel forced to move to another country for a variety of reasons and many do not consent to the idea of abandoning their original identities at all. Again, the issue is much better focused if we consider the immigrants as new citizens, and current society as a diverse one. Policy will not aim at "social integration" of immigrants, but at "managing democratically" the existing diversity. In fact, many of the conflicts or problems we face when debating the position of foreign migrants in the public space are not even cultural debates, but legal problems. The real issue here is the legal meaning of equality and of difference. The main discriminatory factor used so far by the Western nation states has been that of nationality. The problem is that we thought that non-discriminatory and culturally neutral laws were possible, linked as such to abstract and impartial justice. Two useful guiding principles in this respect may be those of reasonable accommodation, and the idea of complex equality: people and social groups have the right to be equal when the differences make them inferior, and have the right to be different when the equality rule makes them uniform (Ferrajoli, Santos and De Lucas).[8]

4. Equality and non-discrimination in a pluralist society

When it comes to the concrete issue of the access to rights and services by specific groups of people (for example, migrants), there is always an ideological tension between the principle of specificity in the social or cultural treatment of minorities (in a broad sense), and the principle of normalisation, by which they are canalised through the existing general services. According to the former, it would be a case of building specific services or specifically oriented services for particular groups, based on their differences and/or disadvantages. The normalisation process would roughly consist of incorporating all users in the same services, regardless of their belonging to specific groups, emphasising the function of integration. The tension between these two principles can be confusing to some extent, and it can also hide a real debate on the implementation of the principle of equality that must be present in any democracy.

In reality, normalisation of access to a particular service is not opposed to specificity as regards the contents of the service. Services related to social or cultural rights must be flexible and adaptable to the different situations and identities, since identity is a crucial factor of social integration, as was already mentioned. But as a general principle, it must be done through normalised institutions offered to all citizens. Here, a distinction must be made between groups or situations that deserve a specific response because they suffered particular disadvantages, and groups which claim a different response because they are different in identity. Being culturally different cannot be taken as a disadvantage in itself. In other words, the aim of any democratic state should be that cultural differences do not create real disadvantage. Therefore, the different response needed is not something different from the "normal response", but another kind of "normal response", at the same level as that offered to the majority.

This debate is also translated into legal consequences when we discuss protection of minorities (including migrants) through specific or general

---

8. See J. de Lucas, "Managing Multicultural Society Democratically: Identities, Rigths, Citizenship", in R. Dunbar and E. J. Ruiz Vieytez (eds), *Human Rights and Diversity. New Challenges for Plural Societies*, Humanitarian Net, Bilbao, 2008, p. 58. L. Ferrajoli, *Derechos y garantías. La ley del más débil*, Trotta, Madrid, 1999.

human rights. The practical consequence of the principles of plural citizenship and complex equality would not be the recognition of specific rights for minorities, but a new reading of the contents of universal fundamental rights. Therefore, it is necessary to de-nationalise the interpretation of human rights in the particular national contexts. The universalism of human rights assumes that there is a universal truth, that is, a common, even minimal, understanding of human dignity. Multiculturalism seems opposed to such a view. However, a common truth or minimum standards do not imply that they must be equally implemented by everybody. On the contrary, the reconciliation of the equality principle and that of different treatment must be founded on the basis of both multiculturalism and human rights theory.

In fact, the principle of equality does not imply uniform treatment of all situations, but, on the contrary, it ensures different treatment in different situations. Thus, the non-discrimination principle is violated when the authorities, without any objective and reasonable justification, treat equally clearly different situations. The principle of non-discrimination has thus been evolving under the influence of multiculturalist debates. Even the European Court of Human Rights has occasionally shifted its traditional interpretation of non-discrimination to incorporate this more pluralistic perspective:

> The Court has so far considered that the right under Article 14 not to be discriminated against in the enjoyment of the rights guaranteed under the Convention is violated when States treat differently persons in analogous situations without providing an objective and reasonable justification .... However, the Court considers that this is not the only facet of the prohibition of discrimination in Article 14. The right not to be discriminated against in the enjoyment of the rights guaranteed under the Convention is also violated when States without an objective and reasonable justification fail to treat differently persons whose situations are significantly different.[9]

The case referred to constitutes the most relevant statement by the Court in this respect, but it is not the only one, since the Thlimmenos doctrine has been used (with different results) in certain other cases by the same Court. A similar development is also present in the so-called discrimination

---

9. *Thlimmenos v. Greece*, Application No. 34369/97, judgment of 6 April 2000, paragraph 44.

directives adopted by the European Community in 2000.[10] They embrace the concept of indirect discrimination, include harassment under the concept of discrimination and require positive action to combat discrimination. In other cases, some human rights bodies have limited the state's margin of appreciation when dealing with identity differences.[11] This is also the case in the framework of protection of traditional minorities under the two main European instruments implemented in this field.[12]

In a nutshell, equality in its purely traditional formal sense is not sufficient for the management of today's pluralist societies, since there exist some groups and people which find themselves in a structural minority position. The role of the law consists in balancing the democratic criterion (majority rule) through corrective measures aimed at overcoming structural and permanent minority positions by highlighting the pluralistic dimension. For this reason, the equality principle cannot be merely interpreted in its formal dimension, namely treating all citizens in the same way. Consequently, equality cannot be evaluated in the perspective of a numerical majority. In this context, the regulation of procedures to determine ways of access to and enjoyment of rights and services is crucial. Thus, open and wide participation (even on the basis of identity) of both individuals and groups becomes thus a key concept in deepening the democratic foundation of society. In any case, the renegotiation of access to the public space and services must be based on a proper extension of the implementation of the equality principle to all citizens, and not on the need to recognise specific rights for concrete collectives or minority groups.

---

10. Directive 2000/43/EC implementing the principle of equal treatment between persons irrespective of racial or ethnic origin, OJ L 180/22; Directive 2000/78/EC establishing a general framework for equal treatment in employment and occupation, OJ L 303/16.

11. For instance, the European Court of Human Rights: *Cyprus v. Turkey*, Application No. 25781/94, judgment of 10 May 2001; and *Bessarabian Metropolitan Church v. Moldova*, Application No. 45701/99, judgment of 13 December 2001. United Nations Human Rights Committee: *J.G.A. Diergaardt (late Captain of the Rehoboth Baster Community) et al. v. Namibia* (Communication No. 760/1997), decision of 25 July 2000, CCPR/C/69/D/760/1997; *Ignatane v. Latvia* (Communication No. 884/1999), decision of 25 July 2001, CCPR/C/72/D/884/1999.

12. The European Charter for Regional or Minority Languages (1992) and the Framework Convention for the Protection of National Minorities (1995).

PART C – REASONABLE ACCOMMODATION
IN A FRAMEWORK OF DIALOGUE, NATIONAL EDUCATION AND TEACHING OF COMPETENCES

Resistances to cultural diversity: anti-pluralist rhetoric and other common objections

François Fournier[1]

For the past 15 years or so in Western societies, the intensity of defensive reactions has been commensurate with immigration. These anxieties are evident in the purport of certain debates, the consolidation of populist movements, the direction of state policies, as well as several opinion polls. Over two thirds of Americans, Canadians and citizens of several European countries think that immigration should be restricted and controlled more (PEW 2007); a majority of Europeans think that too many migrants reside in their country (Novatris/Harris Interactive 2007). To at least a quarter of the citizens in five European countries, immigration is a curse rather than a blessing (TNS Sofres 2007). Nonetheless, other opinion polls indicate that the young people in the Western countries, increasingly socialised under conditions of diversity, are less fearful of cultural melting-pots and of otherness.

This article sets out to present some of the perceptions and arguments that besprinkle "cultural resistance" to diversity and pluralism.[2] These are not all, but have been selected according to their prevalence in most Western countries, which are living through the immigration phenomenon virtually without exception. These utterances are not always free of

---

1. Consultant on socio-political issues, Senior Analyst with the Bouchard-Taylor Commission (2007-08)

2. This expression is borrowed from a Quebec writer, Jacques Godbout, who appeals for "cultural resistance" and argues that the fans of multiculturalism (and of anti-racism) confuse racism and cultural resistance. Racism is discrimination founded on race; cultural resistance is founded on the common good. Jacques Godbout, "Continuons le débat, il ne fait que commencer", *Le Devoir*, 23 September 2006.

intolerance or ignorance, but often remain genuine heartfelt appeals that should be heeded and addressed.

Indeed, one has to reckon with these doctrines, which does not mean yielding to them but taking them into account, whether to refute them convincingly and repeatedly or to ponder the real problems which they raise. To ignore them entirely would give populism an open road to exploit insecurity in a demagogic fashion, to pervert the official policies with our acquiescence. Dialogue is always necessary, even with intolerance.

This survey of anti-pluralist rhetoric has no claim to exhaustiveness since, for example, it does not delve into each national situation and does not register the philosophical objections to cultural pluralism. The matter analysed comes from diverse sources, in particular national and international opinion polls. But one source was singled out because of its wealth, the proceedings of the commission advising on accommodation practices linked with cultural differences (Bouchard-Taylor Commission), which conducted consultations throughout Quebec (Canada) in 2007. The commission's analysts scrutinised the 900 briefs submitted, a task whose outcome, *inter alia*, is a typology which catalogues the arguments for, against or non-committal about immigration, integration and reasonable accommodations (Roy and Lavoie-Talbot 2007). The typology served as raw material from which various categories were compiled for the purposes of this essay.

The arguments surveyed in it do not represent the voice of the majority in host societies and do not even necessarily form coherent discourses of the majority, although they often profess to uphold its interests and do originate within the majorities. It is important to remember that these majorities are also found to have a far more overt discourse which must be heeded in the same way as that of the minorities, for the urgent purpose of enriching the pluralist rhetoric.

1. Anti-pluralist rhetoric and other common objections

Two preliminary remarks:

Objections to diversity and pluralism as presented here are in many respects disparate, some more emotional, others more structured; some more radical, others more qualified; some mainly attacking the sociological process of cultural diversification in our societies, others more opposed to pluralism, that is the general approach underlying the policies of diversity. Besides, the varied nature of the objections bears witness to the range of objectors: readers will discern the arguments of those who champion Christian civilisation, or who propound every brand of secularism, and the anxious perplexity of ordinary uncommitted citizens.

This presentation of perceptions and critical arguments is bereft of any national background despite the accepted fact that each objection is embedded in a specific national reality, to a greater or lesser degree depending on the features of states' national histories and their socio-political, economic and cultural context (portrayal of immigration, *inter alia*). As an example, the debates over secularity in Quebec have a particularly sensitive side in that the secularisation of the public institutions there is a comparatively recent phenomenon.

Anti-pluralist rhetoric is classified under three headings: general expressions of unease, diagnostic elements and proposed solutions.

1.1. Unease: What is wrong?

This is principally in the register of emotion and general impressions. Six interlocking themes have been singled out:

- The sense of becoming alien to one's homeland. This is the theme of invasive difference, both visible and audible, in which the known references vanish.

- The impression of lost unity, erosion of social cohesion, ending of collective aspirations. So many differences and contrasts spell the end of a certain uniformity. The common interest disappears, to be supplanted by incompatible interests. In these circumstances, the world that we share will soon be no more, becoming permeated with disparities so that there is no more common impulse, no more common direction. Cultural differences are perceived as being more problematic, possibly as more threatening and outrageous, than socio-economic distinctions (inequalities).

- The perception of a beleaguered national identity, that we are finished. The entity that "we" were is no longer appreciated, no longer counts; "our" national past is rejected in favour of the present. The national identity, in the sense of memory, past and (often ethnic) uniformity is felt to be under combined attack from diversity and pluralism. There is the sense of a brutal hiatus, of disconnection of past, present and future. On the horizon looms breakdown and extinction for us – because of them.

- The fear of threat to common values (and practices). There is fear of regression, of being infiltrated by retrograde values, especially of a religious kind. In Quebec, for example, the entire legacy of the "Quiet Revolution" (secularity, gender equality and French language) is purportedly endangered in this way.[3]

- A feeling of personal insecurity. Immigration and the presence of visible minorities is firmly associated in some people's minds with the rise of social tensions, violence and crime.[4]

- The sense of an uncertain future. This is loss of faith in the future.[5] In Quebec, we suffer from a recurrent syndrome of our own possible disappearance, periodically heralded as imminent.[6]

---

3. The "Quiet Revolution" in Quebec in the 1960s was a period of intense and very rapid modernisation of the institutions and values.

4. In Belgium, North Africans are more extensively blamed for the increase in crime problems (56%), followed by east Europeans (52%), Turks (48%) and sub-Saharan Africans (38%) (Centre for Equal Opportunities and Combating Racism and IPSOS 2009).

5. "The United States and Europe are divided by a common culture of fear. On both sides, one encounters, in varying degrees, a fear of the other, a fear of the future, and a fundamental anxiety about the loss of identity in an increasingly complex world. ... What unites all these fears is a sense of loss of control over one's territory, security, and identity – in short, one's destiny. Such concerns contributed to the no votes of the French and the Dutch last year on the referendum on the proposed EU constitution. They also explain the return of strong nationalist sentiments in many European countries ... Some of the same sense of loss of control is present in the United States." Dominique Moïsi, "The Clash of Emotions", *Foreign Affairs*, January/February 2007.

6. This rhetoric of possible disappearance is recurrent in Quebec and associated with its demographic characteristics, with its minority position within an English-speaking continent, and with immigration. Which disappearance is meant? That of the majority group (French Canadian born and bred, and disappearance of the French language). Some 20 years ago in 1989, a documentary was produced by a leading light of the national movement in Quebec, Lise Payette, former minister and a respected public figure. The documentary caused a great stir, its title was *Disparaître*. In it, the claim was made that within 25 years at the most, according to the forecasts of certain demographers, the French Canadian nation would be moribund and would then become extinct – unless it began to produce children in larger numbers and only took in immigrants really wanting to integrate. Three years ago, an important Quebec writer, Jacques Godbout, expressed anxiety about the possible disappearance of Quebec's French culture in a time-span of three generations. He said it must be understood that within three generations, Quebec's cultural heritage, creativity, originality and memory would be either consolidated or forfeited (Jacques Godbout, "Continuons le débat, il ne fait que commencer", *Le Devoir*, 23 September 2006).

- On balance, what predominates in this pessimistic not to say alarmist picture is the sense of being caught up in a process of far-reaching transformation: immigration is expected to change the profile of who and what "we" stand for, to transform the destiny of "our" societies; we are headed for a future that does not look bright.

1.2. The diagnosis: How did it come to this?

Here, I have brought together the arguments that purport to give a diagnosis, or explanations, for the unease expressed by part of the population. These schemes of argument are divided into two complementary blocks: those centred on the shortcomings of the host society ("our fault"), then the arguments directed at the attitudes of ethnic minorities ("their fault").

1.2.1. "Our fault"

"Our fault" certainly, but above all the fault of the elites and those in government, severely condemned by part of the population, a tendency confirmed, for example, by the finding of a comparative study: "in most countries there is a disjunction between public opinion and the dominant view of political elites, which tend to be more favourable to immigrants" (Citrin and Sides 2008).

The points of reproach are thus as follows:

Unsuitable policies

- Governments are too tolerant, do not stand firm, prefer to seek votes (pandering to minorities) rather than attend to the common good.

- Immigration policies are not selective enough. Immigration has become too diversified, too many immigrants unlike us are accepted.

- Citizenship policies are too liberal, too permissive.

- Integration policies are a failure, not strict enough on immigrants. Multiculturalism too (in the countries which have adopted it) is harmful to integration in allowing minorities to live on the fringe of society and in encouraging reasonable accommodations.

Laws and courts for the benefit of minorities

- Charters (or anti-discrimination laws) give every right to the minorities and nothing to the majority. They protect sexist religions.

- Reasonable accommodations are in fact unreasonable[7] because:

  - They reinforce fundamentalism of various kinds. Those who demand them are fundamentalists. Why encourage fundamentalism and reinforce reactionary groups?[8]

  - They are harmful to integration in encouraging the maintenance of cultural differences.

  - They confer privileges on minorities, under a parallel legal system which circumvents the law and allows any number of exceptions to be made. Reasonable accommodations place the rights of migrants above those of the majority, which is unfair.

  - They run counter to the common values, permitting the return of religion to the public sphere and beating back secularism and gender equality.

  - They are costly.[9]

---

7. In December 2006, 59% of Quebecers thought that their society was too tolerant regarding reasonable accommodations. In the autumn of 2007, 65% of Quebecers were of the opinion that Quebec had granted too many accommodations (Girard 2008).

8. "The accommodations demanded by the hard-line practitioners are affronts to the values of Quebec and Canada. ... The more room is made for accommodations, the more fundamentalism, which feeds off them, is condoned. It is a Trojan horse in the culture of a people seeking to bolster the principles of equality and respect" (Marie-Andrée Bertrand, criminologist, International Centre for Comparative Criminology, Montreal University, in "Les accommodements raisonnables: des affronts aux valeurs communes?", Forum, Vol. 41, No. 9, 30 October 2006, Montreal University, Montreal).

9. "Our political system enables various groups to be granted privileges which, while highly advantageous to them, are expensive for society. Not only expensive in monetary terms but also because they create insecurity and frustration in the population. And that is essentially what happens with the granting of the accommodations termed reasonable" (Pierre Simard, professor at Enap-Québec, and Jean-Luc Migué, Senior Fellow with the Fraser Institute, "Accommodements volontaires plutôt que 'raisonnables'", Le Soleil, 10 October 2007).

- The courts and judges interpret the bills of rights too broadly and at all events have too many powers and encroach on the power of the elected representatives.

Excessive and self-destructive tolerance

- Rather than assert and uphold "Western values", our elites internalise the Westerner's uneasy conscience and yield to the siren song of cultural relativism, cosmopolitanism, political correctness and pluralism.

- There is a collective attitude of abdication (Quebec): the people are limp, apathetic, fearful, defeatist, characterless, unassertive, always give in, accept humiliation, cast off their culture and identity.

- Fewer and fewer children are born.

1.2.2. "Their fault"

This type of contention is made by us against them:

Minorities do not want to integrate

- They do not learn our language. They do not respect our usages and customs, they impose theirs on the majority, and show no interest in us, our language, our history and struggles. They want to keep their own company and reproduce the lifestyle and values of their place of origin.[10] All things considered, they themselves create the obstacles to their integration.[11]

Migrants are opportunists

- Migrants supposedly take advantage of the host societies' generosity while giving nothing in return. Typically, "More than 4 out of

---

10. Almost one out of two Belgians (48%) thinks that most people belonging to a minority ethnic group do not want to become full members of society (Centre for Equal Opportunities and Combating Racism and IPSOS 2009).

11. An opinion poll by TNS Sofres/France 24 indicates that some 60% of Europeans regard immigrants as having difficulties with integration, and over half (69% in the United Kingdom) think that it is primarily the immigrants, not the host country, that do not acquire the capabilities for integration (TNS Sofres/France 24 2007). The same survey indicates that the Europeans polled mention different lifestyles (language, culture: 31% to 67%) and religious differences (35% to 57%) among the main problems associated with immigration.

10 Belgians think that North Africans, Black Africans, East Europeans and Turks come to Belgium to take advantage of the social security (respectively, 48%, 43%, 43% and 44%)" (Centre for Equal Opportunities and Combating Racism 2009).

The problems are caused by religious minorities

Here the simplistic motif of clash of civilisations is quite explicitly present:

- Certain minorities especially bring the religious factor back into the public sphere, and turn back the clock.[12]

- Religions are harmful and disrespectful to our values, and demeaning for women especially.[13]

- Religious minorities are very exacting, abuse the legal system, try to circumvent the law, reject the rules, and make improper use of accommodations for religious reasons, all in order to preserve their retrograde patriarchal and fundamentalist practices.

- Minorities are intransigent. They refuse compromise, impose their lifestyle upon us, and their attitude to reasonable accommodations is proof of the fact.

- While the historical majority religion stands back, the minority religions seek to take its place.

- Islam is an archaic, anti-egalitarian religion, a violent and intolerant religion; the Islamic headscarf and veil betoken the rejection of our values, they isolate and demean women; Christianity has been modernised, not so Islam.[14]

---

12. Some 40% of Quebec's French-speaking population consider that their society is threatened by the arrival of non-Christian immigrants. When Quebecers are asked which values they wish to pass on to their children, 21% say "religious faith or spirituality", a percentage that rises to 58% among newcomers to Quebec (Girard 2008).

13. Whereas three Quebecers out of four consider that their society fosters gender equality, only 40% consider that migrants do likewise. Moreover, the same survey indicated that 94% of Quebecers see their society as recognising children's rights, while 69% think that migrants do so to the same degree (Girard 2008).

14. Some 40% of French speakers have a favourable opinion about Muslims, 60% about Jews and 88% about Catholics ("Quebec Newcomers Should Forfeit Their Culture: Survey", Gazette, 22 May 2009).

1.3. The "solutions": How to set things right?

The standard arguments, here too, have been divided into two categories: the solutions to be applied by the host society, then the ones requiring changes in attitudes and values of the minorities. It is not surprising that the "solutions" put forward to reverse the trend are a back-to-front reflection of the diagnostic elements above.

1.3.1. What "we" should do

Adopt more restrictive policies

- A more selective immigration policy needs to be adopted, choosing immigrants who have similar values to ours, people who resemble us culturally and linguistically (not to mention the calls for a halt to immigration, or a moratorium).[15]

- The integration procedures must safeguard secularity and gender equality, and discourage the maintenance of obtrusive cultural practices, at the very least in the public sphere.

- Citizenship is a right to be earned, and policies on access to citizenship must be conditional. A minimum requirement is knowledge of the national language.[16]

- A core of non-negotiable common values must be defined. The values of the majority must outweigh the values of minorities where the latter are incompatible with the former.

---

15. "In May 2007, with the congressional debate on the Bush-backed legislation under way, a New York Times poll found that 90% of the public believe that US immigration policy should either be 'completely rebuilt' or needs 'fundamental change'" (Citrin and Sides 2008). "Two Belgians out of three think that Belgium has reached its limits; problems will arise if the number of people belonging to minority ethnic groups keeps increasing." Besides, "54% of Belgians are of the opinion that immigration must be halted if a country is to reduce tensions" (Centre for Equal Opportunities and Combating Racism and IPSOS 2009).

16. Some 72% of Quebecers are in favour of future immigrants being required to have an elementary knowledge of French in order to vote or stand for election in Quebec. Among those who speak French, 76% are in favour compared to 54% among those who do not (Girard 2008).

Change the legal framework

- Religious observance must be private and the legal framework must be adapted accordingly.

- The state should prohibit reasonable accommodations on religious grounds because religious beliefs are a matter of personal choice which ought not to be imposed on society as a whole (as opposed to the ground of disability, for example, which is not a choice but a condition). The law must be the same for everyone; all citizens must obey the same rules in the same way.

- There must be rank-ordering of the fundamental rights in the charter, giving freedom of religion second place to gender equality in particular. Freedom of religion is less important than the other rights.[17]

- Religious symbols must be prohibited in the public sphere, at least in public institutions, and at the very least for state and public service employees.[18]

Display a firmer collective attitude

- The majority should stop negating itself and assert its values.

- Two recent examples in Quebec demonstrate this assertive stance to differing degrees:

  a. Quebec's Liberal Party government adopted in autumn 2008 "Measures for intensifying the action of Quebec on migrant integration". One such measure is to make migrants sign a declaration on the common values of Quebec's society. By setting their signature to it, they certify that they have acquainted themselves with these values and declare that they wish to live in the framework of and in accordance with them and to learn French if they do not already speak it. (The values are as follows: "Quebec is a free demo-

---

17. Some 75% of Quebecers and 65% of Canadians in other parts of Canada wish to amend the Charter of Rights and Freedoms so that gender equality outweighs freedom of religion (Girard 2008).

18. Only 23% of the French speakers in Quebec think that Muslim women should be entitled to teach in the state schools while wearing hijab; and 29% that Muslim girls should be entitled to wear it in state schools (Jack Jedwab, "Enquête sur le Rapport de la Commission Bouchard-Taylor", Association for Canadian Studies, 11 June 2008).

cratic society; political and religious powers in Quebec are separate; Quebec is a pluralistic society founded on the rule of law; women and men have the same rights; individual rights and freedoms must be exercised with respect for those of others and for the general well-being".)[19]

b. The main opposition party, the Parti Québecois, in 2007 moved an amendment of the province's Charter of Human Rights and Freedoms in which the Parti Québecois proposed an interpretative clause to be inserted into the charter forthwith in order to affirm the historic heritage and the fundamental values of Quebec as a nation, and specifically the predominance of the French language, the protection and advancement of Quebec's culture, gender equality and secularity of public institutions. This clause would allow "clear guidelines founded on our identity" to be established. NB: nowhere does the Parti Québecois define what it means by "Quebec's culture". It may be supposed that such a grading of the cultural (and religious) ingredients in the Charter of Human Rights and Freedoms is intended to afford a legal basis on which to refuse, for example, demands for accommodation or adjustment.[20]

1.3.2. What "they" must do

It is up to the minorities to adapt to the usages and customs of the host society and not vice versa

- Accordingly, religious believers should adapt to secular society and profess their religion in the private sphere and in their own places of worship.

---

19. Department of Immigration and Cultural Communities, Government of Quebec, *Affirmer les valeurs communes de la société Québecoise*, 2008.

20. This kind of measure underlies a "reference culture" that rules without (too much) concession. Cultural expressions of a minority, and especially religious type, would not automatically gain acceptance. An advocate of this "law on identity" explains that "Quebec is not a blank page, and migrants' integration with the national identity is not so much a matter of bills of rights as of allegiance to a community of memory and culture. From this standpoint, most importantly, *not all religious symbols are equivalent in the symbolic register*, and it should not be considered discriminatory towards cultural communities to combine a certain secularity with the defence of Quebec's historic heritage" (my italics) (Mathieu Bock-Côté, "Décriminaliser l'identité nationale", *La Presse*, 21 May 2009).

- Minorities should discard their traditions and customs.[21]

Minorities must abide by our laws and values

- Minorities should give up practices that treat women as inferiors and comply with the secularity of the host societies.

Ethnic minorities should refrain from living for themselves in ghettos

On balance, these critical statements, which, let us remember, only represent the opinion of some citizens in Western society, disclose the sense of a qualitative transformation of the universe of reference, founded on the perception that all the symbols of social and national cohesion are crumbling; a historical caesura is felt, besides which, in relation to religious minorities, there is the sense that religiosity is coming back into its own or that the values won by sustained struggle are losing ground or under threat (secularity and gender equality especially).

---

21. Slightly over half the people in Quebec (56%) agree with the statement "newcomers should discard their traditions and customs and become more like the majority of the Quebecers" (Jeff Heinrich, "Generation Accommodation", *Gazette,* 8 September 2007).

    The survey by the Centre for Equal Opportunities and Combating Racism and IPSOS (2009) indicates that 55% of Belgians consider it better for a country that almost everyone share the same habits and the same customs. It is observed that most Belgians approve of the idea that a person belonging to a minority ethnic group must distance him/herself partly if not completely from its specific character to be able to integrate.

    On the whole, there are nearly as many Belgians for as against (37% to 40%) the opinion that persons belonging to a minority ethnic group must give up their culture and assimilate Belgian culture to be fully accepted by the host society (ibid.). Some 58% of the Belgian population think that to be fully accepted by the host society, persons belonging to a minority ethnic group should if necessary give up certain cultural rites like wearing veils or sacrificing sheep.

    Some 78% agree or emphatically agree with the statement that persons belonging to a minority ethnic group may retain their culture but only in family life. In public areas (school, street, work, etc.), they must adapt to Belgian lifestyles.

2. Fears that must be heard, heeded and allayed in an ongoing dialogue

What is to be done with these arguments, misgivings and fears, which undeniably bring pressure to bear on official policies on immigration, access to citizenship and integration?

The worst course would be to disregard them and refuse dialogue on the pretext of unwillingness to legitimise what is considered xenophobic or racist talk. Whether founded or not, these fears are quite real. Indeed, the cultural diversification of our societies ousts certain firmly entrenched social representations, and various citizens greet these changes with considerable apprehension, hence the need for an ongoing social dialogue on such important issues.

This conversation on a national scale must not be confined to the parliamentary arena, to colloquies or to the media alone; let us hope that it can be held in all strata of society and everywhere in the public sphere, including neighbourhoods, workplaces and schools at local level, and also that the tone of public debate, over-charged with emotion on these subjects, may tend towards reasoned and reasonable dialogue.

Admittedly, the chief benefit of ongoing dialogue would probably not be the appeasement of all discords, but at the very least it would give a say to those who seldom have the opportunity to speak, and it would get the citizens thinking about the diagnoses to be made and the solutions to be provided for the challenges facing us as regards cultural diversity and pluralism.

2.1. Questions to address

In the context of a social dialogue like this, certain questions are plainly inescapable, such as:

2.1.1. Concerning integration procedures

The current criticism of multiculturalism is wholesome, but some try to take advantage of it to make a clean sweep of pluralism and promote a retrograde outlook. Rather, the scrutiny of multiculturalism should be an occasion to shore up the pluralist perception, find solutions to inter-community tensions and divides, identify common values and collective agendas to be furthered, and lastly to develop a stronger sense of national solidarity (Cantle 2006). In that respect, the avenue of interculturalism as a mode of integration is promising (Bouchard-Taylor 2008; Rocher et al. 2007; James 2008).

2.1.2. Cultural diversity and pluralism are not to blame for all the ills of our societies

Some schemes of argument make cultural diversity and pluralism scapegoats for social fragmentation, the source of breakdown of all symbols of the common good and social cohesion (national identity, social state, collective solidarity, "cultural heritage", common values), or a deterrent to communal aspirations. Actually the diversification of our societies is very far from being the sole factor that robs the traditional landmarks of stability. Globalisation, the internal crisis of the social state, the awakening of national minorities or European construction, but also re-privatisation, consumerism, altered configurations of the couple and family, the crisis of education, ageing of the population, environmental problems, all these are phenomena the combined effect of which is to permeate the entire Western world with longing for a uniform and less hectic but largely imaginary past, and apprehension about the present and future.

2.1.3. Accommodations and adjustments

These are much discussed in the present book. Suffice it to recall that to grant ethnocultural and religious minorities accommodations and adjustments does not negate the fundamental values of the host society making the concessions, but on the contrary expresses those values in a certain way through the inclusion of difference for the sake of social cohesion and the right to equality.

These accommodations do not compete with or gainsay the host society's values, but mark out an area for the exercise of freedom of religion. Before they are made, they must be tested by the yardsticks of excessive constraint, bills of rights, the spirit of the national laws, and the scheme of secularity that applies. All demands that do not measure up to these tests are refused. It is therefore incorrect to claim that accommodations and adjustments are granted unconditionally and thoughtlessly; what happens is the exact opposite.

It does of course happen that some managers, in complete good faith, commit errors of judgment in granting adjustments. These errors are not the rule, though; they remain the exception and can be quickly rectified.

It would be highly profitable, to inform public debate, if a list were made of the accommodations and adjustments most commonly granted (or refused) in the various Western host societies, and if understanding of their concrete rationale was cultivated. Ignorance of this encourages rumours and distortions, and facilitates the work of demagogues.

Finally, the debates on accommodations and adjustments illustrate the desirability of addressing the related questions such as schemes of secularity, and above all the role of courts and bills of rights in our societies. Since these legal instruments are sometimes suspected of helping only minorities, to the detriment of the "majority", it is important to propose a more balanced viewpoint.

2.1.4. The Muslim question

Discussions in the West of religious freedom make quite an issue of Muslim religious practices. The Islamist attacks in North America and Europe obviously have something to do with it. Allegations of "growing Islamification" in Europe or even in America are obtrusive enough in public debate to arouse anxiety. Islamophobia is comfortably established. To reverse direction, create a calmer climate and allay the fears on either side, host societies and the Muslim leaders and communities within them must tighten the links and define common strategic actions.

2.1.5. Common values

This is a very trendy theme. How are our "common values" to be defined without entrapment by a definition so rigid that it becomes a device for banishing and forbidding any practice that does not fit in? To what extent, and how in practice, could cultural diversity weaken or threaten common values as some claim? Are there true common values beyond the common public democratic values (that is the principles embodied in our laws and public institutions)?[22]

---

22. Concerning the distinction between common values and common public values, it is found that for some people, common values are the principles that have been carried into law, namely into bills of rights and freedoms, statutes, government policies, etc. From that standpoint, common values are those which public institutions seek to foster; they are common public values or, according to the terms of the Quebec charter, "democratic values". For others, common values also embody the values and practices of the majority, that is the norms, conventions and demeanour espoused by the many but lying outside the ambit of law and public institutions (Bouchard-Taylor Commission 2008, p. 164).

2.2. Some concepts to be used with caution in public debate

Again in the spirit of a reasoned and reasonable dialogue on cultural diversity and pluralism, the use of certain words, because of their connotations and ability to turn into bombshells in public debate, should be approached with the utmost circumspection. Here I am thinking primarily of the concepts "majority", "we" and "national identity". The anti-pluralist persuasion makes ample use of them to peddle its ideas.

While the theme of "dictatorship of minorities" was in style in certain circles 20 years ago (Granjon 1994), "affirmation of the majority" now holds sway. The minorities had their moment for the last 25 years, but "the moment of the majority" has now come: "the majorities demand that something be done about them, their identity, and their place in the complex society which has grown up around them".[23]

According to this stance, the majority should stop feeling guilty (about its colonial history, whiteness and wealth), it should no longer acquiesce to all demands of ethnic minorities, it should become aware of itself, unashamedly be itself, assert its values and aspirations and defend its permanence, doing so via the adoption, if need be, of binding policies in respect of minorities.

This type of contention has gained some prominence in Quebec, but is also present elsewhere, especially England, where Pathak (2008) calls this "mounting majority" phenomenon majoritarianism:

> By majoritarianism I mean a popular backlash against the indulgence of national minorities and doctrines of minority rights, as per multiculturalism. But unlike multiculturalism, majoritarianism is incoherent and inchoate. In Britain it's more apparent as a trend than

---

23. Lisée (2007) says that "it is not a case specific to Quebec. Majority unease is perceptible in France, England, the Netherlands and the United States. Whether their government is left, right or centre, these societies, like Quebec's, have moved on in time. The last quarter of a century has been the minorities' moment, the moment for redress of wrongs. It is not completely finished, far from it; in our social transformations, it was at the centre of debate. It also required the majorities to adapt to, yield to, model themselves on these new realities. They did so, not always willingly or enthusiastically, but with a sufficient level of consent for the change to occur. The democratic and social gain is significant for the visible minorities, whether religious or sexual. Now the day of the majority is dawning. I do not claim to understand all its mechanisms and manifestations, but it is due to the majorities' demand that they, their identity, and their place in the complex society which has grown up around them should now receive attention."

a movement .... It's a trend that connects populist tirades against Eastern European immigrants in the tabloid press, essays that indict immigration for withering social bonds, and government green papers that propose making citizenship earned and exclusive. ... It manifests itself, overall, as a weakened commitment to the principles of multiculturalism and the practice of minority rights. (Pathak 2008.)

"Majoritarianism" according to Pathak is sustained by a conservative or new-wave liberalism typified by its dismissive attitude to liberal rights and its conservative inclinations regarding immigration and ethnic relations.

On the cultural plane, the majority should thus defend its heritage, affirm its "majority culture" (never explicitly defined, being indefinable), and this includes states not acknowledging any majority culture a priori. In the United States, for example, a survey (Citrin and Sides 2008) indicates that:

While 64% [of respondents] described the United States as a country made up of "many cultures and values that change as new people come here", 62% felt the country should have a "basic American culture that immigrants take on when they come here". Only 39% of immigrants expressed this normative position, a gap that arguably feeds concern about the cultural threat posed by large-scale immigration. (Citrin and Sides 2008.)

This concept of "majority", at least as used by its proponents, is problematic in three or more ways: first, it postulates the existence of a seamless majority, ethnically, culturally and/or ideologically homogeneous; second, it suggests that the democratic institutions adopted by society, namely the bills of rights and the protections extended to minorities, are not an emanation of the majority but a kind of alien excrescence imposed by the "elites"; third, the insistence on talking in terms of majority and minority causes an "us" against "them" polarisation. The "us" re-emerges moreover in public speaking,[24] expressing at a more emotional level the desire to regain a lost unity, an "us" without "them" (or an "us" augmented by a "them" stripped of its otherness).

If fact, like the concept of majority, majority culture and the "we" entity, the concept of national identity also has strong connotations. How is a nation to be represented in the context of a society which is becoming culturally diversified? Some consider the nation under threat of deliquescence precisely because of this diversity. In the appeals for "preservation" or "perpetuation" of national identity, nostalgia for a certain national uniformity is discernible. National identity in such hands, just like the concept of "majority culture" furthermore, is not a progressively evolving reality but becomes more of a museum piece which above all must not be desecrated by the present: the new must stand aside for the past and nothing but the past. So according to this outlook, the main undertaking is not to incorporate diversity but to make every effort to resist transformations of the national identity in order that it forever remains in the possession and in the image of the "founding group".[25]

Overall, these rhetorical patterns serve various ideological functions. They operate to remind minorities who is the legitimate collective player (the majority, "us") and set limits to the changes brought by cultural diversity

---

24. Pauline Marois, head of the Parti Québecois, the principal opposition party in Quebec, says "For the last ten years or so, we have been afflicted with a kind of uneasy conscience that prevented us from saying 'we' or 'us', as if the word was taboo. As if to utter it or lift a finger to defend our identity was tantamount to racism and intolerance. As if the desire to exist and to live in our own language and culture was an ethnic agenda or a flight of folklore. ... we should no longer be embarrassed or afraid to say that in Quebec, the French-speaking majority wants recognition and is the heart of the nation" (address on the occasion of the party's nominations assembly at the Beaupré Community Centre, 29 August 2007). Note: this usage of *nous* (we) in Quebec has two meanings (at least partly coinciding, however): firstly a "we" standing for Quebec and its sovereignty and striving to distinguish itself not only from the rest of Canada but also from Quebec's federalist forces; secondly, a "we" whose core is the ethnic majority of French-Canadian ancestry, striving to assert the permanence of "Quebec's culture", and of the French language in particular (see note 38).

25. In an interview, Mathieu Bock-Côté, the Quebec apostle of a primal and totally unabashed nationalism, aptly personifies this mindset of cultural resistance to diversity and pluralism: "In Quebec, upholding the national identity is a task of conservation. There is a historical legacy to preserve. Nationalism and conservatism must now join forces, drawing sustenance from a Quebec in the midst of collective reconstitution" (Elias Levy, "La majorité refoulée" (the downtrodden majority), interview with Mathieu Bock-Côté, *Voir*, 20 September 2007).

(the "majority culture" and the traditional landmarks of national identity must remain unchanged and central to the nation). They also send out another message to minorities, welcoming them in so far as they become almost identical to "us", namely when their difference has become ineffectual folklore, when they have given up the more obtrusive marks of their cultures, when they join "our" ranks, including support of our schemes.[26] The requirements for inclusion are in fact on an upward trend in several Western countries.[27] These rhetorical patterns spell out conditions of inclusion whose purpose is to neutralise the differences (firstly, cultural) personified by minorities; they seek to demonstrate the need to lay down more restrictive conditions of access to citizenship, or even to legitimise prohibitions (on reasonable accommodations, notably).

The notions of "majority", "we" and "national identity" have indeed become the ideological mainstays of anti-pluralism and a new conservative rectitude as regards diversity and pluralism. That is why they are to be used with caution.

At the end of this essay, all that remains is to restate the need for the present resistances to cultural diversity and pluralism to be seriously addressed by setting up permanent mechanism for dialogue in the public sphere.

---

26. In Quebec that means, for example, showing solidarity with the pro-sovereignty aspiration of a (generally narrow) majority of French speakers. "If the Franco-Québécois have no qualms about taking upon themselves the memory that is theirs, why should the newcomers refuse to go along with it and be associated with the steadfast progress of a people whose likeness is found everywhere in world history?" (Jacques Beauchemin, "Souveraineté. Miser sur Stéphane Dion?", Le Devoir, 9 December 2006). Likewise, Pauline Marois, head of the Parti Québécois: "To say 'we' is actually to assert two things: that there is a majority in Quebec which history has fashioned in its distinctiveness and originality, and that this majority rightfully aspires to self-assertion in the name of an identity, a language and values which it perceives as its own. To say 'we' is also to invite everyone who does not identify with four centuries of history to join the majority in its hopes and in building an open democratic society in America" (address by Pauline Marois, National Conference of Presidents, "Quebec Identity Bill", 20 October 2007).

27. See in particular: Denise Helly, "The Breakdown of Legitimacy? Immigration, Security, Social Cohesion, Nativism", Centre Urbanisation, Culture et Société, Institut national de Recherche scientifique, Montreal, 2008.

References

Bouchard-Taylor Commission (2008), "Fonder l'avenir. Le temps de la concil-iation", Commission de consultation sur les pratiques d'accommodement reliées aux différences culturelles, Government of Quebec, www.accommodements.qc.ca/documentation/rapports/rapport-final-integral-fr.pdf.

Cantle T. (2006), "Parallel Lives", www.eurozine.com/pdf/2006-11-03-cantle-en.pdf.

Centre for Equal Opportunities and Combating Racism and IPSOS (2009), "Survey: How tolerant are Belgians towards ethnic minorities?", Belgium, www.diversiteit.be/?action=publicatie_detail&id=70&thema=2&setLanguage=3.

Citrin J. and Sides J. (2008), "Immigration and the Imagined Community in Europe and the United States", *Political Studies*, Vol. 56, pp. 33-56.

Girard M. (2008), "Résumé de résultats de sondages portant sur la perception des Quebec relativement aux accommodements raison-nables, à l'immigration, aux communautés culturelles et à l'identité canadienne-française", Commission de consultation sur les pratiques d'accommodement reliées aux différences culturelles, www.accommodements.qc.ca/documentation/rapports/rapport-6-girard-magali.pdf.

Granjon M.-C. (1994), "Le regard en biais. Attitudes françaises et multi-culturalisme américain (1990-1993)", *Vingtième Siècle. Revue d'histoire*, Vol. 43, No. 43, pp. 18-29.

James M. (2008), "Interculturalism. Theory and Policy", Baring Foundation, UK, www.baringfoundation.org.uk/interculturalism.pdf.

Lisée J.-F. (2007), *Nous*, Boréal, Montreal.

Noiriel G. (2007), *À quoi sert l'identité "nationale"?* Agone, Marseille.

Novatris/Harris Interactive (2007), "Une étude Novatris/Harris Interactive pour Le Talk de Paris, France 24 et l'*International Herald Tribune*", broad-cast on France 24 on Friday 25 May 2007; published in the *International Herald Tribune*, 25 May 2007, www.harrisinteractive.fr/news/pubs/Novatris_France24_2007_0525.pdf.

Pathak P. (2008), "The Rise of the Majority",
www.journal-online.co.uk/article/3222-the-rise-of-the-majority.

PEW Global Attitudes Project (2007), "World Publics Welcome Global Trade – But Not Immigration",
http://pewglobal.org/reports/display.php?ReportID=258.

Rocher F. et al. (2007), "Le concept d'interculturalisme en contexte Québécois: généalogie d'un néologisme", report presented to the Bouchard-Taylor Commission (CCPARDC), 21 December,
www.accommodements.qc.ca/documentation/rapports/rapport-3-rocher-francois.pdf.

Roy A. and Lavoie-Talbot E. (2007), "Typologie générale: Analyse du contenu", Commission de consultation sur les pratiques d'accommodement reliées aux différences culturelles, Liste des documents produits par la commission, Document No. 9, 2 August 2007.

TNS Sofres/France 24 (2007), "Les Européens et l'immigration",
www.tns-sofres.com/etudes/pol/131107_immigration-europe.htm.

"Ha da passa' 'a nuttata": reasonable accommodation, a tool for defending coexistence based on respect for rights in a pluralist society

Emilio Santoro[1]

1. Democracy and pluralism of identity

Liberal democracy and the nation state are inseparable: the rules of democratic decision making are based on the assumption that agreement on many things is pre-political and will never require political decision, not even one taken democratically. Towards the end of the last century this point was made by many communitarian authors, first among them Michael Sandel and Michael Walzer.[2] Their accounts contain important insights, even though they may have a tendency to place too much emphasis on the pre-political nature of the background agreement. The people's unity – which I would call a unity of identity – on which the nation state, and hence democracy, rests, mostly results from a political operation, a never-ending effort by the elites of the state concerned. As it implies these processes, albeit without ever explicitly mentioning them, Ernest Renan's definition seems closer to historical reality: in his view "a nation is ... a large-scale solidarity, constituted by the feeling of the sacrifices that one has made in the past and of those that one is prepared to make in the future. It presupposes a past; it is summarised, however, in the present by a tangible fact, namely, consent, the clearly expressed desire to continue a common life".[3]

The means for building pre-political unity, or what Renan called a common past and the desire to continue a common life in the future, are the myth of the nation (with the nation state as its expression) and discipline. These two devices made it an academic question whether citizenship

---

1. Associate Professor of Philosophy of Law, University of Florence (Italy).

2. Cf. M. Sandel, "The Procedural Republic and the Unencumbered Self", in S. Avineri and A. de Shalit (eds), *Communitarianism and Individualism*, Oxford University Press, Oxford, 1992, pp. 12-28; M. Walzer, *Spheres of Justice*, Basic Books, New York, 1983.

3. E. Renan, "What is a Nation?", Sorbonne lecture, 1882.

presupposes a community which citizens are members of or, on the contrary, the community is created by citizens who exist independently of social bonds. If, as Thomas H. Marshall wrote in his classical work, citizenship is "a kind of basic human equality associated with the concept of full membership of a community",[4] different "peoples" can be said to have been built since the 18th century through extremely skilful use of the myth of the nation and disciplining, each one understood as a group of individuals who are able to make appropriate use of the rights bestowed upon them by liberal regimes (and then liberal democracies). The democratisation of the nation state (the extension of enfranchisement) goes hand in hand with the disciplining of the people and the establishment of the myth of the nation. The processes of inclusion within the nation, namely within the people, and disciplining made democracy possible, that is, the gradual attribution of ever larger sets of rights, starting with the right to choose the government. From this perspective democracy is itself connoted as a device of inclusion/disciplining.

As democracy becomes established, so does the belief that individuals' use of their rights should conform to standards that are both moral and rational (for 18th and 19th-century Enlightenment contractarianism, the two adjectives were largely synonymous): "discipline" shapes individuals according to the standards of the order in which they are placed. Tocqueville's is perhaps the best description of how the nation state was born and established through a slow process in which the granting of new rights went hand in hand with building a population with the requisite competence to use the powers conferred on its members by rights themselves. In his *L'ancien régime et la révolution*, referring to England – the country where this process took place more gradually than anywhere else, and without any sudden revolutionary leaps forward – Tocqueville emphasised how the granting of rights, and hence the establishment of democracy, took place as a slow process through which every individual came to be acknowledged to have the competence of a gentleman:

> There had not been, for a long period of time, any nobility at all in England, in the old circumscribed meaning of the word. The revolution that destroyed it is lost in the night of time, but the English tongue is a surviving witness of the change. Many centuries since, the meaning of the word "gentleman" changed in England .... Follow, for instance, the meanings of the word gentleman throughout its

---

4. T. H. Marshall, *Citizenship and Social Class*, 1950.

career. Our word "gentilhomme" was its father. ... Century after century, it was applied to lower and lower classes in the social scale. The English at last bore it with them to America, where it was indiscriminately applied to all classes. Its history is, in fact, that of democracy.[5]

Today the sovereign "people" has taken on a new connotation quite different from that assumed by liberal democratic theories in the second half of the last century. It is now more than (just) a place where class differences arise and are resolved, as it used to be around the turn of the 19th and 20th centuries. In the space of a few years, a society that was culturally relatively homogeneous has become a pluralist society. Today's "people" is first and foremost an aggregation of particularities, cultural differences, communities, ethnic groups, religions, in a permanent tension between border security and the integration of new souls, diverse identities, strong migratory flows, heterogeneous factors of segmentation. In an era of globalisation and mass migration, differences tend more and more to cluster around "cultural" vectors and fault lines, and generate conflicts in terms of both identity and values which are connected with the search for meaning. Individuals try to regain feelings of community membership by reasserting their loyalty to traditions alien to those of their host state: regionalism, the growth of what are to a greater or lesser degree religious sects, religious fundamentalism, suburban gangs of young people are all phenomena that, beyond their specificities, clearly show the decline of the great inter-class solidarity within which national identity had been structured.

This situation seems to have frustrated liberal democracies' capacity for order and inclusion, and individuals' interests often appear to be irreconcilable. Within societies that are now multi-ethnic, the presence of many culturally differentiated groups virtually prevent not only an agreement on the "common good", already relegated by Joseph Schumpeter to the status of a 19th-century myth,[6] but also the legislative mediation advocated by procedural theories of democracy.[7] It is the democratic model

---

5. A. de Tocqueville, *L'ancien régime et la révolution*, 1856, English Translation: *The Old Regime and the Revolution*, Harper & Brothers, New York, 1856.

6. J. A. Schumpeter, *Capitalism, Socialism and Democracy*, Unwin University Books, London, 1954.

7. For a procedural conception of democracy see H. Kelsen, *Vom Wesen und Wert der Demokratie*, JCB Mohr, Tübingen, 1929, and "Foundations of Democracy", *Ethics*, CXVI, 1955.

itself that seems inappropriate to the situation of present-day European societies. Majority-minority dialectic, central to democratic decision making, was appropriate in 19th and 20th-century societies characterised by bipolar oppositions based on ideologies or interests. Today, however, it seems too rigid for the complexities of societies in which cross-party or "transversal" fronts emerge about every issue that arises.

The only minorities which have the right of citizenship in a democracy are temporary minorities that hope to become majorities in the medium or even short term. There is no room left for minority identity groups charac-terised by radical difference from the majority, and neither intending nor having any opportunity to assimilate the majority. Pluralism of identity makes the idea of majority decision making unviable, for there are many interests that minorities consider to be fundamental to their identities (cultural, religious or other), leading them to refuse to submit to the majority's judgment. Indeed, to accept a democratic decision on such issues would be to give the majority a right to suppress the minority as a group with given characteristics. Conversely, no majority is willing to run the risk of being ruled by members of a minority identity group: no majority is ready to accept rules considered alien to its tradition. During the 20th century, liberal regimes characterised by the presence of strong identity groups had to develop decision-making techniques that greatly limited the scope of "democratic" government: examples are Switzerland, in the European context, and those regimes defined by political scientists as "consociational democracies",[8] such as those of the Netherlands and Belgium in the second half of the 20th century. However, the history of the closing years of the 19th century shows that social fragmentation and the large number of often intertwined identities within any community complicate the survival of consociational regimes themselves.

As Tocqueville clearly saw, democracy exerts strong pressure to conform and involves the criminalisation and institutionalisation of those who are "too different". Already in a context such as that of the United States,

---

8. The phrase "consociational democracy" was created by Arend Lijphart (*The Politics of Accommodation: Pluralism and Democracy in the Netherlands*, University of California Press, Berkeley-London, 1968) to indicate those political regimes in which any social group, being unable to impose its own values, is forced to make an alliance with the component parts of the society that seem ready to provide the best conditions for defending its interests. In the last years many multi-ethnic states based upon a con-sociational agreement have experienced secession, as in former Yugoslavia or former Czechoslovakia. Also significant is the current crisis in Belgium, a country hitherto considered to be, like the Netherlands, a prototypical consociational democracy.

with broad scope for expansion, those who were deemed to lack competence to use their rights were consigned to dark penitentiaries and denied the chance to choose the country's rulers. In *De la démocratie en Amérique*, the underlying rationale of disciplinary institutions emerges as a structural feature of liberal democratic regimes. In his chapter on the tyranny of the majority, the French philosopher emphasises that, however paradoxical it may seem, a democratic republic like the United States, which considers law and order to be the embodiment of the people's will, treats disobedient minorities with greater severity than did monarchic regimes which completely ignored their subjects' will. It would not, therefore, seem to be a coincidence that modern disciplinary institutions originated in the United States, namely the first large country to adopt republican government. As Thomas L. Dumm emphasised, disciplinary institutions are shown in Tocqueville's account to be a constituent part of the American liberal democracy project:

> The American project, a system of self-rule, involved not only the establishment of representative government with an extensive suffrage, but also the establishment of institutions that would encourage the internalization of liberal democratic values, the creation of individuals who would learn how to rule their selves.[9]

According to Dumm, Tocqueville was the first to realise that the network of disciplinary institutions "formed the epistemological project of liberal democracy, creating conditions of knowledge of self and other that were to shape the political subject required for liberal and democratic values to be realised in practice".[10]

Since the end of the 18th century, it became clear, first in the United States and then little by little in Europe, that a stable liberal democratic society requires a range of disciplinary institutions – from penitentiaries to asylums, hospitals, schools, etc. – capable of producing the kind of citizen fit for the new political system. Thus a system of social control was needed that was expressly designed to reinforce, or to create if necessary, individual responsibility. With the Industrial Revolution, there emerged a population characterised by high social mobility outside the control of the family, farm life, or guilds. In this context, the first aim of building up a network of disciplinary institutions applying varying degrees of coercion

---

9. T. L. Dumm, *Democracy and Punishment: Disciplinary Origins of the United States*, University of Wisconsin Press, Madison, 1987, p. 6.

10. Ibid.

was to reinforce a binding system of belief that was able to make citizens' everyday life meaningful and to guide their use of their rights, first among them their right to choose their rulers. The weaker classes were driven (forced?) to adapt to new social conditions through preaching and the institutional implementation of a civic virtue capable of replacing the traditional virtue that had by then reached crisis point. It was a commonplace that belief in free will and personal reliability and the associated imperative of self-discipline, once embedded in institutions and social practices, would help many to put up with the impersonal conditions of life in an urban industrial society.

2. The end of inclusive disciplinary devices

When we say that rules in liberal democratic societies are and should be neutral, we do not mean that they should be absolutely neutral, but neutral in relation to the specific range of world views/cultures under consideration. Most of Europe's constitutional arrangements derive from a wish to achieve a neutral position in terms of ideologies – particularly between the liberal and the socialist ideology – as well as, in some cases, a neutral position in relation to the different forms taken by Catholicism. They are not designed to be neutral in relation to radical cultural differences. Now this is becoming clearer every day. The new world views/cultures that have arrived in many European societies have brought to an end belief in the neutrality of the rules that had until recently seemed neutral. Neutrality seems now an unachievable myth: it would be better to say that it is clear that neutrality rested upon a pluralism that was limited, possibly as a result of disciplining and the myth of the nation state that cannot be reproduced today. It is worth emphasising that, like the presumption of the neutrality of the normative framework, the possibility of an "objective" definition of discrimination is itself ruled out. Even identifying an instance of discrimination requires a balancing of values: allowing Catholics to celebrate Sunday but not allowing Jews to celebrate Saturday is considered discriminatory, but allowing Catholics to celebrate the rite of transubstantiation and to eat the body and drink the blood of Christ, while forbidding any anthropophagic religious rituals, is not.

The list of constitutional rights is just one tiny part of those elements about which democratic decision is ruled out, namely that part which has been the subject of political controversy. Only when a nation state is breaking down and coming into contact with alien points of view does the unspoken agreement hitherto taken for granted come more into the light, and often become problematic, but the problems that emerge cannot, by their very nature, be solved democratically. Even the rights that can be used to allow for the most radical differences in a pluralist social context are being questioned and limited, for some of their uses are deemed unacceptable: the rights laid down in European constitutions were originally acknowledged on the assumption that individuals would tend to use them in a certain way. When we encounter completely unexpected usage of rights, when – to use Tocqueville's terms – it is not "gentlemen", but "barbarians", who are using them, numerous problems arise. Many European states accept that women's right to health, including psychological health, justifies abortion, and that an individual's right to psychological health justifies surgical transformation of his or her genitalia from male to female, or vice versa, although epidemiological research shows that people who have undergone such surgery may encounter significant problems in terms of psychological balance. But no European state accepts that this right justifies the mutilation of female genitalia known as infibulation. This is because, if we look beyond the issues relating to surgery and personal injury, abortion and sex change are recognised to have a liberating value, as expressions of personal autonomy whereas infibulation is thought to imply a form of cultural oppression of women. It is worth emphasising that the differences leading to a limitation of the use of rights are not only cultural ones imported by migrants, but also others which develop endogenously within society: use of the right to refuse medical treatment tends to be regarded as illegitimate when it turns into a means of suicide. The issue is further complicated by the fact that differences do not exist solely in respect of values, and do not stem solely from different conceptions of values, but often relate to the connotations of things: the conflict is often a descriptive, rather than a normative, one. Today, particularly but not only in Italy, there is a heated debate about whether the forced feeding of comatose people should be considered as a "treatment". Similar debates have taken place, and are continuing, about the "appropriate level of care" that parents should provide to their children, a problem that most frequently arises when Gypsies who are still minors are sent out to beg, namely, this occurs in the context of a radically different culture. A similar problem occurs, however, in respect of the sensitive issue of the relationship between parents' directive power and respect for minors' autonomy, of the decisions to be taken on abortion for minors, of parents' right to enrol their 14-year-old child at a denominational school, and so on.

The disappearance of "the people" as a relatively homogeneous actor is closely related to the crisis of inclusive disciplining devices: today the population is no longer built, as it used to be in the 19th century, but selected. When, following the establishment of the Westphalian order, the world was shaped as an arena for competition between states, the main problem became that of the techniques enabling each individual state to develop its forces: enrichment through commerce was expected to encourage growth in terms of population, workforce, production and exports, making it possible to set up strong and numerically large armies. State power came to be based on the assumption that every state has a given population, which it should deal with by regulating the mechanisms of birth and death, providing suitable living conditions and giving its members an identity. Disciplinary techniques and science of police were meant to secure the population's well-being, thereby ensuring the power of the state. The welfare state is but the latest transformation of these technologies, the latest technological instrument used by states to look after their population in order to increase their own economic (and military) power. The apparatus of the welfare state was born when the belief emerged that prerequisites of population management were a reduction in child mortality, the prevention of epidemics, the provision of sufficient medical facilities, and influence on individuals' living conditions through the enforcement of rules relating to food, environmental management and urban organisation. The welfare state is rooted in the gradually emerging need for states to take responsibility for managing their population in order to secure for it well-being, thereby increasing their own economic and military power. The direct link between the shouldering of responsibility for the population and state power clearly emerged when Britain, at the time the leading colonial power, had such a difficult time coping with Afrikaner settlers during the two Boer Wars (1880-81 and 1899-1902). Unsurprisingly, it was in Britain itself that, towards the end of the 19th century, the first structures of the welfare state began to emerge. In Bismarck's Germany, too, the first moves towards a welfare state were made under pressure from aggressive Prussian policies at the end of the 19th century. During the 20th century this kind of population management seemed able both to meet states' need for power and to "manage" workers' demands. Thanks to this ability, it developed throughout Europe with the two world wars and was consolidated as an essential device of economic reconstruction after the Second World War.

For as long as the market was able to develop through government intervention guided by reasons of state, its development coincided with that of a given population's well-being, thanks firstly to the science of police, and secondly to state welfare. The power of the state was linked to its capacity to implement inclusive citizenship policies based on a steady extension of rights and social welfare to new segments of the population. Now that mass migratory movements have been affecting European countries for several decades, the population is no longer a predefined set of individuals to be controlled through regulation of births and deaths and to be given an identity, an endowment of competences needed to use their rights. States can no longer "govern" their population, which can now be constantly redefined through the acceptance and expulsion of migrants and the marginalisation of nationals. This change brings with it a radically different problem in terms of social and political order. Migration has made populations much easier to manipulate. States can select their population much more easily, and by using a number of devices of inclusion and exclusion, they can build a population of individuals capable of entering the market, without any need to "discipline" the members of a supposedly predetermined population. It is no longer necessary to create "good citizens", for it is enough to select individuals according to contingent needs.

Since the population is no longer viewed as a given resource that needs to be cultivated and taken care of in order to increase state power, the prospect is that of a society where politics ceases to take responsibility for individuals and groups, to provide them with an identity, to nurture or set up an environment for their transformation, but is limited to filtering and selecting them. This change brings with it a traumatic failure of the liberal political and social order as we have known it for over two centuries. We are facing "a historical/political crisis" that has, at least for the time being, left us without any models by which social integration could be guided. For the first time, European liberal democratic societies appear dominated by a satisfied majority whose well-being depends only minimally on the integration of excluded people, who are therefore perceived as a threat much more than a resource. In Europe, but also throughout the northwestern world, the perception is spreading that the age of ever-increasing wealth to be shared with more and more people is coming to an end, and that we are now in transition towards an age of steadily reducing wealth to be shared with more and more people.

In the picture just described, politics is pulling back and, almost everywhere, dropping all its ambitious aims of building a homogeneous and socially cohesive population: its goal now seems to be the security of a restricted *demos* living in a democratic *polis*, limiting market-generated risk. The perception, bolstered by the ideology of globalisation, that the resources which states can use for social purposes are inevitably scarce makes it a commonplace that securing rights for "native" majorities entails the exclusion of migrants (and, next in line, of "undeserving" nationals) from these rights. What most European voters care about is not the inclusion of newcomers within the population of a given state, possibly through severe disciplining, but the prevention of uncontrolled admission of migrants to citizenship rights, which may result in a considerable reduction of their own traditional social security. To put it more crudely, we might say that European citizens, believing that social rights are a zero-sum game, fear that granting migrants the benefits of social welfare may further decrease their own benefits, which are already being reduced as a result of economic and financial globalisation. In this context, democracy becomes a purely exclusive device, defending the wealth of, not even all citizens, but often only one section of them, as demonstrated by the secessionist tendencies occurring in richer areas (in this respect, movements like the Northern League in Italy are both popular and democratic).

3. Reasonable accommodation as a tool for constitutional protection of individual interests

Hence the pluralism of our societies and the current global economic and political context necessitate a radical rethink of the categories we apply and the political and institutional language we use. The only possible path suggested by our history is the one that led to moderation of democratic government and the birth of constitutional rights, although we only arrived at this point after such apocalyptic events as the Nazi and Stalinist extermination campaigns and the Second World War. Over a period of two centuries, we have learnt that we should not allow the majority to decide on the individuals' rights that we consider fundamental. After reaching this point, we thought we had set very strict and narrow boundaries for democratic power, but instead, we have now come to realise, in the latter half of the 20th century, that constitutional courts are continuously redefining and broadening the scope of the area not subject to democratic decision making. Today, there seems to be only one viable way of preserving that respect for people and their freedom that we considered obvious in the narrow pluralism of liberal democratic societies, in the light of our cultural, political and legal heritage: another reduction in the scope of democratic government, through an expansion of those areas, similar to those defined by basic rights, within which courts can protect individuals specifically from democratic decisions. If a minority within the state considers an aspect as constitutive of its identity, this aspect should be removed from the scope of majority decision making.

Eduardo De Filippo, that great Neapolitan writer of comedies, used to say: "ha da passa' 'a nuttata", meaning that the night must come to an end. One can get through the night if there are courts, or at any rate quasi-judicial bodies, which redefine the local balances between new needs and all that used to be called pre-political (all that was built up by the myth of the nation and by disciplining). This balance cannot be for democracy to achieve, for this would require imposition of the way of life of the best protected people and criminalisation of the those most troublesome or different. Bearing this in mind, reasonable accommodation should be a tool for constitutional protection, not of multiculturalism or of other cultures, but of individual differences. This technique of government should be used until such time as a new inclusive citizenship project appears on the horizon.

I emphasise that this should involve constitutional protection of individual differences, not of cultural, religious or collective differences. Canadian experience seems to point in this direction, not only because the concept of reasonable accommodation, born in the United States and exported to Canada, developed in the framework of a common law system, but chiefly because it is of judicial making. The individual, rather than the multicultural, connotation of reasonable accommodation is supported by its use to protect the rights of disabled people. People with disabilities by no means form a minority identity group. They do not question the majority's values and standards, but simply ask to be enabled to live a life which includes all the activities engaged in by other individuals. In their view, the problem of reasonable accommodation is mainly an economic one: how much can reasonably be spent to enable them to engage in a given activity? Of course, values matter in this respect as well: it seems more reasonable to spend on certain essential activities or to secure some basic rights than to make pointless or secondary activities possible, but the values invoked to justify the reasonableness of spending are those shared by the whole community.

Where identity-based minorities are concerned, on the other hand, it is important to avoid reifying "cultures", for this would make any reasonable accommodation impossible. As soon as we start discussing the main constitutive elements of a culture from the point of view of that same culture and its strict preservation, any kind of "accommodation" seems unreasonable, for it changes the culture concerned and turns it into a different one. In this context, the association of cultures with religions is a very dangerous tendency, for religions as such do not lend themselves to any kind of accommodation; it is often heretical, from a religion's viewpoint, to refer to the possibility of accommodation. Unfortunately, however, this is quite a strong tendency in Europe, either because, as Weber taught us, many features of cultures can easily be traced back to different religions, or because the one difference that Europeans historically are ready to accept and tolerate is a religious difference. When we are faced with a difference in value or viewpoint, that is, either a normative or a cognitive difference, this leads us almost instinctively to regard it as a religious difference when we consider whether or not it is acceptable.

All anthropologists emphasise, in contrast, that cultures change on a daily basis, and often evolve unnoticeably but steadily through everyday interaction between their members (or, to use a better term, holders). Changes are often unspoken, or not explicitly discussed without the question being raised of their adaptation to a contingent situation. When the matter is considered, changes are usually justified with reference to a whole range of ad hoc considerations. Reasonable accommodation decided on a case-by-case basis fits in with this dynamic (or I might say interactionist) approach, allowing decisions not to be viewed as a threat to a culture – whether of the majority or of a minority – but as a reasonable solution to a personal problem. As Cass R. Sunstein wrote,[11] courts' decisions can achieve a high degree of legitimacy because they are "incompletely theorised agreements", that is, decisions that do not play any part in the ideological controversies of culture or value that often underlie a specific case. An individual, casuistic and pragmatic approach enables the concept of reasonable accommodation to be successfully applied to different kinds of problems: the case of disabled people who, as we have seen, do not question the values and viewpoints shared by the majority, but instead appeal to and reinforce them; the values and viewpoints of cultural minorities; the values and viewpoints which arise endogenously within our pluralist societies, and which, as is clear from cases relating to abortion, decisions about the end of life, and bioethics issues in general, are no less disruptive than those raised by other cultures.

Where the new minority identity groups resulting from immigration are concerned, an individual, casuistic and pragmatic approach is also facilitated when migrants' problems are viewed by the host societies, and often by the migrants themselves, as individual rather than political problems. This is likely to be the case for a long time, for what has traditionally turned individual problems into political problems has been

---

11. *Legal Reasoning and Political Conflict,* Oxford University Press, Oxford, 1996, pp. 35-61.

the responsibility for those problems taken by the disciplining agencies of social inclusion. Since these agencies are gradually disappearing, especially for the migrant population, and seem to be targeting nationals in particular, migrants and large categories of citizens who are suffering social marginalisation increasingly regard the courts as the only public authority to which they can refer their "private" problems.

It is no coincidence that, as Saskia Sassen remarked, the judiciary in the Western countries that are destinations of major immigration flows has assumed a "strategic role" "when it comes to defending the rights of immigrants, refugees, and asylum seekers".[12] Indeed, the "individualist" connotation of recourse to justice is especially important for those who are in a given country after following an immigration path and lack many citizenship rights. For they have a very hard time (we shall use C. Wright Mills' well-known words)[13] making "individual troubles" into "public issues": even something that is for nationals an unquestionably public issue (social security, safety in the workplace, housing, the very chance to have one's case heard by a court) is for migrants an essentially "individual trouble", and one that often has to be dealt with in almost complete solitude. While migrants are not the only ones for whom recourse to justice is virtually the only means to initiate a proceduralised conflict in accordance with the rules of the law, it is they who derive the greatest benefit from the supranational character of many normative sources that judges, as we have seen, may apply, and from the emergence of new supranational judicial bodies. These two elements are indeed crucial in breaking the link between access to justice and nationality and citizenship.

After all, given the widespread perception that influencing the legislative process is impossible, the chance to take part in it by expressing one's will is no longer such a significant legitimising factor. As Jürgen Habermas remarked, what seems important is "the general accessibility of a deliberative process whose structure grounds an expectation of reasonably acceptable results",[14] and only courtrooms seem to allow this process. Through recourse to a judge, all who feel dominated and excluded can

12. S. Sassen, "Regulating Immigration in a Global Age: A New Policy Landscape", *The Annals of the American Academy*, No. 570, 2000.

13. C. Wright Mills, *The Sociological Imagination*, Oxford University Press, New York, 1959.

14. J. Habermas, *Die Postnationale Konstellation*, English Translation: *The Postnational Constellation*, MIT Press, Cambridge, MA, 2001, p. 110.

regain a comforting sense of being "legal subjects". As Antoine Garapon argues:

> Justice seems to offer a chance for action that is more individual, closer, more permanent than classical political representation, which is discontinuous and distant. ... In a courtroom, the fate of a claim is not dependent on the relative strength of two political entities – e.g. a trade union and the government – but on the ability of a fighting individual to win against the state, for both are – fictitiously – placed on the same footing.[15]

The fact that recourse to justice could be compared to the "sling" which made it possible for David to fight Goliath is an element that should not be underestimated in societies whose fragmentation makes it difficult to find other individuals who are in the same situation and have the same specific interests, and where individuals often come up against the interests of the same big corporations and conglomerates, which often drive the legislative process. To many individuals recourse to justice seems to be one of the few elements of actual empowerment in a society in which, as Danilo Zolo argued:

> not only the fulfilment of social expectations but the very protection of each citizen's fundamental liberties risks being dependent less on his or her entitlement to citizenship rights than on his or her potential for corporate affiliation ... lack of capacity for affiliation ... means de facto (and sometimes de jure) exclusion from citizenship.[16]

This picture tends to obscure the collective dimension of politics. Even when their demands concern political issues or widespread interests, individuals on the margins of, or outside, consociational networks are more willing to express them in legal than in ideological or general terms; claims of individual rights prevail over collective action. Those requesting judicial intervention feel that they are taking action and determining their own fate, and are unwilling to rely on collective action. This results in a judicialisation of political conflict deriving from the individualisation of the issues at stake, and ultimately makes these issues more prominent and accelerates the shift to dealing with all claims and issues in the legal context.

---

15. A. Garapon, *Le gardien des promesses. Justice et démocratie*.

16. D. Zolo, *La cittadinanza democratica nell'era del postcomunismo*, in D. Zolo (ed.), *Cittadinanza. Appartenenza, identità, diritti*, Laterza, Rome-Bari, 1999, p. 23.

4. What does "accommodation" need to make it "reasonable"?

The variety of cultures coming into Europe, the speed of their coming and the rate at which they change on contact with European societies rule out a rationalistic approach *à la* Rawls in which people sit around a table and decide which (aspects of) cultures are compatible or incompatible, how much difference is permissible and which differences are acceptable. However, these factors also make it hard to imagine a solution like a constituent assembly to lay down guidelines for reasonable accommodation. Constituent assemblies could only meet after a 100 years or more of homogenisation of cultural differences by the myths of nation states and by discipline, and of arrangement and comparison of ideological differences. Incidentally, we can emphasise that it is this origin of constitutional rights and of the "civic" competences required to exercise them that today give these rights a certain discriminatory note: they were born to accommodate certain differences (mostly ideological) rather than others.

The rationality guiding reasonable accommodation can only be the systematic pragmatic rationality of common law. In other words, it cannot be based on conformity with a transcendent or immanent *logos*, but only on social sharing of the reasonableness and historical adequacy of its specific solutions to individual cases. Historically the provisions of common law were not validated by reason, but were the product of a long process whose reasonableness was demonstrated as they were continually relied on over a period of time. Their ability to stand the test of time and to be constantly amended in the light of practice derives from the wisdom that they embody. Their reasonableness cannot, and has no need to be, further proven. The persistence of common law over time and its continuing ability to meet the needs of large numbers of people is the sole proof of its reasonableness and goodness. The outcome of this long, and accurate, process is itself the basis for judging the reasonableness or unreasonableness of citizens' actions. It is by common law that rationality is measured, not the other way round. Similarly, the development of reasonable accommodation should only be guided by its actual ability to accommodate individual situations by constructing on each occasion a rhetoric that justifies the decision. This is the only way in which this approach can produce good practices for society and for service managers. These practices need to be flexible and discreet, or even anonymous, to take on the appearance of solutions to individual problems and to avoid raising insuperable resistance. If this happens, they will gradually alter citizens' view of life in general and their measure of reasonableness, which itself may come to encompass reasonable accommodation.

Universality, differences and rights in health and social services in the context of migration, or how can the differences of minorities be made an advantage for all?

Francine Saillant[1]

As elsewhere in the Americas, the territory of Quebec comprises groups of Native American ("First Nations") and Inuit groups and diversified groups from all continents that have populated it intensively over several centuries. Quebec society can take pride in the various contributions to its formation from the migrants who have settled there; it has been a very diverse society from the outset. Although the official account of its foundation, which is tied in with the account of Canada as a whole, refers to three founding peoples – the First Nations and Inuit (indigenous peoples), immigrants from France and immigrants from the British Isles – individuals and groups in addition to those usually mentioned were also present and contributed to its cultural diversity. The majority of the colonising and migrant groups that historically took part in the formation of Quebec society were, nonetheless, from Europe. More recently, as a result of migration policies and the particular characteristics surrounding major migration movements since the 1980s, Quebec society has been marked by a growing process of ethnic and religious pluralisation that began some 30 years ago. Other phenomena, which first appeared in the 1960s, have strengthened that pluralisation, but in other forms: beliefs and lifestyles have gradually diversified under the influence of secu-larisation, social movements and the rise of minority group demands. Although they have different causes, all these factors have had a strong influence on the daily life of the people of Quebec and on institutions, which have had to adapt to these transformations. Quebec society has had to engage in dialogue with the various groups exhibiting difference, including immigrant groups. The rise of demands by indigenous groups has also contributed to a self-conception of Quebec society in terms of diversity, differences and current or future transformations. The diversity that characterised the past, which was for a long time obscured by the dominant conservative ideologies, is now there for all to see, reminding society itself and politicians of the rights and multiple identities of which it

---

1. Department of Anthropology, Célat Université Laval, Quebec (Canada).

is composed. Given this situation, a whole range of legislation, institutional practices and values is being discussed and reviewed in order to address this pluralisation. Public debates on the impact of ethnic and religious pluralisation also intensified when the Bouchard-Taylor Commission was set up (Consultation Commission on Accommodation Practices Related to Cultural Differences, Bouchard and Taylor 2007, 2008). Public services in areas such as education and health and social services were called upon to provide an appropriate response to the different sections of the population, particularly first and second-generation immigrants. Reasonable accommodation between service providers and users, training courses and intercultural programmes and legal accommodation were practical solutions put in place by institutions.

In this paper I shall focus on the adaptation of public health and social services to the situations of migrants. Part 1 deals with the development of the social and health context in the light of migration in Quebec; Part 2 discusses the intercultural approach and its enhancement by broadening the concept of difference and the indissociability of the legal and communications dimensions; Part 3 continues this discussion by going on to broaden the concept of vulnerability, conceived not as an exception but as part of the human condition. The extended intercultural approach also aims to avoid institutional and political resistance to those who are too often relegated to the heading "exceptions".

1. Overview of the Quebec health-care system, immigration, health and well-being

In 2006, the population of Quebec represented 23.9% of the population of Canada; 11.5% of the population was of immigrant origin. In the Montreal area, one of the three Canadian cities regarded as having the highest proportion of immigrants in their territory (the other two being Toronto and Vancouver), one third of the population was of immigrant origin (Battaglini 2007). In some districts of Montreal, the proportion of the population of recent immigration background (two generations and fewer) is now more than 60% (Battaglini 2007) and includes people from more than 100 countries speaking as many languages. In 1951, immigrants accounted for 5.6% of the population of Quebec; by 2001 they accounted for 10% of the population. This means that in a 50-year period, between 1951 and 2001, the level of immigration had leapt by 4.4% (Ministère des Relations avec les citoyens et de l'Immigration, 2004b).[2]

The Quebec health-care system is a universal, free system that in principle offers public health and social services to all citizens living in the territory, whether or not they hold Canadian citizenship. Therefore Canadian citizens, people legally living in Canada with landed immigrant status and public refugees (selected by Canada in their countries or in a third country) in principle have the same rights with respect to use of public services, including those of the health-care and social system. Since 2001, however, landed immigrants and public refugees have had to wait three months after their arrival for the Quebec health insurance card that gives them access to these public services. Those who are able to do so therefore have to take out private insurance during this waiting period (Munoz and Chirgwin 2007). Nevertheless, access in principle to health-care services once this waiting period is over does not mean that these public services are completely open to the needs of such people.

Asylum seekers, in other words people who do not have landed immigrant status and are awaiting a legal status, are in a different situation. They have a right to health care under the Interim Federal Health Programme (IFHP)[3] (Munoz and Chirgwin 2007).

---

2. These findings do not reflect the real ethnic pluralism of Quebec. They concern only the proportion of the population of Quebec born abroad. Children with an immigrant background born in Quebec are not counted because they are not considered to be immigrants. They, nonetheless, display difference. Quebec immigration statistics do not make it easy to give an accurate figure for the proportion of the population with an immigrant background. However, the Canadian data from the 2006 population census provide a table of the population of Quebec according to ethnic origin. Respondents were able to tick more than one box relating to their ethnic origin. By calculating the total number of single replies regarding respondents' subjective identification and excluding Native Americans, the census findings put the proportion of the population of Quebec belonging to one or other of the ethnic minority groups at 28.4% (Statistics Canada, "Ethnic origins, 2006 counts, for Canada, provinces and territories – 20% sample data", www12.statcan.ca/english/census06/data/highlights/ethnic/pages/Page.cfm?Lang=E&Geo=PR&Code=24&Data=Count&Table=2&StartRec=1&Sort=3&Display=All&CSDFilter=5000).

3. This official document is to be found on the following website: www.cic.gc.ca/english/refugees/outside/resettle-assist.asp.

The Canadian Health Act[4] makes no provision for health services adapted to immigrants and refugees. Conversely, the current Quebec Act respecting Health Services and Social Services[5] states clearly that the agency must "facilitate accessibility to health and social services in a manner which is respectful of the characteristics of those cultural communities" and must do so in their language and in the localities in which there are large immigrant groups.

Generally speaking, all users have the right to receive public health and social services in either of the country's two official languages, French and English. On the other hand, despite the legislator's intentions, immigrants of all categories who do not speak either of these two languages cannot usually receive these services in their mother tongue. Although the Quebec health and social system allows for this type of accommodation, it does not have all the necessary resources. In spite of limited resources, some practice environments in highly pluricultural areas, such as the Côtes-des-Neiges district of Montreal, nonetheless offer services that take language and culture into account, using interpreting and cultural mediation services. Services of this type are not available throughout the territory of Montreal and are not systematically available in cities other than Montreal, although some (Quebec City and Sherbrooke) are also affected by the increase in the immigrant population.[6]

Landed immigrants and refugees have to comply with Canadian and Quebec laws and use services in accordance with the existing provision, which is always universalist. The social situation is such that the majority of health and social services provided which take cultural particularities into account, including those for first-generation immigrants, are dispensed under programmes developed within initiatives specific to a particular service environment and to the professionals and researchers working in them, who have the authority and expertise to establish and build on them. The initiatives being taken in various fields (paediatrics, standard care, psychiatry) in the public services have been greatly facilitated by the existence of an explicit and favourable legal framework.

---

4. This official document is to be found on the following website:
    www.parl.gc.ca/information/library/prbpubs/944-e.htm.
5. www2.publicationsduquebec.gouv.qc.ca/dynamicSearch/telecharge.
    php?type=2&file=/S_4_2/S4_2_A.html.
6. In the late 1990s, the Government of Quebec decided to "regionalise" immigration, in other words to promote the settlement of immigrants in cities other than Montreal.

Landed immigrants and public refugees have access not only to public services but also to a whole range of community services (voluntary sector) distinct from the public network but which collaborate with it through front-line services whose aims include directing people towards the various Quebec institutions and introducing them to local cultural and civic values (Saillant 2007; Rojas-Viger 2008). Voluntary sector bodies act as leading mediators.

Quebec has an immigration policy that respects the multicultural nature of Canada and emphasises interculturality.[7] The essence of this policy is to foster the reception and adaptation of immigrants to Quebec society, with due regard for local rules on diversity. In line with this policy, immigrants are considered a source of cultural, social and economic enrichment of Quebec society; they are invited to contribute through their culture and their efforts to such enrichment. Under this policy, adaptation to Quebec society is said to be dependent upon efforts to guide and support immigrants so that they become integrated as harmoniously as possible and on the efforts of the immigrants themselves, so that their actions tie in with those of the host society. It has to be understood that the openness of Quebec society to immigration is conditional on immigrants' willingness and capacity for adaptation and integration, respecting the culture and laws of the host society; what is called interculturality could be expressed by the neologism "enculturality": the values of interculturality should in a sense serve integration and therefore the gradual "enculturation" of immigrants.

It should be emphasised that one of the particular characteristics of Quebec society as compared with other Western societies lies in the range of efforts made for immigrants to foster their adaptation, although those efforts are conducted from the specific and foreseeable standpoint of the host society. The possibility for immigrants to be able to refer to accredited associations (community groups) for support in their efforts (seeking employment, French language courses, guidance and referral, legal assistance) has few equivalents in the world and has beneficial effects. At the level of health and social services, community group efforts can only be limited, however, in view of their terms of reference, which limit responsibilities to supporting and assisting people in their dealings with public services, and to providing information and guidance. Community organisations do not have sufficient financial resources and expertise to provide

---

7. See www.micc.gouv.qc.ca/publications/fr/planification/PlanAction20042007-integral. pdf (available only in French).

health and social services comparable to those provided by the public services. They may, however, guide people towards those services, for example in cases of psychological distress. It should also be pointed out that several of these services are offered by people who speak one of the users' languages and are also closely linked with ethnocultural associations playing a positive role in providing new arrivals with identity-related and material support. In this way "the burden of adaptation" is to some extent divided between civil society and the public services. In the adaptation of public and community services, the values of interculturality serve as an ingredient in the ideal adaptation desired, but they are not compulsorily mobilised in the public services throughout Quebec, only where specialised services have been developed. They do, however, come into play where there is a large immigrant population and in environments that assume responsibility for adapting their services.

A major exercise in collective examination of the issues of immigration, cultural adaptation and diversity recently took place in Quebec. In particular through its discussion of reasonable accommodation, the Bouchard-Taylor Commission (op. cit.),[8] which, during its hearings, held over a period of several months, attracted hundreds of civil society groups, institutions, individuals and observers from various environments. The question of the cultural adaptation of health services was not systematically examined during the commission's hearings or in the various reports submitted to it. Only 2% of the reports submitted to the commission in the Montreal region dealt specifically with health, and these were reports prepared for the most part by public services already providing adapted health services. There are three interesting facts here. First, no report dealing with health was submitted to the commission from any region of Quebec other than Montreal. Second, the report submitted by public services specialising in interculturality recommended flexible forms of adaptation set up through local arrangements rather than based on legal accommodations. Third, it is hardly surprising that the people who submitted the reports were ardent defenders of the adaptation of services to immigrant groups and pointed to the significant advances made in Quebec as a result. Over the last 30 years huge progress has been made with regard to the provision

---

8. See the report used for the public consultation and the final report published after the consultation: www.accommodements.qc.ca/documentation/document-consultation-en.pdf and www.accommodements.qc.ca/documentation/rapports/rapport-final-integral-en.pdf.

of adapted services in Quebec, although there are still improvements to be made in terms of both quality and quantity.

2. The approach to immigration and interculturality in public health and social services

A number of considerations need to be borne in mind regarding the provision of health services to immigrants and refugees. In Quebec, first-generation immigrants are more vulnerable to mental health problems than the general population, while those of the second generation present higher levels of physical morbidity than those of the first. Vulnerability to health problems also differs according to the point in the migration trajectory (Zunzunegui et al. 2006). Other factors also have to be taken into account: the health conditions, stress and violence of pre-migration contexts, some seriously affecting the health of individuals, such as refugees (Rojas-Viger 2008); conditions of settlement in the host country (culture shock) (Lacroix 2004); aggravating factors such as poverty, unemployment and isolation (Leduc and Proulx 2004); problems of access to services (whether or not they have insurance) (Oxman-Martinez et al. 2005); whether or not they speak the language or experience cultural barriers (Leduc and Proulx 2004, p. 23;[9] Lai and Chau 2007; Asanin and Wilson 2008); and, lastly, the characteristics of individuals, such as whether they belong to groups that suffer particularly from racism, for example from regions such as the Middle East, Africa and the Caribbean.

The conventional intercultural approach could be defined as all the practices that stress the cultural adaptation of the health and social services of a host society for immigrants and that take into account the language of the services provided, treatment practices and ways of life that are difficult to incorporate into the national health system, relating to conceptions of the body, the health and illness of migrants, conceptions that are usually embedded in worlds with religious meaning and family and community structures. Health and social services based on the intercultural approach are supposed to take into account the specific health conditions of immigrants, mental health in particular, such as cases of post-traumatic stress among refugees. Poverty, isolation and the consequences of adaptation problems experienced by immigrants and their families are also factors to be taken into account in establishing culturally adapted services. The

---

9. See also for similar American data, Derose, Escarce and Lurie 2007; Snowden and Yamada 2005.

cultural factors involved in immigrants' refusal to use or resistance to using public services, as was observed in the Montreal psychiatric services (Kirmayer et al. 2007; Whitley, Kirmayer and Groleau 2006), are also concerns fundamental to the development of adapted services.

The intercultural approach presupposes practical knowledge and training in the fields of anthropology and intercultural relations connected with health. Little time is usually devoted to such training in the curricula of training schools (for social services, nursing and medicine, for example). In most training schools, basic training is limited to about 50 hours of class in a three-year course. Moreover, the intercultural approach has inherited a corpus of knowledge that generally favours pairs and small groups, based on postulates drawn from communication and clinical sciences. These postulates assume that, in order for intercultural values to be instilled – values such as recognition of others and their individuality, and affirmation of diversity and universality – the protagonists need communication tools such as interpreting, effective knowledge of the other's culture and its particularities, and the requirements and conditions connected with migrant and refugee experiences. In the health and social field, this is conceived as having to be part of the clinical field and professional practices. This same model still tends to be imperfectly integrated in institutional frameworks (policy and philosophy of hospitals and public bodies) and national health legislation. And yet the virtues of the model have been demonstrated in numerous experiences of cultural adaptation of health services in the world (DePlaen 2006; Fortin and Laudy 2007), particularly in Quebec, despite the fact that, like all models, it has limitations. For example, no clinician can become a specialist in all cultures in all their variations and expressions. Some health problems experienced by immigrants and refugees sometimes require more than communication skills on the part of health workers: they require specialised anthropological, psychoanalytic or medical knowledge and necessitate mastery of several disciplines, but this cannot be expected of every clinician. Some cultural resistances to the norms and values of health institutions in the host country will not always be able to be addressed within them (DePlaen 2006; DePlaen et al. 2005). Furthermore, the question of available resources is central: the provision of culturally adapted services should take into account the capacity and limitations of services, in particular their human, cognitive and financial resources.

Health and social services virtually throughout the world are faced with economic restrictions connected with the neo-liberal movement that imposed upon them particular management choices and a rationalisation of services. This leads institutions to develop uniform and increasingly standardised services that cater less and less for particularities, whether those of ethnocultural communities or of other communities, such as people with disabilities, women or gays; the costs engendered by services adapted to or that take account of particularities (cultures, lifestyles, specific conditions in terms of age, gender, place of residence, income, etc.) are considered exorbitant at a time when everyone is being asked "to do better with less"; lastly, little is known about the ability of training institutes to give appropriate training in line with an intercultural approach. It may be assumed that when courses are taught there are problems such as lack of qualified staff and lack of available time in curricula in view of other needs regarded as just as important. It also has to be asked to what extent the values of the conventional intercultural approach can truly be integrated in large cities more marked by cultural plurality than the presence of a miscellany of clearly defined "ethnic" communities alongside an (ethnic) majority that is also clearly defined (Hall 2007; Bibeau 2000). What is at issue is the transformation of migration situations in major cities: we now talk less and less about small ethnic neighbourhoods, although they still exist, and more and more about a pluricultural, cosmopolitan, hybrid urban fabric which as a result makes the reality of diversity more complex. A high degree of diversity may make the intercultural ideal difficult to put into effect in the clinical field since it may become difficult to respond to all the needs of all the immigrant members of a society of this type. The cosmopolitan Indian or African of the diasporas in major European cities probably does not much resemble the Italian or Pole who migrated to New York or Montreal in the 1940s.

Over and above these considerations, societies have no choice but to take account of the immigrants and refugees they receive because of their commitments under international conventions (humanitarian law and the Geneva Conventions, human rights law) and the fact that such people should be considered as full citizens in the broadest possible sense of the concept of citizenship, with its political, social and economic dimensions. If the state has the power to protect its citizens, it should in the first place do so at the social and health level because illness and the conditions of fragility associated with it are vulnerability factors that are added to other factors associated with the experience of migration and refugee status. The difficult economic conditions in which most immigrants and refugees find themselves, especially in the early years, are also factors that influence people's physical and psychological health, which means that even greater attention should be given to this group of citizens.

Interculturality in health services – or, as I prefer to put it, taking into account cultural diversity and individualities in the provision of services – cannot be justified politically or in practice solely by approaches based on a vision favouring communication, cultural mediation and translation, in other words by a conventional intercultural approach. We have just seen that other problems arise: the transformation of the migratory fabric in major cities that leads diversity to be thought of less in terms of groups of communities than in terms of a diversified, plural multitude; the difficulty for staff of possessing all the tools and all the knowledge concerning all the cultures they encounter, even though there is a need for interculturality-based professional skills; the importance of including intercultural values in broader models, including questions of law and citizenship. It may also be important to take a broader view of diversity so that it is not only immigrants and refugees who bear the burden of difference in the host society. Such is the case for democratic values. Western societies, such as that of Quebec, have diversified in the last 30 years, not only as a result of migratory flows, but also as a result of the identity-specific movements they have witnessed (Fraser 2004). The increasing pluralism characterising our societies should be thought of in broader terms and incorporate all facets of culture and all the groups that contribute to it. I am thinking here of all the groups that display difference, whether they are ethnic, religious, sexual, gender-specific or related to functional abilities. We should also consider difference not as something that enters institutions (public services) from outside, but also that operates and must be addressed within. Internal differences affect professional, health and social and institutional cultures. This is an important point because it may be easy for a state to relegate the needs of migrant groups to categories of "particularities" that are too expensive, thereby limiting its responsibilities to a significant proportion of its citizens. The renewed and enhanced intercultural approach I am advocating views difference as multidimensional (open to dimensions other than, but including, the ethnic dimension) and to be situated in multiple locations (in institutions and public services, in the groups served). This enhanced intercultural approach includes the basic precepts of the conventional intercultural approach at the level of communication, but has the advantage of opening up difference in the aim of serving the greatest number of users. It does not make immigrants the sole bearers of the burden of difference. It also has the advantage of taking into account the major social transformations that have contributed to the pluralisation of Western societies. Its cross-sectoral power is a most valuable advantage at the level of policies and programmes. The question of difference, which is at the heart of intercultural values, should also be linked to another question, that of law. It is essential to point out that immigrant users of services have rights: in this sense, states must provide their services according to their legal and moral obligations to this category of citizens. The provision of services adapted in line with an enhanced intercultural approach embedded in the public domain must include both the right to equal treatment (rights to services, geographic, economic and physical accessibility) and the taking into account of difference (adapted services, cultural accessibility).

3. Bringing about an enhanced intercultural approach

At this point, we need to look in greater depth at enhancement of the conventional intercultural approach. In order to strengthen the argument, it is crucial to consider two concepts: vulnerability and diversity.

It is through the body that the subject enters the world and culture. The codes and symbols of a culture pass through the body that experiences them. Culture acts as a fount of signs, symbols and metaphors. Human language and capacity for language make it possible to interpret and appropriate these symbolic resources; it is also through language that cultural, personal and collective meanings are constantly developed and recreated. The cultural experience, which is also a physical experience, is continually mediated by language (Geertz 2000; Csordas 1990).

The body is the locus of the development of language, of language made experience by speech; it is also subject to vulnerabilities. The body is vulnerable in itself because human experience is relational: the experience of socialisation at an early age involves dependency on a person occupying the place of mother, father or a close relative, and this dependency is the first experience of vulnerability in human life after birth (Honneth 1995). In adult life, the human subject, as a relational being, is also constantly affected by others, and the emotions, encoded by cultural and personal experiences, are experienced through the intermediary of the body. Culture is in a sense embodied and language is the means of dialogue between inner experience and the external world (Butler 2004). The body is also the object of violence: human subjects, fundamentally relational, address others but are also addressed by others and by people who have power over them. The fact of being human necessarily means being more than oneself by making of oneself what is beyond one, being socialised and humanised, therefore formed through the transmitted memory of those who have preceded us and of the memory transmitted by those who are also interacting with us in the present. Human beings are relational in their genealogical, interactional, cultural and memory-related dimensions (Ricoeur 1990, 2000). Culture provides the frameworks of meanings and the frameworks of social behaviour. Our condition is one of vulnerability as subjects with bodies and as beings of language, indebted as we are to the experience of dependency, first on our parents or people performing their role, and then on the resources of an unknown environment charged with meaning, the signs, codes and symbols of which we have had to learn through and with others. Let us consider this vulnerability to be normal and part of a shared human condition.

"Difference" is among other things inscribed in the body because it is naturally observable and culturally reconstructed: on the basis of difference, societies have elaborated strong and complex symbolic systems, part of the profound dimensions of cultures, at an elementary level (the individual body, for example, left and right), and at more complex levels (between bodies: gender, "race", age). The most ancient symbolic systems were developed on the basis of observations of discernible differences that were used as references for organisational and cultural interpretation models, for example, myths and religions. Differences were the basis for hierarchical and discriminatory classifications of people and groups of a naturalist and essentialist kind leading to discriminatory ideologies, such as racism, sexism and ageism. Skin colour and belonging to a gender or age-group may be classifying factors unfavourable to the people in those groups, and the ideologies that allow such classifications are important factors contributing to social inequalities and observable forms of vulnerabilities (Lacroix 2004). Although such differences are too often pretexts for social inequalities and contested, contestable and debatable cultural elaborations, they are at the heart of human life in society.

We have just seen that the human condition is made of vulnerability; the normal vulnerability that dependency brings in its train is also that of everyone who is introduced to another culture because that human being, foreigner and migrant, must again place himself or herself in a situation of dependency and vulnerability, unlearn part of what he or she knows and learn the symbolic and social resources of a new environment. A migrant who is ill may experience this situation of vulnerability even more strongly since the unknown then takes several forms, the experience of the new society, along with the experience of illness. We should not forget that illness, particularly serious or chronic illness, brings with it a number of consequences: redefinition of self and identity, redefinition of life projects, anguish and anxiety, fear, stigma, etc. (Saillant and Genest 2006).

All societies in history and all different cultures have their way of responding to the health problems of their communities according to the meanings of the normal and the pathological, the evaluations they make of the gravity of problems, and of course of their available resources (values, economy, technology), including knowledge about health (biomedical, ethno-medical and alternative approaches). They do so because illness is part of the human condition, its existence is inevitable and no society can completely suppress it. They intervene with the aim of keeping alive those they consider worthy of life. In some cases, societies consider that it is not useful, necessary or effective to intervene, or they are simply unfamiliar with the problem that is presented. It is not only the various medical systems that offer responses to illness; there are also ritual and symbolic forms that at their level have their own effectiveness, forms that are not always systems in the sense of Ayurveda or Chinese medicine; from birth to death, religious and spiritual practices fall into this category.

Modern states also play a role in the management, organisation and focus of public health and social services based on science, biomedicine and the health professions. By providing or withholding services, they make judgments about people's worthiness or unworthiness and their right to life, to live well or to die, just as traditional medicine does. The responses to sick people are constrained by factors such as available technologies, existing knowledge, values, health and social policies, to name but a few. It is normally part of the role of states to protect the people on their territories, to promote health through access to public services and the values of adaptation and equality. The action of health and social services on citizens' well-being is a way of giving some expression to social rights and social citizenship.

Categories of differences other than those referred to above are also inscribed in the body but are unequally distributed among human beings: states of illness. All societies have a given number of people who have to live with a condition that limits their autonomy to varying degrees. Obvious examples are disabilities, chronic illness and many other conditions that result in some degree of incapacity. Many such conditions are consequences of social inequalities or are aggravated by them, and make some groups more vulnerable than others, in particular where inequalities mean unequal distribution of wealth. Illness can be discussed in terms of an experience of difference, particularly when people have to adapt their whole life to an illness: this is the case with Aids, some forms of mental illness and certain types of disability. In these cases, these observable differences are once again the basis on which inequalities are embodied in discriminatory practices of various forms: stigma, negligence, refusal of treatment, etc. Such differences, when linked with other categories of differences, in particular those referred to above, be they causes or consequences, and according to combinations specific to individuals, groups or communities, produce social vulnerabilities.

Certain categories of differences do not always take the body as locus and centre of development. Some cultural groups experience differences that are both embodied (by "visible minorities") and expressed by codes and traditions (for example, wearing a veil or a turban). Groups from India and the Middle East are examples of this. In the context of migration, such groups have to relive the experience of vulnerability that is involved in relearning the codes of a society of which they will become full members, at least that is what is expected and desirable. They also have to confront potentially discriminatory experiences based on the difference they represent at cultural level, a difference that may be accentuated according to whether it is linked with other differences, such as age or gender. In this respect migration and taking refuge are strong experiences of difference often inscribed in inegalitarian social relations. The vulnerability of individuals and groups experiencing these differences and inequalities is accentuated in such circumstances.

Public health and social services constantly have to come to terms with differences, inequalities and vulnerabilities. As a matter of principle they must enable inequalities based on difference to be reduced through appropriate services, such as measures on access, non-discrimination and humanisation, as well as the cultural adaptation of services.

The function of the public health and social services of modern societies, in particular those established since the Second World War, is to reduce morbidity and mortality, promote health and prevent illness. They also have particular responsibility for people and groups affected by health inequalities, giving them special attention, making treatment economically and culturally accessible to them, and developing prevention/promotion programmes that take into account their particular situation, regardless of age, culture of origin, gender, religious belief or ethnicity.

Public health and social services were much criticised in the 1970s, 1980s and 1990s for what was seen as their over-standardisation. This criticism was made through movements in favour of de-medicalisation (of perinatal care and mental health, for example) and choice in styles of practice (alternative medicine). The criticism concerned the anomie of relationships in services, the reification of individuals and the scant importance attached to both the particularities of users and medical practices other than those of biomedicine. Following on the heels of these criticisms and movements for autonomy in health, various social movements, preceding the intensification of worldwide migration movements in the globalisation process, advocated diversity in services provided in a manner sympathetic to difference, despite the strong trend to centralise and operate according to a standardised and standardising model: examples are services combining soft medicines and biomedicine, the movement to de-medicalise childbirth, the midwife movement and the palliative care movement. These services have served the greatest number, although at first sight they seem to come from very specific quarters. These different social movements have exerted pressure for health and social measures that are more adapted to the needs of, for example, women, gays and people with disabilities. Although they have not always had the expected outcomes, the development of adapted services that take difference and particularities into account have taught us a number of things. For example, the transformations in the environments of people with disabilities have also been useful for many other social categories: ramps are also used by pregnant women and the elderly. The adaptations women have requested in delivery rooms have enabled men as well as women to experience the time of birth more harmoniously, not to mention the benefits this has had for children. The development of a humanised vision of health and social services in this sector has been a sort of inspiration for other sectors. The criticisms of asylums and places where people with mental health problems were confined had an impact on other places: environments for the care of the elderly have also benefited now that the sort of confinement seen 30 or 40 years ago is no longer acceptable to current sensitivities. The movement to combat Aids and the various forms of community self-help developed by gays have become models that have inspired a whole range of interventions in the chronic illness sector. The palliative care movement, which began in the United Kingdom, has spread to all Western countries and now benefits millions of people: it has changed the way in which care is conceived and death experienced. No one would ever have imagined that the experience of a small British clinic run by volunteers would influence health-care workers throughout the world. We should perhaps add to this list the experiments to de-institutionalise people suffering from mental illness conducted in Italy in the 1960s and 1970s, which then influenced Western countries and spread to other groups, such as the elderly and people with disabilities. What has to be understood here is that demands made by a few experts or user movements that initially appear to be costly special cases for public systems can often be of benefit to a great many people, in addition to the groups intended at the outset. Could this not also be true of services for immigrants? Does not an approach to treatment that makes allowance for cultural sensitivities and differences in lifestyles and values have its place in a world that can only become increasingly pluralist? An approach to public services open to diversity in the broadest sense of the term and to accessibility viewed as a right would make it possible – at least it is hoped that it would – to avoid the institutional and political resistance to those who are too often relegated to the heading "exceptions".

4. Conclusion: health, rights, diversity and democracy

In Quebec, public health and social services have diversified their provision for immigrants and refugees in certain localities. Some observers believe that these services are still inadequate; this situation is decried by the voluntary sector, experts on migration issues and those working in specialist practice environments, familiar with these questions. It is, however, the role of public health and social services to serve the population and take care of the most vulnerable sections and therefore those who are marked by the experience of difference against a background of inequality.

Accessibility (geographic, economic and cultural) to public health and social services is one of the social rights of citizens and people who are legally in the countries of the European Union and countries such as Canada and Australia. It is also a responsibility incumbent upon states deriving from humanitarian law in respect of asylum seekers. This responsibility, which is set out in international charters and conventions and reflected in national legislation, is not always truly respected, in particular as regards cultural accessibility and the rights of migrant communities. Asylum seekers are in a still more precarious situation because they may be deprived of the documents that give them access to free treatment; moreover, where they do have a right to it, their access may be limited and subject to conditions. More generally, immigrants from non-European or non-Euro-American cultures have greater problems of access for reasons connected with racism and discrimination, as we saw above. They are more likely to experience the effects of the inequalities of which they are victims, in view of their difference and the way it is dealt with in host societies. From this point of view, the question of the integration of minorities and their rights in public services, of course including health and social services, should be considered a question of citizenship and a question of democracy. Accordingly, expressing the question of difference only in the terms of conventional interculturality (communicational approach) may not be the only way for states to open up to providing culturally adapted services relevant to the needs of the populations concerned through their policies and health and social systems. Adaptation of services according to an enhanced intercultural approach could be seen as a way of contributing to the development of a society with full rights enabling immigrant communities to enjoy the advantages of full citizenship. It would make it possible not only to respond to the needs of immigrant populations, but also to the needs of other groups who display difference and to historically highly marginalised groups, such as indigenous peoples and the Roma. However, it is perhaps time to attribute to the term "interculturality" the enhanced meaning given to it here. At this stage in the discussion I suggest that interculturality and citizenship, together and indissociably, can guide the principles for developing the services for the greatest number, at the lowest cost and taking cultural differences into account. Moreover, cultural differences can also be taken into account by avoiding seeing difference only from the point of view of culture in the ethnocentrist sense of the term, but rather in terms of diverse lifestyles and values and therefore of the intrinsic plurality of modern societies. When all is said and done, focusing on the conception of a plural citizenship could serve to conceive of public health and social services that respond both to the requirements of difference imposed by the context of migration in contemporary societies and to the requirements of the greatest number in a society with full, pluralistic and democratic rights.

References

Asanin J. and Wilson K. (2008), "'I Spent Nine Years Looking for a Doctor': Exploring Access to Health Care Among Immigrants in Mississauga, Ontario, Canada", *Social Sciences and Medicine*, 66, pp. 1271-1283.

Battaglini A. (2007), *L'intervention de première ligne à Montréal auprès des personnes immigrantes: Estimé des ressources nécessaires pour une intervention adéquate*, Agence de la santé et des services sociaux de Montréal, Montreal.

Bibeau G. (2000), "Vers une éthique créole", *Anthropologie et Sociétés*, 24, 2, pp. 129-148.

Bouchard G. and Taylor C. (2007), "Accommodation and Differences. Seeking Common Ground: Quebecers Speak Out", Consultation Commission on Accommodation Practices Related to Cultural Differences, www.accommodements.qc.ca/documentation/document-consultation-en.pdf.

Bouchard G. and Taylor C. (2008), "Building the Future. A Time for Reconciliation", Consultation Commission on Accommodation Practices Related to Cultural Differences, www.accommodements.qc.ca/documentation/rapports/rapport-final-integral-en.pdf.

Butler J. (2004), *Precarious Life: The Power of Mourning and Violence*, London.

"The Canada Health Act: Overview and Options", www.parl.gc.ca/information/library/prbpubs/944-e.htm.

Citizenship and Immigration Canada, "Financial Assistance and Loans", www.cic.gc.ca/english/refugees/outside/resettle-assist.asp.

Csordas T. J. (1990), "Embodiment as a Paradigm for Anthropology", *Ethos*, 18, 1, pp. 5-48.

DePlaen S. (2006), "Travailler avec les jeunes issus de l'immigration: vers une pratique pédopsychiatrique culturellement sensible: L'ethnopsychiatrie", *Santé mentale au Québec*, 31, 2, pp. 123-134.

DePlaen S. et al. (2005), "Mieux travailler en situations cliniques complexes: l'expérience des séminaires transculturels interinstitutionnels", *Santé mentale au Québec*, 30, 2, pp. 281-299.

Derose P. K., Escarce J. J. and Lurie N. (2007), "Immigrants and Health Care: Sources of Vulnerability", *Health Affairs*, 26, 3, pp. 1258-1269.

Fortin S. and Laudy D. (2007), "Soins de santé et de diversité culturelle: comment faire pour bien faire?", in Jézéquel M. (ed.), *L'obligation d'accommodement: quoi, comment, jusqu'où? Des outils pour tous*, Yvon Blais, Cowansville (Quebec), pp. 289-317.

Fraser, N. (2004), *Qu'est-ce que la justice sociale?* La Découverte, Paris.

Geertz C. (2000), *Available Light: Anthropological Reflections on Philosophical Topics*, Princeton University Press, Princeton.

Government of Quebec, An Act Respecting Health Services and Social Services, www2.publicationsduquebec.gouv.qc.ca/dynamicSearch/telecharge. php?type=2&file=/S_4_2/S4_2_A.html.

Hall S. (2007), *Identités et cultures. Politiques des Cultural Studies*, Amsterdam, Paris, 2007, pp. 57-70.

Honneth A. (1995), *The Struggle for Recognition*, Polity Press.

Kirmayer L. J. et al. (2007), "Use of Health Care Services for Psychological Distress by Immigrants in an Urban Multicultural Milieu", *Canadian Journal of Psychiatry*, 52, 5, pp. 295-304.

Lacroix M. (2004), "L'expérience des demandeurs d'asile: vers l'élaboration de nouvelles pratiques socials", *Nouvelles pratiques sociales*, 16, 2, pp. 178-191.

Lai D. W. L. and Chau S. B. (2007), "Effects of Service Barriers on Health Status of Older Chinese Immigrants in Canada", *Social Work*, 53, 3, pp. 261-270.

Leduc N. and Proulx M. (2004), "Patterns of Health Services Utilization by Recent Immigrants", *Journal of Immigrant Health*, 6, 1, pp. 15-27.

Ministère des Relations avec les citoyens et de l'Immigration (2004a), "Des valeurs partagées, des intérêts communs, Plan d'action 2004-2007", www.micc.gouv.qc.ca/publications/fr/planification/PlanAction20042007-integral.pdf, accessed 9 October 2009.

Ministère des Relations avec les citoyens et de l'Immigration (2004b), "Population immigrée recensée au Québec et dans les régions en 2001: caractéristiques générales", Government of Quebec, Quebec.

Munoz M. and Chirgwin J. C. (2007), "Les immigrants et les demandeurs d'asile: nouveaux défis", *Médecin du Québec*, 42, pp. 33-42.

Oxman-Martinez J. et al. (2005), "Intersection of Canadian Policy Parameters Affecting Women with Precarious Immigration Status: A Baseline for Understanding Barriers to Health", *Journal of Immigrant Health*, 7, 4, pp. 247-258.

Ricoeur P. (1990), *Soi-même comme un autre*, Seuil, Paris.

Ricoeur P. (2000), *La mémoire, l'histoire, l'oubli*, Seuil, Paris.

Rojas-Viger C. (2008), "L'impact des violences structurelle et conjugale en contexte migratoire: Perceptions d'intervenants pour le contrer", *Nouvelle pratiques sociales*, 20, 2, pp. 124-141.

Saillant F. (2007), "Vous êtes ici dans une mini-ONU", *Anthropologie et sociétés*, 31, 2, pp. 65-90.

Saillant F. and Genest S. (2006), *Medical Anthropology. Regional Perspectives and Shared Concerns*, Blackwell, Maiden.

Snowden L. R. and Yamada A. M. (2005), "Cultural Differences in Access to Care", *Annual Review of Psychology*, 1, pp. 143-166.

Statistics Canada, "Population and dwelling counts, for Canada, provinces and territories, 2006 and 2001 censuses – 100% data", www12. statcan.ca/english/census06/data/popdwell/Table.cfm?T=101.

Statistics Canada, "Ethnic origins, 2006 counts, for Canada, provinces and territories – 20% sample data", www12.statcan.ca/english/census06/ data/highlights/ethnic/pages/Page.cfm?Lang=E&Geo=PR&Code=24&Dat a=Count&Table=2&StartRec=1&Sort=3&Display=All&CSDFilter=5000.

Statistics Canada, "Selected trend data for Quebec, 2006, 2001 and 1996 censuses", www12.statcan.ca/english/census06/data/trends/Table_1.cfm ?T=PR&PRCODE=24&GEOCODE=24&GEOLVL=PR.

Whitley R., Kirmayer L. and Groleau D. (2006), "Understanding Immigrants' Reluctance to Use Mental Health Services: A Qualitative Study From Montreal", *Canadian Journal of Psychiatry/La Revue canadienne de psychiatrie*, 51, 4, pp. 205-209.

Zunzunegui M.-V. (2006), "Community Unemployment and Immigrants' Health in Montreal", *Social Science & Medicine*, 63, 2, pp. 485-500.

Two successful examples of reasonable accommodation and intercultural mediation in the health-care sector

A. The case of the Tree of Health

Fabrizia Petrei[1]

1. Introduction

This study will deal with migration in the Italian city of Prato and the surrounding area[2] from the standpoint of the problems and critical situations that may be encountered regarding migrants' access to and use of the public health-care service, with particular emphasis on women.

The chief factors which show that female migrants in the Prato area do not enjoy the best possible health, including in terms of "global health",[3] are listed below:

- a high risk index during childbirth, frequently owing to pregnant women's delayed access to health care (often when their pregnancy is already at an advanced stage);

- inadequate coverage of women's health-care needs in the period following childbirth;

- a high number of, often repeat, abortions;

- scant recourse to preventive oncology.

---

1. Graduate in Public, Social and Political Communications, University Alma Mater Studiorum, Bologna (Italy).

2. For more details regarding the data, situation and health needs of migrants in the Prato area see Appendix A.

3. The concept of "global health" refers to an undivided, indivisible good linking the health of the individual with social networks and the environment, aimed at fostering mutual knowledge, relations and exchanges between persons of different origins, genders and social, cultural and linguistic backgrounds living in the same territory.

The purpose of this study is to identify the crux of the problems underlying these behavioural trends, highlighting the existing difficulties and critical situations, so as to point to the directions to be taken by action aimed at overcoming these problems, through the presentation of guidelines and a number of good practices existing at the local level. Convinced that, to this end, an open relationship, on an equal footing, with public health-care services can provide a fundamental strategic stimulus, the author bases her approach on the theoretical foundations of the discipline of public communication, showing how the latter can play a vital role in improving the handling of these issues.

2. The migrants' point of view: types of assistance/ mediation requested

(Exchange between Ling,[4] a young Chinese woman, and Lai Fong, while the other members of the group were speaking among themselves)

Ling: "I had a miscarriage last time, now I am three months' pregnant. I am very worried it is going to happen again. I don't know why I miscarried"

Lai Fong: "Have you not asked these health professionals here?"

Ling: "No, it is very difficult to ask about these things, I can't speak Italian and they [glanced up at the health-care staff across the room] don't understand me or us, and our ways. For example, I have so much that I wanted to ask them, such as whether I should be drinking the 'ginger and vinegar broth' after the birth or before the birth. I know it is beneficial to birth mothers and is a very important thing to consume in our culture but I am not sure how to go about preparing it. I am here all on my own [without my extended family], and cannot consult anybody. I am so afraid and I don't know what to do."

From a conversation between Lai Fong and Ling during a meeting held with members of the Chinese community in Prato, Italy, at the initiative of the organisation L'Albero della Salute, May 2006

Firstly, an attempt will be made to present the standpoint of the migrant population in Prato. The above brief conversation already embodies all

---

4. Ling is a pseudonym.

the difficulties with which a young woman of foreign origin may be confronted when seeking to address a personal health-care need. The aim here is to make an analytical study of these problems.

The analysis can be situated on two levels: the first concerning the access barriers to health care and the second the obstacles encountered when the person benefits from the service.

With regard to the first level, there are a number of aspects that impede, or in any case restrict, access to health-care services for foreigners living in the Prato area.

First and foremost, it must be borne in mind that health is not a standardised concept, in that a person's perception of his/her state of health/sickness changes in space and time and is closely linked to personal attitudes and ways of thinking, habits, beliefs and the entire range of factors that make up the culture of a community and of the individual belonging to it.[5] For example, a different concept of pregnancy, based on the teachings of traditional Chinese medical science, also entails a different way of experiencing this condition and hence different expectations vis-à-vis the health-care service.

In addition to this cultural factor, there is the key role played by the lack, paucity or incompleteness of information experienced by migrant women, who struggle to find their way around a health-care system that is often very different from those of their countries of origin. Their difficulties in pinpointing and consciously assimilating and handling the information needed to access health-care services concern:

- their right to health, and the legislation safeguarding that right, even for those who do not have legal migration status;

- the very existence of these services;

- the means of accessing them (whom to contact and how).

Their ill-informed state can also be linked to the sometimes vulnerable social and economic position of migrant women, a situation which does not permit them to develop to the full their potential and ability to take care of their own health.

---

5. For a more detailed discussion on this theme see E. Colombo, "Le culture della salute", in Bucchi and Neresini 2003.

At the same time, the difficulties in accessing health-care services encountered by women migrants are also tied to certain specific structural and organisational characteristics of the services themselves: for example, many women say they are unable to access health-care services because their hours of work are incompatible with these services' opening hours or because they find it difficult to travel to the places where the services are situated.

As regards the second level, which concerns the obstacles encountered by women while benefiting from the services, the following problems have been noted:

- difficulties in expressing their own health-care needs, on account of linguistic and/or cultural differences, particularly in situations of emotional and/or psychological stress (for example, in the case of women seeking an abortion or undergoing oncological examinations);

- difficulties in understanding oral information provided by staff due to the lack of a linguistic and/or cultural mediation service and a vague impression that these staff members are prejudiced, have preconceived ideas and are not open to dialogue;

- difficulties in understanding written information due to the complexities of the language used in structural, syntactic and lexical terms and to the scant availability of certified translations;

- consequent difficulties in following the health-care procedure indicated and being fully in control of the situation (doing the right thing, in the right place and in the right way);

- difficulties in following instructions and medical indications (for example keeping appointments, returning for a follow-up examination after childbirth, an abortion, etc.).

To overcome these kinds of legal, administrative, organisational, cultural and linguistic barriers it is desirable not to assume that migrants are seeking to be received differently or to be given preferential treatment as compared with Italian nationals, but that they simply wish to have the possibility of accessing the information and basic services to which they are entitled. The first step in dealing with this problem therefore consists in showing that these health behaviours are not typical of any given nationality and that we are not confronted with a unitary, in itself homogenous phenomenon – migration – which presupposes that migrants are different from us but identical to one another. Quite the contrary, what needs to be underlined is rather the potential influence of certain health determinants,[6] such as personal behaviour and lifestyle, social factors, living and working conditions, access to health-care services and general socio-economic, cultural and environmental conditions. Migrants are, in fact, not seeking anything more than a service adapted to their own particularities, which are often not very far removed from those of Italian citizens with language difficulties or of an advanced age, who are not well integrated in relational and social networks, have poor health literacy and are, accordingly, scarcely capable of finding their way around the services proposed. Improved access for migrants would accordingly lead to an improvement in the quality of service provision in general and therefore better access and assistance for all members of society.

3. The staff's point of view

The high number of migrants present in the Prato area and the gradually growing awareness of their atypical profile as regards access to and enjoyment of health-care services has already led to the implementation, for a number of years now, of many measures and initiatives designed to facilitate relations between health-care staff and migrants themselves. Although many members of staff consider that this has improved service provision for migrants as compared with the past, they nonetheless mention a variety of problems, often causing genuine emergencies, the nature of which varies, mostly according to the neighbourhood under consideration. For example, in the western part of the city there is a high concentration of service users of Chinese origin and the resulting urgent communication and management problems cannot be understated.

---

6. Health determinants are the range of factors that interact to establish, maintain or alter one's state of health in the course of one's life. They include strictly personal elements (gender, age, genetic heritage), socio-economic factors (economic conditions, occupational status, the sociocultural context), environmental factors (air quality, place of residence), lifestyle elements (nutrition, smoking, physical exercise, substance abuse) and access to services (the education and health-care systems, social services, transport, leisure activities).

3.1. Are staff capable of the appropriate responses?

"I work as a replacement doctor and have recently noted that the majority of the non-EU children I see have expired health-care cards. Are these cards not issued free of charge? Do children also need to have a residence permit?"

The above statement by a doctor who works in Prato is one of many examples of the informational, and hence operational, uncertainties with which many social services, health-care and administrative staff have to contend in their daily work. How can a doctor devote all the necessary time to receiving patients, taking care first and foremost of the relational aspects, as recommended, if he or she instead has to deal with administrative and procedural matters such as an expired health-care card? Above all, how is it possible for a doctor who works with migrants on a daily basis to be unaware that health-care cards are replaced free of charge and not to realise that the problem is in fact due to the difficulties of applying for renewal of the card, which has an expiry date linked to the period of validity of the parents' residence permit, but which has to be re-issued by another specific office, which is always overcrowded?

Staff shortages, the frequently irrational distribution of human and financial resources, the inadequate presence of linguistic and cultural mediators and the complexity of certain bureaucratic procedures make the staff's work particularly difficult, and service quality all too often depends on the individual staff member's goodwill and ability to deal with stress rather than on structural characteristics of the service being supplied.

To give an example of the importance of the institutional environment in which the staff member works, over and beyond his or her own good intentions, the immigration service can be cited.

The immigration service is the place where all migrants in Prato, whether present legally or illegally, have to go to obtain the issue or re-issue of their health-care card, necessary to obtain access to all health-care services in the area. For organisational reasons, the service recently moved, but the information provided on its new location was unclear. This led to much confusion among the foreigners who use the service, above all immediately after the transfer. The service's new premises comprise a bare waiting room, with insufficient seating for the large number of foreigners it receives every day, many of whom have to wait their turn outside the building, even during cold weather. A big sliding door divides the waiting room from the "front office" desk, behind which only two staff members are present to respond to users' requests without any kind of linguistic and cultural mediation. Accordingly, when users (this occurs above all with Chinese and Romanian migrants) do not speak or understand Italian they usually pass over their turn until someone else of their nationality arrives who knows Italian and who is willing to provide an improvised, rudimentary translation service. As can easily be imagined, despite the staff members' great availability and dynamism, organisational limitations such as the shortage of staff, the inadequacies of the premises, the mass of people to be dealt with and the lack of linguistic and cultural mediation prevent them from devoting enough time to listening to the migrants and providing them with full information on the health-care system. In addition, the service lacks information materials in foreign languages, a situation which it is currently seeking to remedy, although a request for a screen, on which videos providing information on consultations and health issues for migrant women could be projected, made three months ago to the local health authority, has not yet met with a response.

3.2. Difficulties (obstacles/restrictions/problems) encountered by staff

The Prato area has undoubtedly managed to find many effective solutions for managing the migration phenomenon at the level of its public services, including, but not only, in the health-care field. Nonetheless, there are still many obvious difficulties with which health-care staff have to contend in meeting the health-care needs of members of the migrant population and responding to their requests for assistance.

These problems can be divided into two categories: those of a technical nature and those of a cultural order.

The chief technical difficulty which staff encounter is scant or incomplete knowledge of the rules governing management of migration in Italy, whether in general terms or with particular regard to access to and enjoyment of social and health-care services. In Italy, immigration is indeed a field where the legislation is constantly evolving and is the subject of numerous decrees and circulars which supplement, amend or cancel sections or articles of the legislation in force. Furthermore, although immigration policy is a national competence, health-care management is a regional one. Besides, since immigration is a topical theme in Italy and an issue that is fiercely debated in both the political arena and public opinion, the whole question is in the media spotlight, although the media sometimes have difficulty finding sufficient space to publish information helping to clarify legislative changes in the pipeline and in the end even add to the confusion surrounding such initiatives.

This situation places a burden on staff who have the responsibility of applying the rules in force on a daily basis. Lack of knowledge thereof, or incomplete or erroneous knowledge, involves a tangible risk of discretionary administrative action or of unequal treatment of the same request depending on the service dealing with it and the employee on duty at the time. Owing to a lack of clarity of administrative practices concerning means of action, processing of requests, who is responsible for what, time frames and migrants' rights, the staff complain of not insignificant difficulties in extricating themselves from this bureaucratic labyrinth and being able to guarantee the optimum balance between clarity, that is the legislation's legibility and intelligibility, and precision in applying the law. Another factor is the often uncalled for complexity of the drafting, from a structural and linguistic standpoint, of the forms and papers they are required to complete or to have users fill out.

Improved co-ordination between the various entities involved, simplification of the procedures and language used, more effective internal communication between services and an investment in training are absolutely essential to cope with these kinds of obstacles and guarantee transparency and the quality of service provision.

Difficulties of a cultural order can lead to incomprehension and misunderstandings, very often experienced as conflicts or threats, whether on the part of migrants or of staff members. Staff are often ill-prepared to cope with diversity. Male and female migrants indeed often have both a concept of health shaped by their culture and some knowledge of traditional medical science that can lead them to make use of multiple forms of treatment. This must be perceived as a sign of belonging to two different cultures and of a multiple identity and, as such, should not constitute a source of conflict but be valued as a particular resource of cultural diversity.

Emotional stress and a feeling of being unable to cope with diversity can, however, also result in cases of prejudice, feeding stereotypical, preconceived ideas. In one instance, when confronted with a Chinese couple who had come to the local health authority's help desk, the employee assigned to front office duties assumed, without giving the young man time to explain the situation in his somewhat halting Italian, that they were seeking an abortion for the wife, when it was in fact the husband who needed to undergo further clinical examinations. This staff member thus gave tangible form to the stereotypical belief, which has been the subject of a number of studies in the region, that stigmatises Chinese women as being likely to seek an abortion rather than becoming devoted good mothers for their children.

To ensure that similar episodes do not reoccur, it is necessary rapidly to find a solution to the apparently trifling day-to-day conflicts that tend to become a strain on staff, who are always running against time, to the point of causing genuine states of tension and frustration. Investing resources in language training for staff members, who sometimes say they do not understand or speak even one foreign language, and in the linguistic and cultural mediation service can be considered the first step to be taken.

4. Staff training

Starting from the premise that an organisation or service exists thanks to and through the actions and attitudes of its staff, fundamental importance must be attached to the latter's training so that they acquire the intercultural skills that can provide a basis for the development of migrant friendly[7] public services geared to empowerment[8] and networking.

With regard to the training's content, it should cover a range of fields and disciplines. Although it is no simple, straightforward matter to determine the type of training needed and develop staff's intercultural skills, which can undoubtedly vary depending on the context and the specific service to which they are assigned, it is nonetheless possible to identify certain thematic directions in which the training should be oriented. In particular, training should be specific and focus at least on the following:

- *legislation*, whether general, concerning the management of migratory flows in Italy and other European countries, or more specific to the social and health-care management aspects. The aim of this training should be to clarify subjects that are all too often a

---

7. For more information on the concept of migrant friendly services see Chiarenza 2008.

8. As a means of promoting and safeguarding migrants' health, an empowerment strategy aims to foster their cognitive and social skills, skills which determine their motivation and ability to obtain access to the services and make use of the available information, while at the same time enhancing the specific knowledge and skills transmitted within the migrants' own culture, as possible further health resources.

source of confusion and to provide the staff concerned with practical tools that enhance their operational know-how and assurance;

- *foreign languages*, so that staff, above all those assigned to front office duties, are not completely ill-prepared to deal with people unable to understand or speak Italian. This training should give staff a basic knowledge of at least one foreign language, especially English;

- *management of diversity and of multicultural relations*: this entails an understanding of the migration phenomenon in all its variety, spanning numerous subjects and differing points of view: constant updating of data on migrants' presence, movements and health needs at the national and local levels; knowledge of migratory systems in Italy and the region concerned from the historical, economic, socio-logical, psychological and anthropological angles; consideration of the health determinants of relevance to migrant populations; study and constant comparison of good practices existing at the national and international levels regarding the management and organisa-tion of culturally sensitive, migrant friendly public services; social analysis of organisational cultures and the risk of "burnout" when conditions are psychologically stressful for staff; training in conflict management and respect for diversity, helping staff to take on board viewpoints differing from their own, in theoretical and practical terms; knowledge of bioethical and public ethics principles;

- *public communication*: the staff who breathe life into the public service must be familiar with and assimilate the basic principles of this discipline, so they are able to put it into practical effect in their day-to-day activities. Transparency of the public service, the social responsibilities they bear, simplification of procedures and termi-nology, the importance of in-house communication, of listening and of relationship-building, the capacity to communicate with others, migrants' rights in their dealings with the public authorities – all are elements which are vital to ensure that the organisation progresses from an attitude of communicating rules to one of communicating values.

With regard to the methodology to be followed to ensure that the training is effective and achieves the desired results, it should be targeted and continuous and accordingly capable, firstly, of specifically remedying the deficiencies noted and, secondly, of permitting a long-term training approach rather than one confined to ad hoc sessions limited in time.

Training should be perceived from the very top to the very bottom of the organisation as a strategic element of change, a strength for generating and bringing to the fore a new professionalism. To achieve this, staff should be made aware that the service's performance is essentially based on its own internal know-how and the skills acquired and developed over time. A training effort conceived within such a strategic framework will be capable of turning to account a staff member's individual potential and redefining organisational roles, where necessary, so as to vest them with greater autonomy and responsibility.

A useful methodology in this connection could be peer-to-peer cascade training: this involves running a dedicated training scheme for a limited number of staff, who will then be asked to pass on what they have learned to colleagues in their own sector, thus bringing into being a process of ongoing production and enhancement of knowledge, conferring greater responsibility on the individuals concerned, and establishing a more aware, more knowledgeable staff network. Training capable of inculcating conceptual and methodological skills should indeed also enhance networking through the exchange of experience with staff of other services or other regions and the implementation of joint projects. To this end, it may also be useful to experiment with innovative solutions such as online forums or social networks, which promote contacts between the participants and place their relations on a continuous, lasting footing.

5. Solutions, guidelines and good practices

The principal obstacle to be tackled can be seen to be of a cultural nature and concerns the capacity of society as a whole and of public services in particular to manage change and to function in a dynamic manner in tune with modern times. This, therefore, necessitates an awareness that migration is no longer a passing, urgent phenomenon, which one may be for or against, but a structural trend that is essential to our society and, as such, needs to be managed in an ordinary, increasingly knowledgeable manner. It is accordingly of key importance that a renewed impetus should first of all be given to the reform process initiated in the Italian public administration since the 1990s[9] so as to overcome the resistance, still very present in some services and departments, to change, innovation and the pursuit of an equal, two-way, transparent relationship with the public in general and with migrants in particular.

---

9. For more details on this subject see Grandi 2001.

In the light of these observations and the critical situations that have emerged it is be hoped that the local health-care service in the city of Prato will move in the following directions:

- a reorganisation of the services that will make it possible to expedite administrative tasks through a simplification of procedures and administrative language and through staff training, leaving more leeway for contacts with migrants and for listening to their needs;

- effective planning of in-house communication;

- a service approach based on the requirements and particularities of migrants using the services: this is what may be called an active services offer, meaning the services' capacity to reach out to migrants in a way that departs from their own traditional operating frameworks, for example through the organisation of information sessions on health and use of health-care services in places frequented by the migrant communities, involvement of migrants' associations and the active participation of public service staff;

- allocating resources to the linguistic and cultural mediation service;

- investing in staff training;

- effective planning of the distribution of information materials;

- effective planning of written communication and adaptation of the institutional language used;

- investment in translation processes.

Some brief comments on these last two points: Italy has a long-standing, and still not easily surmounted, tradition of tending to use so-called "officialese" in the public administration, that is to say a complex language characterised by the lack of sub-divisions in a text, lengthy sentences with many parenthetic and subordinate clauses, sentences containing too much information, complex sentence structures, use of passive and negative forms ("not being acquainted with", etc.), use of nouns instead of verbs ("to be by chance in a state of recovery of one's senses"), choice of terms with too high a register ("render oneself", "effect", etc.), and the prevailing use of specialist terminology even where not necessary and in any case without explaining the technical terms used. Good written communication of social relevance must, however, eradicate these complexities so as to bridge the distance that often characterises relations between the authorities and the public and move towards a civic, democratic culture which regards openness in interaction between stakeholders in society as a constitutional obligation. In addition, in the health field, good communication concerning health matters reflects the principles of the universality of health care and of human solidarity. A simplification of the language used should also go hand in hand with an effort to translate the information materials and administrative forms into the main lingua francas in use in the region. The standard of the translation work should be guaranteed by using suitably qualified translators, whose abilities are tested beforehand and whose translations are revised before the materials are distributed, to ensure that the translations are correct and comprehensible for native speakers.

In the Prato area many experiments and initiatives have been undertaken in the above fields. Two examples of particularly relevant good practices are described below: the Albero della Salute, the reference body for cultural mediation in health-care matters in the Tuscany region, and the website Pratomigranti.it.

The Albero della Salute (Tree of Health) is an inter-institutional organisation, which had project status from 2001 to 2004 and in 2005 became the reference body for cultural mediation in health-care matters in the Tuscany region. The organisation deals with institutions, health-care authorities, the public, whether Italian or foreign citizens, doctors, social and health-care staff, teachers and students within a space for discussion of and training in health matters. It operates at the regional level but has its headquarters in Prato. Its objectives are to promote recognition and enhancement of the plural views of health and illness that characterise individual and cultural identities, to strive to bring down the barriers that can prevent migrants from enjoying their right to health care within the services, to foster cultural awareness at local level and within social and health-care services, to facilitate debate on various forms of mediation in the health-care field and support recourse to such mediation in social and health-care services. These objectives are pursued through a joined-up range of activities: promotion and organisation of training courses for social and health-care services staff and for linguistic and cultural mediators; ongoing research and monitoring of data on migrants' health-care needs and on the issues they raise from a sociological, communicational and ethical standpoint; publication of scientific documents; promotion of and participation in regional and international projects (an example being the Mum Health project of the region of Tuscany, focusing on the empowerment approach, with the principal aim of raising migrant women's awareness of their own rights to health and to good quality care, of the social and health-care services linked to pregnancy, childbirth and the period post childbirth, of the use of contraceptive methods, to enhance their decision-making capacity and reduce recourse to abortions, and of health screening programmes for women); the design and production of traditional and multimedia information materials and of online communication products; the translation of information materials brought out by the region of Tuscany and local health-care authorities; advice and counselling activities.

Pratomigranti.it is a local website for migrants in the Prato area. The project came into being thanks to the work and resources of a number of sponsors and funds providers in the Prato area; the municipality of Prato, the province of Prato, the prefecture and the chamber of commerce. At the initiative of the local immigration council, a collegial body attached to the prefecture, a memorandum of understanding was recently approved and signed between these public authorities, which participate in various capacities in the management of migration in the Prato area, the aim being to provide a flow of information that is as fluid and up-to-date as possible so as to meet the information needs of the migrant population in the Prato area. The Pratomigranti portal is a multilingual website which publishes news items of interest to the migrant population on local initiatives, services and relations with administrative agencies. The portal's aim is to provide a source of general information on immigration issues and a site where male and female migrants can find useful information of relevance not only to their health but also to their day-to-day lives, studies, work and the opportunities the area has to offer. The website's graphic design and documents are conceived so as to be clear and easy to navigate, allowing users to search for and retrieve the information they need in an intuitive way, thanks to a sub-division into chapters dealing with specific themes, for example "living in Prato" (associations, accommodation, work, health care, education, transport and so on); "services for migrants" (training offers, reception and support facilities, information points, and so on); "documents" (residence cards and permits, Italian citizenship, family reunification, and so on); an "observatory" (data banks, studies); useful guides for migrants; broadcasting of a multi-ethnic TV news programme; photo galleries;

news updates; events and initiatives in the spotlight, etc. Apart from Italian, the site can be accessed in Chinese, Arabic, English and French. This initiative is a good example of co-ordination and co-operation between different bodies, of information exchange and facilitation of information flows, of activation of local resources, not least through the involvement of local associations, and of the key importance attached to the circulation and communication of information in developing a pluralist society open to diversity.

6. Conclusions

Knowledge and pooling of experience at the local, national and international levels can be seen to be essential to deepen understanding of migration and allow a constant improvement in public services. In conclusion, it can be underlined that the desired processes of change must have their starting point in a new debate on the effectiveness of institutional communication from the standpoint of cultural awareness and cultural mediation. The goal to be aimed for, above all in health-care matters, is to bring the public service to review the significance it attaches to enhancing self-efficiency and user empowerment through a continuous, permanent process of capacity-building targeting migrants themselves.

Appendix A

The area concerned by this study is that of Prato, a city with slightly more than 185 000 inhabitants in Tuscany, Italy.

From the standpoint of migration, the province of Prato has two fundamental demographic characteristics: firstly, it is the Italian city with the highest percentage of foreigners in its total population (11.4%, compared with 7.5% in Tuscany and with the Italian average of 5.8%); secondly, it has a high concentration of migrants from the People's Republic of China, who alone represent 40.7% of the entire foreign population of Prato (followed by Albanians and Romanians). This population group includes 47% of women, most of them young.

Foreign population living in the province of Prato as at 31 December 2007, top 10 nationalities					
	Male	Female	% of women	Total	% of foreign population
Chinese	6100	5270	46	11370	40.7
Albanian	3007	2369	44	5376	19.2
Romanian	923	1187	56	2110	7.5
Pakistani	1322	524	28	1846	6.6
Moroccan	1135	671	37	1806	6.5
Bangladeshi	335	213	38	548	2
Nigerian	236	276	60	512	1.8
Polish	67	331	83	398	1.4

Filipino	135	195	59	330	1.2
Tunisian	130	103	44	233	0.8

Source: ISTAT 2008.

The presence of minors, in particular second generation (foreign citizens born in Italy), has been chosen by the CNEL (National Economics and Labour Council) as an indicator of settlement in an area. Here, too, Prato is a national leader:

	As at 31 December 2006				As at 31 December 2007			
	Foreign minors present	% of foreign residents	2nd generation	% of foreign residents	Foreign minors present	% of foreign residents	2nd generation	% of foreign residents
Prato	6806	26.1	4633	**17.7**	7441	26.6	5339	**19.1**
Tuscany	50847	21.7	30082	**12.8**	58339	21.2	34609	**12.6**
Italy	665625	22.6	398205	**13.5**	767060	22.3	457345	**13.3**

Source: Caritas/Migrantes 2008.

Non-Italian pupils by schooling level – Academic year 2007/2008								
	Infant		Primary		Lower secondary		Upper secondary		Total
Prato	983	15.0	1934	17.5	1122	17.6	931	10.3	4970
Tuscany	8541	9.3	16864	11.1	10101	11.2	9737	6.6	45243
Italy	111044	6.7	217716	7.7	126396	7.3	118977	4.3	574133

Source: MIUR 2008.

Attention can also be drawn to the overall increase in the migrant population in recent years. Between 2007 and 2008, Tuscany scored a percentage increase of 17%. The steady increase in the number of foreign citizens noted in recent years merely confirms the region's attractiveness; in all the provinces the trend for the period 2001 to 2007 was an increase in the number of registered foreign residents equal to or exceeding 90% (ISTAT 2008).

As can be seen from the data set out below, the migrant population is of considerable importance in the health-care field. By way of example, consideration is given here to the reproductive health of women, in particular to the data on childbirth and abortions.

Within Prato local health authority 4, the number of births in 2007 totalled 2 779, of which 1 271 concerned women without Italian citizenship. ISTAT reported that, in the province of Prato, the percentage of foreign births compared with the total was 30.8%, noting that this was the highest percentage in Italy.

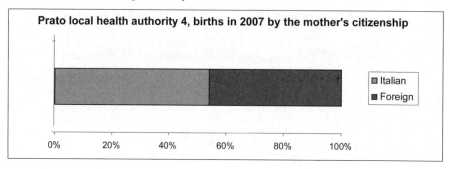

In 90% of these births to mothers without Italian citizenship, the nationalities broke down as follows:

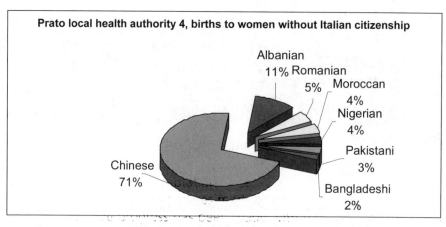

Source: regional archives, birth attendance certificates. Region of Tuscany – Directorate General for the Right to Health and for Solidarity Policy.

As the report used for the public consultation and the report after the consultation: www.accommodements... consultation-en.pdf and www.accommodements... rapport-final-integral-en.pdf

On the other hand, within Prato local health authority 4, in 2007 the number of abortions totalled 650, of which approximately 62% concerned women without Italian citizenship.

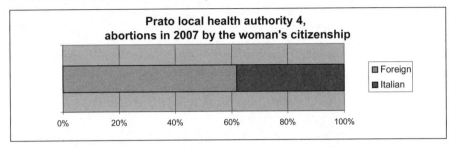

Prato local health authority 4, abortions in 2007 by the woman's citizenship

In 85% of these abortions of women without Italian citizenship, the nationalities broke down as follows:

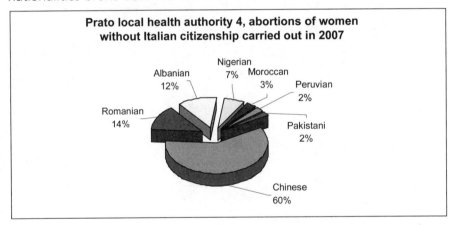

Prato local health authority 4, abortions of women without Italian citizenship carried out in 2007

Source: regional archives, abortion statistics. Region of Tuscany – Directorate General for the Right to Health and for Solidarity Policy.

As can be seen, the city constitutes a privileged laboratory for observing needs and problems of access to public services, with particular emphasis on health-care services, which, albeit to differing extents and in different ways, are of relevance for the entire region and characteristic of Italy as a whole.

The principal characteristic of migration, not only in Tuscany but in Italy in general, can already be inferred from the few data provided: this is the constant growth in the phenomenon, which for a number of years now has become a structural feature of Italian society. Hence the absolute need to manage this phenomenon, at the public policy and administrative levels, no longer through emergency measures and improvisation but via a more conscious, wider-ranging approach.

The above observation is all the more valid in the case of migrants' right to health and access to and utilisation of health-care services, since the state of health and the well-being of entire communities depend on these factors.

Appendix B

The bibliographical sources referred to in the present study are listed below.

The data set out in Appendix A were obtained from the following sources:

- regional archives – birth attendance certificates;

- Caritas/Migrantes (2008), "Immigration Statistics 2008", IDOS, Rome;

- CNEL – National Economics and Labour Council (2009), "Indicators of Immigrants' Integration in Italy, 6th Report", p. 13;

- ISTAT – national statistical institute;

- MIUR – Ministry of Education, Universities and Research;

- Region of Tuscany – Directorate General for the Right to Health and for Solidarity Policy.

For the theoretical and practical foundations of public communication policy and institutional language see:

Cortellazzo M. A. and Pellegrino F. (2003), *Guida alla scrittura istituzionale*, Editori Laterza, Rome-Bari.

Civil Service Department – Office of the Prime Minister (2004), "Il piano di comunicazione nelle amministrazioni pubbliche", Edizioni Scientifiche Italiane, Naples.

Civil Service Department – Office of the Prime Minister (2006), "La gestione per competenze nelle amministrazioni pubbliche", Rubbettino Editore, Soveria Mannelli.

Fioritto A. (2007), "Il linguaggio delle amministrazioni pubbliche", in Fiorentino G. (ed.), *Scrittura e società*, Aracne, Rome, pp. 289-309.

Franceschetti M. (2007), *Comunicare con l'utente*, Carocci Editore, Rome.

Grandi R. (2001), *La comunicazione pubblica. Teorie, casi, profili normativi*, Carocci Editore, Rome.

Mancini P. (1996), *Manuale di comunicazione pubblica*, Editori Laterza, Bari.

Raso T. (2005), *La scrittura burocratica*, Carocci Editore, Rome.

Rovinetti A. (2002), "Diritto di parola", Il Sole24Ore, Milan.

Rovinetti A. (2006a), "Comunicazione pubblica Sapere e fare", Il Sole24Ore, Milan.

Rovinetti A. (2006b), "Fare comunicazione pubblica. Normative, tecniche, tecnologie", Comunicazione Italiana, Rome.

For studies on access to public health-care services, the assistance requested by migrants, the problems encountered by staff and the guidelines and good practices applied in the Prato area, see:

Bucchi M. and Neresini F. (eds) (2003), *Sociologia della salute*, Carocci Editore, Rome.

Chiarenza A. (2008), "Servizi sanitari migrant-friendly ed aperti alle diverse culture: l'esperienza dell'Azienda USL di Reggio Emilia", in Baraldi C., Barbieri V. and Giarelli G. (eds), *Immigrazione, mediazione culturale e salute*, Franco Angeli, Milan.

CORECOM Emilia-Romagna (2006), "Immigrati da informare", Minerva Edizioni, Argelato.

Formez – Istituto Piepoli SpA (2006), "Progetto per la formazione continua dei funzionari della Pubblica Amministrazione addetti ai servizi agli immigrati", La ricerca.

Petrei F. (2007), "Immigrati e Istituzioni. Ruolo e obiettivi della comunicazione pubblica", thesis published on the Internet.

Tognetti Bordogna M. (ed.) (2004), *I colori del Welfare. Servizi alla persona di fronte all'utenza che cambia*, Franco Angeli, Milan.

Reference was also made to studies and analyses carried out in the context of my own co-operation activities with the reference body for cultural mediation in health-care matters in the Tuscany region – L'Albero della Salute – and to a number of interviews with staff of the Prato health-care authority and with local migrants.

B. Intercultural mediation in Belgian hospitals – A successful example of reasonable accommodation in the health-care sector

Lucia Morariu[1]

1. Introduction

The Intercultural Mediation programme in Belgian Hospitals (hereafter "ICM programme") was identified when looking for examples of good practices in Belgium in the area of institutional change (the adaptation of services) aiming at a reasonable accommodation of migrants' needs in a pluralist society.

The aims of the ICM programme are to improve access and the quality of health care delivered to ethnic minority patients at the hospital, and also to improve communication and responsiveness to the sociocultural and health-care needs of ethnic minority patients.

This article is based on interviews conducted in March 2009 with five intercultural mediators (ICMs) of Moroccan, Turkish and Algerian origin and their co-ordinator,[2] around the following issues: recruitment and training of the ICMs, types of interventions encountered in practice, the role and the powers of the ICMs, personal and institutional difficulties encountered in their professional approaches and possible solutions/ changes needed.

2. History of the ICM programme in Belgium

The ICM programme is a result of the political evolution in Belgium. At the end of the 1980s after a right-wing party with racist, extremist views as regards immigrants obtained a large number of votes in Belgium, the major political parties realised that a new policy was needed on how to

---

1. Doctoral Student in European Law at University of Basel and University of Strasbourg; member of the European Doctoral College, Strasbourg.

2. I would like to thank Mr Hans Verrept for organising the field research. He is the Head of the Intercultural Mediation Unit, Federal Public Service of Public Health, Food Chain Security and Environment, Belgium. Its aim is to co-ordinate and coach intercultural mediation services in Belgian hospitals.

accommodate migrants' needs, especially in the health-care sector. As a result, King Baudouin[3] created a royal commission which was actually an institution linked to the cabinet of the prime minister and under royal protection; this institution had as its task to identify all the problems faced by the immigrants and to write reports presenting solutions on: housing, employment, health care, etc.

For the health-care section, an NGO was contacted (comprising researchers and medical practitioners) to write the report. One of the recommendations was to introduce intercultural mediators in the health-care system, because there was a language problem and cultural differences were affecting the quality of care. Very soon (in 1991) this NGO was asked to start a programme for the training and employment of ICMs in health care. In 1998, the ministers involved decided that this programme should become a structural part of the health-care system and funding should be provided.

As a result, an Intercultural Mediation Unit was created, as part of the administration.[4] Even if it is still a small programme with a small budget (2.5 to 3 million euros/year) in charge of improving intercultural competences in hospitals through the development of all kinds of activities, nowadays there are approximately 80 ICMs and 20 co-ordinators working in around 60 hospitals.

The main goal of this unit is to co-ordinate and coach intercultural mediation services in Belgian hospitals. In other words, to incorporate ICMs in hospitals where there are relatively large communities of migrants, mainly Moroccans and Turks. However, assessing the need in a hospital is a very big problem. It is difficult to calculate the need for mediation in a hospital/community, especially because in Belgium it is forbidden by law to conduct ethnic registration.

One of the first public institutions to incorporate ICMs was Kind & Gezin (Child & Family).[5] This is a public institution/service, with responsibility for young children and families in Flanders. It is actually an agency of the Flemish Government. It started in 1994 with ICMs for Moroccan and Turkish families. The ICMs were trained for three years (similar to others

---

3. For more info see: http://en.wikipedia.org/wiki/Baudouin_of_Belgium.

4. https://portal.health.fgov.be/portal/page?_pageid=56,704702&_dad=portal&_schema=PORTAL.

5. For more information, see: www.kindengezin.be.

working in hospitals). At roughly the same time, this agency also started to work with "experts through experience" (people who themselves have experienced a great deal at the hands of social exclusion and poverty). The reason for introducing ICMs in this institution was the realisation that there was a gap between the people in poverty and the social workers, not only as regards language and cultural background but also level of education, which created barriers. In 1995, ICMs received a structural place in the organisation.

3. Recruitment and training of ICMs

Concerning the recruitment of ICMs, the work was initially done only by poorly qualified people, most of them from the specific community. As a consequence, a special training programme was created, for a period of three years and people interested in participating were paid during this time. However, since 1999 this programme no longer exists.

Nowadays, there are schools (two in Flanders) that provide this training for three years at the level of secondary education. At the end of the training, participants receive a certificate, but not a degree. This represents a problem because a certificate is not as useful as a degree; for example, it does not entitle the holder to a bigger salary.

When the programme became a structural part of the health-care system, another difficulty appeared since the training programme existed only in Flanders but not in the other parts of Belgium. So, while developing legislation, they also had to open up: on the one hand, everyone who had followed the training was eligible; and, on the other hand, other categories of people were also taken into consideration (for example, nurses, social workers, interpreters, etc.); the only condition was that the person should speak the language of one of the targeted groups. An interesting finding was that for example a nurse who had received some training on cultural diversity, and interpreting was actually a better ICM than the ones specifically trained.

The hospitals realised that they needed people to assist the patients of foreign origin. To enable this, from 1999 onwards, the Federal Public Service of Public Health, Food Chain Security and Environment has subsidised hospitals so that they can recruit, train and employ ICMs. As a result, nowadays, hospitals are encouraged to employ ICMs with a certain level of education (for example, nurses and doctors). There is a big advantage in this: the profession is not linked to one training programme; so someone could become an ICM and have higher secondary education. However, this means that the ICMs do not have a professional identity.

The "experts through experience" recruited by Kind & Gezin were people living in the same community, even though it is not always easy to work in your own community. One of the reasons for that could be the fact that the people know you there; it is not always easy to speak with a social worker about what is going on in a family from your community (for example, in the Moroccan communities one of the biggest problems is gambling, but if the ICM speaks about this it could lead to stereotypes). For ICMs loyalty towards their community is important. But they are professionals, they have a code of ethics, they do not share information with others, except the social worker with whom they work.

In 2002, the organisation wrote an extensive report on the problems faced by the ICMs at that time. One of the problems identified was defining more precisely their role in the process of mediating between family and social worker. As a result, it was decided to combine the roles of ICMs and "experts through experience"; the new role was to be known as "family enabler".

Types of training:[6]

- basic interpretation/translation techniques (for example, memorising, taking notes, body language, observation techniques);

- Standard Arabic medical terminology;

- interpretation in a psychiatric context;

- cultural brokerage (how to manage cultural differences/conflict resolution);

- traditional healing methods;

- psychological guidance (difficult case discussions, sharing opinions and experiences with other ICMs; the exchange of ideas and solutions is important especially between old and new ICMs);

---

6. See Hans Verrept, "Intercultural Mediation at Belgian Hospitals", paper presented at the MFH Conference on Hospitals in a Culturally Diverse Europe, in 2004. This was an international conference on quality-assured health care and health promotion for migrants and ethnic minorities. For more details and the text of the paper, see: www.mfh-eu.net/public/conference_-_december_2004/paper3.htm.

- ethical issues (training provided by specialists in medical ethical issues);

- strategies to use in specific cases or how to put some issues into question with the patients (e.g. Arabic patients donating organs);

4. Dissemination

How do patients from different cultural backgrounds get to know about the existence of ICMs?

There are several possibilities for disseminating this information. One of them would be to consult the web page of the programme,[7] but this is hardly ever the case. Another possibility would be directly at the hospital by word of mouth (recently also through posters). Nevertheless, ICMs are considered to be local heroes, so they are very well known in their own community (through family, neighbours, etc.). Unfortunately, sometimes even the doctors do not know about the ICMs' existence (since they stay only short periods of time at one hospital). As a solution, brochures were made to inform health-care providers about what exists in their hospital. In the future, a small brochure will also be available for the patient to receive upon arrival.

At the institutional level, it is also relevant to explain to the hospitals why intercultural mediation is important and why they should rely upon ICMs. There is also a need to explain the importance of being culturally responsive in health care.

A new experiment is the video conference interpreting system, which will make it possible for a small group of ICMs to help more people. The drawback is that the intervention is not so personal. However, with a small amount of money more people can be helped.

In the case of a hospital, normally the administrative service who acquires/registers the patients at the entrance must inform them about the existence of ICMs. Sometimes the doctors tell them during the consultation.

However, the ICM also has a list of all new arrivals and when they see an Arab name on it, for example, they go to visit the patient in the room and offer their services.

---

7. See *supra* note 4.

In the case of Kind & Gezin, the advantage is that mothers are obliged to register their children with a doctor and so ICMs are asked to visit the baby at home. This service mostly works with vulnerable pregnant women or young mothers. It takes the data from hospitals. ICMs make home visits and present their services to the mothers. Most of the mothers agree to enter the service. During the first visit (which usually takes place in the hospital), an ICM can observe how well the mother is integrated into society, how strong is she, how willing she is to integrate, etc. During the second visit, the ICM can see if there are wider problems. One of the barriers encountered is the fear of losing one's own identity by integrating too fast into the host society. But this depends very much on the cultural background (if the person comes from a village, if she/he went to school, etc.); all these aspects make a lot of difference.

5. Types of interventions and the role of ICMs

As regards the typology of requests from the migrants, not only the number of interventions are monitored but also the types of interventions. The job of an ICM depends very much on his/her cultural background. For example, Russian ICMs basically translate/interpret, while Moroccan ICMs carry out a wide range of interventions: completing forms, explaining the health-care system; accompanying patients to the doctor; discussing traditional healing methods and of course interpreting. Why? One of the reasons could be the lower level of education (sometimes even illiteracy) of the Moroccans and Turks.

The most common types of interventions are:

- Interpretation.

- Cultural brokerage/cultural decoding = explaining the culture of the hospital to the patient and the cultural universe of the patient to the doctor.

- Accompanying the patient to the doctor: explaining the procedure, filling the forms, etc.

- Supportive role → listening and advisory work.

- Conflict resolution → ombudsperson.

- Advocacy = defending the rights of the patients in case of discrimination (in theory, the ICM has the power to report cases of discrimination to the authorities, but there is no special mandate for this).

Because of the active advocacy role of the ICM, doctors always think that the ICM is on the side of the patient, but in fact they are neutral. There is a special connection between the ICM and the patient and doctors feel threatened by this connection.

- Preparing the patient for an intervention/surgery → explaining the procedure, the machines, the medicines they will have to take, how to take them, etc. In other words, the role of the ICM is to explain to the patient how to take the medicine, so that he/she can receive the same level of treatment as anybody else.

- Observation/interpreting (not only words but also gestures).

- Reinforcing the position of the patient in the triangular relation: doctor, patient, ICM.

- To increase the trust between the family and the nurse/social worker.

- To provide advice in general.

In conclusion, the types of requests from the migrants differ from generation to generation. The third generation, for example, has fewer problems integrating into society. So, the most important part of the job of an ICM is done with the newcomers: they do not go out, and do not have friends in the new society. One of the roles of the ICM is to advise them to be more sociable, to go out more often, and to have more contact with local people and institutions. An ICM accompanies them to register their children to school, to enrol in language classes, to apply for social benefits, etc.

6. Powers of an ICM

What powers do ICMs posses in order to meet migrants' requirements?

- The most important power of an ICM is their ability to communicate clearly, sensitively and effectively with people from different cultural backgrounds.

- Another important aspect is their power to convince the doctor (for example, on the urgency of a case). Sometimes the role of the ICM is not only to interpret but also to measure the patient's pain and to give their opinion on the seriousness of the pain.

- But the ICM also has the power to convince the patient (for example, on the seriousness of a case) and this is why the doctors sometimes feel they are loosing their powers to the ICM, because the decision sometimes is in their hands.

- Theoretically, the ICMs also have the power to report cases of domestic violence to the authorities, but practically they almost never do so, because this would mean losing the trust of that person and also of the community.

In a case of reported domestic violence, the community blames the ICM. Sometimes the ICM is even in danger because of an angry, violent husband maltreating his wife. In these cases, the co-ordinator usually advises the ICM to keep their distance for some time in that specific area.

Sometimes, during home visits, the ICM sees that there are very serious problems with the children too, not only with the mothers (for example, they do not go to school, the babies do not receive adequate food, the problems of the mother are affecting the development of the children, etc.). If an ICM sends a note to a public service concerning a person, it is always considered to be a serious problem; so ICMs are taken very seriously by other institutions like the police, for example, and this is another one of their powers.

One of the ICMs interviewed is of the opinion that ICMs do not really have powers, but the specificity of their job is that they have access to a population to which unfortunately the health-care providers do not. They can actually help both of them (doctor and patient). In the opinion of this one particular ICM, a consultation is incomplete without an ICM.

There are even economic benefits in using ICMs: for example, a doctor when they are not sure that the patient has understood their explanations on how to take the medicines will keep the patient in hospital for several more days and so the insurance system will have to pay more. However, there are also doctors who refuse the services of ICMs, since consultation times are longer.

7. Difficulties encountered by ICMs

Pressure

In some cases the pressure on the ICM is very great. There are situations in which the ICMs are actually responsible for the urgency of the treatment received by the patient. Sometimes doctors expect more from ICMs and this also represents pressure on them. For example, doctors expect them also to interpret emotions, reactions, etc. Usually an ICM works alone (for example, when passing on news of a death), while the nurses share the difficulties between them, or exchange the difficult patients. In contrast, every ICM has their own patients. Normally, they do not exchange patients between them. It is a matter of trust and it is not good for the patients, especially for those with psychiatric problems.

Time management

Another difficulty for the ICMs is the fact that they have to move from one place to another, and so they lose a lot of time. They do not have an office; they have to move from one floor to another, from one office to another, from one hospital to another. Another time-related difficulty encountered by ICMs is the doctor's schedule (they are always late for consultations). ICMs have schedules too, but they are not taken into account. Because of this, on many occasions bureaucratic rules are put above the patient's need for mediation.

Administrative work

In the last couple of years the administrative work has increased considerably for ICMs. For hospitals, it is important to receive subsidies for ICMs, so filling out the papers is important if they want to continue having them in the following year. Also, recently, there were some very strict internal rules incorporated into the work timetable (ICMs are only allowed to work between 8 a.m. and 4 p.m.). They are not allowed/not paid to work supplementary hours. Once again, bureaucracy is more important than the well-being of the patient. Every time an ICM has to stay an extra hour they have to write a report. But it is because they are needed that they stay longer – the patient cannot see the doctor alone.

Nevertheless, opinions concerning administrative work are divided among ICMs. Some of them say they only have to fill in an annual report.

Spaces for dialogue

An important problem for most ICMs is that they do not have adequate space to receive patients. They actually work in every office/room of the hospital. For some ICMs, however, the idea of having a special place to receive people for consultation is not so appealing. Probably because they realise that people would not come with confidence to such a place, since this would mean recognising that there is a problem with them. ICMs from Kind & Gezin, for example, make home visits together with social workers; they are present during consultations, educational consultations, practical support of the family, counselling, etc. Home visits are friendlier and trust is built more easily. In an average week, for example, an ICM makes five or six visits alone and three or four visits with a nurse/social worker, and participates in five or six consultations.

Changing mentalities

It is also very difficult to change the mentalities of administrative staff (for example, nurses and doctors) as regards the importance/relevance of ICMs. It is very difficult, especially because the personnel change very often and an ICM always has to prove themselves to new people.

Another issue as regards mentality is the attitude of the patient towards an ICM; for example, Moroccans are very shy and they do not always ask for an ICM's help, whilst Russians always demand to have an ICM with them for every consultation (even if the doctor says there is no need).

Using family members as interpreters

It is not advisable to use family members as interpreters, because they hide information from the patient. However, it is rather difficult to make doctors aware of this risk.

Sometimes, an ICM may have problems with a family if they reveal the true diagnosis to the patient. But according to the Belgian law, the patient has the right to know his health condition. In conclusion, another role of the ICM is to make sure that the patient receives the correct information.

Before ICMs were introduced in hospitals, doctors used to rely on cleaning women, family members, etc. for interpreting. In addition to not having the training, they were not bound by a professional code of secrecy. However, after a while, doctors realised that they could no longer use nurses to do the job; they needed specialists.

Lack of human and financial resources

One of the biggest difficulties is the lack of trained personnel and lack of sufficient financial resources. There are not enough ICMs and even if the existing ones extended their contracts, there is not enough money to pay them.

Despite all this, the ICMs interviewed are not in agreement about shortening the time with their patients in order to be able to accompany more patients. As one of them said: "to reduce the time spent with one patient in order to deal with two patients means that you no longer provide the same quality of service".

Because of this pressure, ICMs lose their patience; they tend to be less friendly with patients. Among other difficulties mentioned is the fact that an ICM has to work with different nurses for the same patient/family.

Letting go of a case when it is over is also very difficult for an ICM.

8. Solutions/changes needed

What other solutions should be adopted (by the public institutions/hospital) in order to help ICMs?

One of the ICMs interviewed thought that during all medical training (doctor, nurse, etc.), there should be at least one course on why to use ICMs (what are the advantages of using ICMs, what are the risks of not using ICMs). He also thought that doctors and nurses should understand that immigration is not a passing problem; these groups of different ethnic origins are here and they are going to stay; and new groups are arriving as well (for example, Polish).

Another ICM thought that training should be available for health-care providers in order to change their views of the migrant population.

Would it be wise to promote specialised services for migrants?

The co-ordinator of the ICMs thinks that it is more important to make every health-care institution responsive to diversity in general and ethnic diversity in particular. The risk of trying to offer specialised services would be to provide a lower quality service, for people who are believed to be less important in society (for example, this happens in Romania and Slovakia for the Roma population). He did not think that specialised services would have the desired outcome. In the United States, for example, because of the specialised services, they talk about "ethnic health-care disparities". But it is also true that sometimes a specialised institution is needed to deal with specific problems (for example, victims of torture). However, if the services can be adapted through ICMs, it is for the best.

The ICMs interviewed did not think that specialised networks would help them. In particular, because it would be too difficult to work with only patients who are terminally ill (for example, dying from cancer). It would be too much only to bear sad news; the pressure would be too great for the ICM. So, in this way they can alternate sad news with good news (birth of a child, etc.) Also having specialised services for a specific group of migrants would mean providing them with a lower quality of services. However, as an example of a specialised service, one could mention that at Kind & Gezin they have developed a tool, based on pictures, to teach young mothers who do not speak the language how to feed their babies.

9. Concluding remarks

Nowadays in Belgium, hospitals have to deal more and more with patients who encounter difficulties in expressing themselves in one of the national languages. The cultural and linguistic barriers have a negative impact on accessibility and the quality of health-care services.

The Intercultural Mediation programme was introduced in Belgium with the aim of resolving, first of all, linguistic barriers, but also the sociocultural disparities and the ethnic tensions. ICMs are all specialised in the health-care sector. They are financed by the Federal Public Service of Public Health, Food Chain Security and Environment – DG for the Organisation of Health Care Establishments. Around 80 ICMs are currently working in 16 hospitals. In 2005 for example, they carried out 65 000 interventions in about 19 languages.

The final aim of this programme is to improve access and quality of health-care services for immigrant patients.

As a general conclusion, it can be stated that the deployment of ICMs in hospitals leads to an important increase in the quality of care, improves communication, contributes to the provision of culturally sensitive care and shows positive effects on patient satisfaction.[8]

---

8. For more details on the importance of employing ICMs in hospitals, see Verrept, op. cit.

Intercultural dialogue: a tool and framework for action for opening up to otherness in public policies and social services?

Christoph Eberhard[1]

How are we to approach living together in harmony in our increasingly multicultural European societies? How are we to recognise all citizens equally while acknowledging their diversity? These questions arise more particularly in the spheres of public policy and access to social services. No political, legislative or institutional reform can take place except in the broader framework of intercultural dialogue. At the same time, that framework must be the principal tool to which all institutional and voluntary-sector players as well as citizens must become accustomed.

In Quebec, the concept of reasonable accommodation has served for some decades now as a veritable institutional and social catalyst for this dialogue requirement. Originally imported from the United States, where the concept emerged in law during the 1970s to place an obligation of reasonable accommodation on public and private employers in religious matters, subsequently broadened to cases of discrimination based on disability, it developed in a quite novel way in Quebec. The concept grew into a cross-cutting legal one, also applicable to public services in Quebec and Canada and to cases beyond religion and disability such as questions linked to gender, pregnancy and age. The principle has even broken free of its strictly legal framework and been taken up by players in civil society to cover arrangements of every kind which may result from conflict management. A victim of its own success, the concept was strongly and widely criticised during the "crisis of reasonable accommodations" that reached its peak in 2006 and 2007. It gave rise to real societal discussion about living together in Quebec's cultural diversity. Indeed, in its 2008 report "Building the Future – A Time for Reconciliation", the Bouchard-Taylor Commission had no hesitation in placing the legal obligation of reasonable accommodation in a broader socio-political context, linked in

---

particular to the management of cultural differences.[2] However, it was careful to emphasise that this principle is not a universal panacea and put forward a range of recommendations which both reflect and supplement its dynamic, relating to the learning of diversity, harmonisation practices, integration of immigrants, interculturalism, inequalities, discrimination, French language and secularism.[3]

It is appropriate to inquire into Quebec's experience of reasonable accommodation in order to draw possible conclusions for the European situation. It seems neither possible nor relevant to transplant the concept exactly as it is. Reasonable accommodation is strongly imbued with a common law logic which perhaps facilitates its acceptance in the United Kingdom but renders it rather alien to the continental countries with their civil law tradition. Furthermore, the historical, social and cultural contexts of European countries are very different. But over and above the differences, the concept reveals major issues which it is important to clarify more fully in Europe and which would benefit from being placed at the heart of our institutional and societal debate. These issues, addressed more particularly in this chapter, are those of a more dialogue-based approach and one more linked to the law,[4] understood not merely as the positive law of the state but as that which shapes and sets a framework for the reproduction of our societies and the resolution of conflicts.

Kalpana Das, Director of the Montreal Intercultural Institute since 1979, summarises very well the issues of intercultural dialogue in her introduction to a thematic paper in *Interculture* entitled "Intercultural Mediation?" After recapitulating the various Canadian/Quebec policies developed over the last three decades, such as Canadian multiculturalism, Quebec-type interculturalism, "diversity management", "reasonable accommodation" and "intercultural mediation", she reaches the following finding (Das 2007, p. 6):

---

2. Nonetheless, excluding the important question of the relationship between the Quebec and Canadian nations and native peoples. It is important to bear this in mind when discussing the possible adaptation of reasonable accommodation in European law.

3. On these points, see the chapters by Bosset and Foblets, and by Jézéquel in this publication.

4. For an introduction to the issues and challenges arising from the law in relation to our thinking and for the changes it implies in connection with contemporary approaches to "governance" and "sustainable development", see Eberhard 2009.

In the context of society in general, which is becoming radically diverse, there is much more that remains to be said on the subject and we need to go beyond the integrationist perspective of mediation of conflicts between the culture of the State and its institutions and the cultures of diverse peoples in a given society. In the contemporary context the challenges of pluralism are much more complex and societies are faced with finding new ways of living together by avoiding the mistakes of colonialism, domination, hegemony and homogenization.

She goes on to ask an essential question: "Is diversity or cultural difference only a source of conflict or a source of enrichment and transformation of society?" (ibid.). Confronted with this question, Kalpana Das stresses the need to deal with three key issues, which it will be useful for the reader to retain as a frame of reference for all the ideas contained in the following pages:

1) We cannot reduce the needs of a society as a whole to the needs of institutions. The State and its institutions hold the "managerial role" of society. But people are not the objects of "management". They are subjects that are constantly creating knowledge, traditions and modes of living. 2) Do we then mediate conflicts caused by cultural differences or do we engage in creating conditions for *dialogical dialogue* (see Panikkar 1979) between persons and communities of diverse origins, in order to arrive at mutual discovery and understanding as a mode of living in a pluralistic society? 3) Is it possible to enter into a collaborative framework between the State and its institutions and the grass-roots social spaces without the latter being recuperated by the dominant system?

This paper will deal with these issues of intercultural dialogue in conjunction with the more institutional approaches developed in earlier papers of this publication. As the history of reasonable accommodation has shown, it developed gradually. From being a limited legal concept, it evolved into a cross-cutting legal concept. It even managed to break free of its strictly legal ties to become a principle re-appropriated by all society's stakeholders, and playing a leading part in devising, case by case, approaches fostering dialogic living together within cultural diversity. From being a limited practice, it became a framework for action in Quebec. Since the concept does not seem to be transposable exactly as it stands, it is necessary to clarify the goal towards which it points and which Europeans can adopt in their own ways.

This emergent perspective will be addressed from an anthropological view of law which entails the more intercultural reinvention of our living together and explores more specifically the intercultural issues of contemporary normative changes. These are characterised by a transition from more pyramidal, state-centred forms of government to more reticular, more participative and more dialogic forms of governance,[5] probably contributing also, *inter alia*, to the bringing together and hybridisation of civil law and common law forms.

While examining more in particular the question of interculturality in the field of law, public policy and social services in Europe, it is important not to lose sight of the broader framework into which it fits. We shall then go on to pinpoint certain fundamental issues and identify some fundamental options, and above all to outline a framework for reflection and action. Some practical proposals will be offered by way of conclusion.

1. The framework of current issues

Roderick A. Macdonald (2002, p. 30), writing in a Canadian and Quebec context, states: "In order to imagine law afresh not as an abstract, impersonal, institutional and formal rule imposed from outside by the competent authority, but rather as a meeting place – which seems essential to a reasonable accommodation approach or one inspired by it – we need a new conceptual apparatus. We have to rethink standards, not as rules imposed but rather as rules negotiated. We must rethink decisions, not as the official utterances of a judge but rather as the product of an agreement among those subject to the law. And the decision-maker must be thought of, not as the wise man settling an argument but rather as a facilitator in the context of interpersonal, cultural and social mediation."

European systems of law, confronted with increasingly multicultural or intercultural societies, face the same challenges. There is a gradual awareness of the issues of interculturalism, and more broadly of pluralism, in the collective experience of living together. That awareness goes hand in hand with the reinvention of the legal frameworks inherited from Western modernity. Need one stress that this development is not only

---

5. On this transition, see for example Eberhard 2002b, 2005, 2008a.

Canadian and European, but is taking place over the entire planet?[6] Government based on law that is state-centred, pyramidal, idealistic, objective, universal, stable and independent of other social mechanisms is gradually opening up to approaches rooted in governance. These are characterised by court regulation, network operation, pragmatism, subjectivism, relativism, a process approach, involvement with society by way of participation in its design and application by stakeholders. These developments are giving increasing prominence to dialogue and mediation procedures. In this respect they are closer to the more pragmatic approaches of the common law and an ethic of "reasonable accommodation" or even mutual accommodation.[7] However, it is very difficult to address these issues, which can no longer be tackled adequately by our present-day theoretical, legal and political tools (see, for example, Arnaud 1998, 2003; Calame 2003).

Despite all the challenges of this kind that we face, it is very hard, especially in continental Europe where an idealistic, ahistorical and systemic view of law prevails, to get away from the unitarist, idealist tradition and entertain more pluralist, pragmatic approaches. Given the anthropology of law, that is not surprising. Every system of law, as the phenomenon which shapes and sets a framework for the reproduction of our societies and the resolution of conflicts in fields regarded as vital, is understandable only in the light of the logics and world views of which it forms part. While legislation can be changed quickly, it is less easy to move towards a paradigmatic transition freeing us from over two centuries of legal modernity (symbolically initiated with the human rights declarations and the major codifications of the late 18th century), itself rooted in a deeper European cultural matrix.

The pluralism, interculturalism and pragmatism to which the reasonable accommodation perspective refers involve going beyond mere "management" through familiar tools and require a creative effort of

---

6. Recent studies on law, governance and sustainable development, looking at analyses from the most local to the most global level in fields ranging from urban governance to the invention of world governance via issues of management and conservation of land and natural resources, issues of companies' social responsibility or the refoundation of more endogenic legal systems in Europe's former colonies, show that these changes are fundamental (see, for example, Eberhard 2005, 2008a). Indeed, they can be observed in every field and reveal a veritable revolution in the shaping of our living together throughout the world.

7. See the chapter by Wright in this publication.

imagination which presupposes a willingness on our part to look at things differently.

2. Foundations for a framework to encompass reflection on intercultural skills and "reasonable accommodation" in social services

2.1. Intercultural dialogue makes sense only over the long term

Furthermore, it derives from human exchanges and common-sense constructions which could never be exhausted by procedures but call for real contacts and real sharing. Here the human factor is essential. As was said by a mediation service co-ordinator cited by Jordi Agusti-Panareda (2007, p. 41), "We do not know how to create interculturality in practice … we are all students and apprentices … Discourse is easy to transmit, but far more complicated to put into practice. We have a long way to go and the problem is that we are not ready to learn from others, or to explain ourselves." (See also Eberhard 2008c in this connection.) The same institutions can be used and interpreted in fundamentally different ways depending on the sense perspective in which they exist. Moreover, creating new institutions often poorly disguises the fact that we "go on doing the same thing in different forms". Reasonable accommodation had to be espoused by the various players in Quebec, otherwise it would have remained an empty shell. This process is accompanied by introspection and self-questioning.

2.2. Intercultural reality exists only in concrete situations

So it is fundamentally pluralist. Firstly, there are very different reception traditions in the "host societies" which receive persons from other cultures and are open or closed in varying degrees to dialogue and the prospect of reciprocal adaptation/reinvention. Not to mention the question of internal cultural diversity in every society and the related problem of national minorities, or even the question of native peoples.[8] Then there are different cultural distances depending on the cultures involved. Even between a Parisian and a Corsican, intercultural dialogue can be tricky. It will be even more complicated between a Frenchman and a Swede, who

---

8. On these points, see the chapters by Basta Fleiner and Ruiz Vieytez in this publication.

do not even share a "Latin" background but only a European cultural matrix. It will become harder still between a Frenchman and an Indian, where even the basic matrix is not the same. Finally, intercultural relations are structured by different power relationships. The clandestine immigrant who has fled his country or the historically weakened national minority is not in the same situation as the expatriate company director or the national minority that has been historically recognised and legitimised. Furthermore, different cultures have their own particular histories of "integration". (For a more detailed account of these questions, see Das 1988.)

2.3. All human beings are naturally ethnocentric, both individually and collectively

Their own ways of doing things seem right to them, and those of other people often strike them as curious, incomprehensible or wrong. This is illustrated by the crisis of reasonable accommodation in Quebec in 2006-07. Opening up to others is not straightforward. Questioning oneself is not easy. As François Fournier explains in his contribution to this publication, the intercultural challenge reawakens the feeling of being a stranger in one's own country, of lost unity, of a breakdown in social cohesion, an end to national identity, the end of "us", the fear that common values and practices are under threat, a feeling of personal insecurity and fear of an end to group projects, rendering the future uncertain. To enable the "crisis" to occur in the most positive way possible, one must realise that it is normal because it is closely bound up with every human being's natural ethnocentricity. But modern-day culture has built itself a "universal" ethnocentricity. It has laid down its conception of law, politics, economics, science, etc. as the rational, universal way of approaching them. This makes the crisis of the intercultural shock all the more painful because, according to this view, there ought not to be other legitimate ways of doing or seeing things, all other – even European, but not modern – views being at best relegated to "the past".

The modern view is not just ethnocentric but universalist and evolutionist. As Europeans, it is extremely important to bear this twofold ethnocentricity in mind: not only do our approaches to law, politics, etc. reflect our views of the world, but in addition we perceive them as the unbreachable universal framework within which all cultures should come to join us. Not only does anthropological experience prove the opposite: it is now becoming urgent for us to open up to these other approaches to the world, law, politics and living together, for today we are no longer able to find the answers alone on the basis of our own cultural experience (see Eberhard 2006). Interculturality does not just mean a challenge to modernity. It is not simply a problem to be solved. Cultures possess riches, and there is much to be learnt from intercultural dialogue. While reasonable accommodation opens a window on cultural diversity, it tends to open up to others in order to solve conflicts or manage problems. Perhaps it would be pertinent to make an explicit link between the reasonable accommodation perspective and that opened up by the concepts of governance and sustainable development. The latter do in fact open another window on intercultural dialogue, focusing less on conflicts than on social projects to be devised and implemented collectively.[9] Approaches to "governance" rely on "dialogue" and "participation". Approaches to "sustainable development" seek to implement a more "holistic" and inter-sectoral approach balancing the economic, social and environmental pillars, to which a "cultural pillar" is coming increasingly to be added and which lawyers might be tempted to supplement with an institutional pillar.

2.4. Intercultural reality is a dynamic reality

The discovery of difference and pluralism, often accompanied by models of "ideal types" or even "stereotypes", must not be allowed to conceal the dynamic nature of intercultural relations. The relativist view which regards every culture as a homogeneous and autonomous whole no longer holds water and has been refuted in anthropology. Every culture is dynamic and only exists in an "impure" way in contact with other cultures, through exchanges, confrontations, avoidance, sharing, etc. Addressing interculturality means going beyond recognition of otherness and daring to tackle intercultural relations in all their complexity (see Eberhard 2006; Le Roy 1999). This is one reason why, in order to do interculturality justice, it is necessary to break free of over-idealistic, systemic approaches such as those reflected in the conventional view of civil law cultures. Processes of mediation, dialogue and accommodation become essential and require approaches closer to the logic of common law, where law appears more as a reality emerging from the bottom up, through the intermediary of the courts, than to the civil law logic in which law is created by the state, the court being merely its mouthpiece. That does not mean renouncing

---

9. At least potentially. On the conditions for interpreting "governance" and "sustainable development" in an emancipatory and dialogic way, see Eberhard 2005, 2006 and 2009.

the legacy of the civil law tradition, but opening it up to these more pragmatic and more negotiated forms of reasoning which it has largely eclipsed in the past.

2.5. Intercultural reality has different stages and time frames

Any culture can be represented as a tree.[10] The branches are its most visible parts (morphological level), but its structure is the trunk (structural level) and its base is its roots (mythical level, deep-seated meaning). The morphological level can be changed fairly quickly and fairly easily (for example, certain behavioural habits, use of objects such as "modern technology"). The structural level (organisation of the family, educational, judicial, political social structures, etc.) adapts to given circumstances more slowly if at all. As for the "mythical" dimension, that of the underlying world view which ultimately gives life meaning, changes here occur only very slowly. As we have already observed, the manner in which one conceives the law, life in society, and one's individual and group actions is always profoundly marked by one's view of the world. It must be realised that we are currently in a period of profound transformation. And it has to be borne in mind, especially if we have a tendency to believe that the world is becoming homogeneous as a result of globalisation, that, as Robert Vachon emphasises (1995, p. 59): "At the heart of the cultural tree, there is a matrix (its roots) which does not change as easily as its morphological (the foliage) and structural (the trunk) dimensions. In fact, the mythical matrix (its vehicle: faith) can maintain itself – at times for millennia – while the ideologies and the practices multiply, change and transform themselves constantly in response to external and internal influences. External transformations can sometimes lead one to think that a culture has disappeared, while in fact, it is still very much alive. ... So we should not conclude too quickly that a culture has disappeared because its external forms, its ideologies or even some of its beliefs and intimate convictions are no longer the same. ... Just as reality is not given once and for all, but is constantly creating itself, so is the primordial myth of every culture. Hence the depth of cultural resistance."

And hence the importance of recognising this pluralism perspective for the shaping of our living together – which runs quite radically counter to the modern Western myth which values unity and uniformity, as the

---

10. See Das 1988, p. 37. For a detailed description and its explanation see also Vachon 1995, pp. 58 ff.

foundation and framework of an "ordered society" (see, for example, Bauman 1993). These various levels are illustrated by the example of the development of the reasonable accommodation concept: starting out from the periphery, changes have little by little infiltrated the very core of thinking about law and social projects, and have thus begun to define a new framework for action which itself helps to make us aware of the emergent myth[11] of the pluralism and interculturalism of reality (Vachon 1997). In short, from the morphological level the dynamic of reasonable accommodation has spread to the structural level and is beginning to impinge on the mythical level.

3. Fundamental options and intercultural framework for action

All the concepts proposed and discussed in this collective study, "reasonable accommodation" and related concepts such as "multiculturalism", "complex equality", "plural and inclusive citizenship", "minority rights" and "cultural rights", are responses by modernity and Western postmodernity to the challenges of interculturality. They meet the concern to translate intercultural problems into an institutional language that our institutions can adopt and use. This is quite reasonable and legitimate, especially bearing in mind the close link between law and society, the former emerging from the latter just as much as it transforms it. It is nevertheless important to remember that we are in a period of paradigmatic change in which we are forced to devise a "new common sense" (see de Sousa Santos 1995), a new framework for our thinking and action to address political, legal and scientific questions. So it is important to clarify at least three fundamental positions that may be taken up by host societies and immigrant cultures alike, and indeed by national majorities and minorities (see Vachon 1981 in this connection):

3.1. Assimilation

Assimilation consists in reducing diversity to uniformity. With this option, the policy of the state is to make all its citizens conform to its model. There is a parallel with a large number of immigrants or members of national minorities who seek to wipe the slate clean of their past and rebuild a new life in the host society or the "majority".

---

11. In the positive sense of an invisible framework for our thinking and our action.

3.2. Monoculturalism

Monoculturalism consists in ignoring all other cultures and settling for one's own. From the state's point of view, such an attitude produces the same effect as assimilation because the "only existing culture" is imposed, unconsciously, on everyone. From the standpoint of immigrants or national minorities, monoculturalism refers to people living in a host society or inside a majority while remaining wholly separate.

3.3. Multiculturalism

Multiculturalism consists in accepting the coexistence of different cultures. From the state's point of view, the coexistence of different cultural communities is acknowledged. Public space and citizenship are seen as multicultural. From the standpoint of immigrants, one lives to varying degrees in harmony "with" or "between" two or even more cultures. Living "between" is never easy. It is an individual and collective experience which may prove extremely traumatic and destructuring, or on the contrary highly enriching depending on the ways and the conditions in which it is experienced. It seems to me that individual and collective enrichment comes about when one manages to move on from mere coexistence ("multi") to dialogue ("inter"), namely from multicultural to intercultural.

3.4. Interculturalism

Interculturalism requires progress beyond not only monoculturalism and assimilation, but also multiculturalism. It means no longer seeing other people as a "problem to be integrated while recognising them" and calls for a commitment to "reasonable accommodations" on both sides. While these are important dimensions, interculturalism aims at an approach of real mutual discovery making it possible to devise projects for society together, from the most local level (neighbourhood, district) to the most global level.

4. Some practical proposals for legislative frameworks to promote interculturality in Europe

The most important point appears to be a change of attitude. This is illustrated by the Quebec experiment in "reasonable accommodation", which lies at the root of this collective thinking about interculturalism in Europe.

It is a judicial response to reality, inspired by a sensitivity to diversity which – this is the interesting thing – is linked in our Western imagination to the sensitivity to universality embodied in human rights: as we are all equal in dignity, we are all also equal not only in our shared humanity but also in the human diversity which we reflect in our particular being. So neither universalism nor relativism, but pluralism, appears as our frame of reference. The problem is that we tend to try to conceive and organise that pluralism in the light of our modern, idealistic, ahistorical, unitarist and universalist judicial experience. The following are a few practical pointers to help in translating the pluralist view into concrete action.

4.1. Enhancing intercultural dialogue in public services

Dialogue between institutions and users calls for translators and go-betweens. The logic of reasonable, mutual, accommodation relies on a capacity for dialogue. Therefore, the role and status of "intercultural mediators", of "dialogue facilitation agents", must be given real value. As already pointed out, all dialogue is potentially a source of crisis. So there must be competent intercultural go-betweens to recognise areas of agreement and friction and provide a peaceable framework for dialogue. These mediators must be able to act as genuine go-betweens for different worlds, which means that their status must be clearly defined, recognised and enhanced, and that they are enabled to work on a long-term basis, employing methods which are not invariably those of institutions but must be allowed, when necessary, to draw on the approaches and procedures of the other culture present. However, the role of these mediators can be properly performed only if institutions in general develop an intercultural sensitivity, which is possible only if their staff receive the right training.[12]

4.2. Enhancing intercultural action going beyond bicultural action

Most mediators are, in the nature of things, specialists in mediating between two cultures (that of the state and an immigrant culture). Most of the time they are engaged in building bridges, reaching accommodations, between the "institution" and a category of users. There are also many contact initiatives between particular communities. Setting intercultural action free of the "me and the other person" gridlock by introducing a "third party", recognising that intercultural action means accepting a

---

12. See, for example, the experiments described in Younès and Le Roy 2002 and in INTERculture, No. 153, entitled "Médiation interculturelle?".

more fundamental and broader pluralism than the current relationship, makes it possible to create wider areas for joint exploration and action. The recognition of a broader perspective of pluralism and interculturalism shared by everyone is the key to escaping from "self/other" dichotomies and essentialising excesses, and embarking on dynamic intercultural dialogue approaches in which the players involved not only reveal themselves to each other but transform each other through their interaction. That is what appears implicitly to have happened in the development of reasonable accommodation in Quebec, when it moved on from the status of a legal concept of limited application to that of one with a cross-sectoral scope, and indeed mutated into a general principle of "good living".

4.3. Recognising the limits of institutions and the wealth of community knowledge and know-how

Institutions, social services, will never be able to cater fully for the needs of all citizens, even if that is the great modern dream. Many communities have their own support and mutual aid structures. It is perhaps healthy to recognise that institutions should not necessarily set out to be used by all cultural groups, nor by all the members of a given cultural group. One major concern is to reflect on the dovetailing of these services (which do not necessarily take the form of modern institutions but may, for example, entail family, community and religious solidarity) with those of the state. The accommodation perspective is dynamic, not static. The aim is not to apply accommodations in such a way that they are institutionalised, locking our interactions into a permanent pattern. The objective should be to bring about the conditions for continuous application of the "logic of accommodation", so as to contribute to a pacified framework within which to constantly reinvent our ways of living together.

4.4. Avoiding politicisation of the issues while recognising the complexity of situations

At a certain level, every question is of course political. A project for an intercultural society is itself a political choice. However, care must be taken not to over-politicise questions of cultural difference. This being a very profound question at the private, personal level as well as at group level, it is all too easy to fall for emotional approaches. So it is all the more important in this sphere to try to bring about the conditions – not always an easy matter – for the emergence of dialogue that will afford knowledge of oneself and of others (see, for example, Eberhard 2008c). This is an absolute precondition for the emergence of genuinely pluralist and intercultural projects for society. Pragmatic issues often become ideological battles in which concrete problems are masked and drowned in discussions which ultimately yield little, such as the endless debates between "progressives" and "traditionalists", between "universalists" and "relativists", etc. As already noted, without discarding the achievements of the civil law tradition, we must take care not to lapse into its idealist excesses which all too readily transform the questions addressed into ideological battles.[13] A typical example is the manner in which the Muslim headscarf issue was dealt with a few years ago in France. Avoiding hasty politicisation means familiarising oneself with the issues and accepting their complexity. It is also a basis on which to begin conducting politics "differently".

The complexity of situations and the length of time for which those involved in intercultural dialogue commit themselves makes it necessary to enhance the responsibility of stakeholders.[14] While such concepts as "reasonable accommodation" or "multicultural citizenship" can play important roles as general principles of action, it would be counterproductive to over-proceduralise them, as has happened with the implementation of many governance procedures. Under the guise of more dialogic, more participative, more intercultural procedures, one ultimately dilutes the responsibilities of those involved further and further, to a point where the procedures in question lose all meaning. One might take inspiration here from traditionally African rights: the important thing is not to legislate for the future by trying to anticipate every situation, but to pass on ways of addressing questions of living together and the construction of consensus in situations increasingly characterised by pluralism.

For the underlying aim of the framework defined by the concept of reasonable accommodation, and the whole question of intercultural

---

13. The human rights and cultural diversity debate showed the danger of focusing on a "cultural whole". While it is important to take otherness into account, it must not be essentialised. We must avoid seeing all the problems through a solely cultural prism and address situations in all their complexity, with cultural aspects seen in conjunction with economic, political, social, etc., ones (see Eberhard 2002a). Moreover, focusing on cultural diversity runs the risk of obscuring the problems of differences of language, social class, economic category, etc., with which the law also has to concern itself.

14. On this huge question, see Eberhard 2008a, 2008d.

dialogue in public policies and social services in Europe, is to contribute to the emergence of cultures of peace which do not impose themselves on us despite our differences, but build upon them. While it is difficult to take the full measure of them, it is possible – as Robert Vachon (1995, p. 10) argues – that "accord and concord do not necessarily require a formal, ideological, doctrinal unity, a universal theory, or a common (that is, homogeneous) culture, where differences disappear or are watered down. On the contrary, concord calls for differences (that are irreducible to each other or to a third), but in non-duality. Hence, it calls for neither monism nor dualism, but mutual acceptance of differences (in non-duality). Differences not only enhance the quality of the accord/concord, but are a precondition for harmony. The result of concord and peace is harmony, *not in spite of,* but *in and because of* our differences."

Select bibliography[15]

Agusti-Panareda, J. (2007), "La promesse interculturelle de la médiation", *INTERculture*, No. 153, pp 41-58.

Alliot M. (2003), *Le droit et le service public au miroir de l'anthropologie. Textes choisis et édités par Camille Kuyu*, Karthala, Paris.

Appadurai A. (2001), *Après le colonialisme. Les conséquences culturelles de la globalisation*, Payot, Paris.

Arnaud A.-J. (1998), *Entre modernité et mondialisation – Cinq leçons d'histoire de la philosophie du droit et de l'État*, Collection Droit et Société, No. 20, LGDJ, Paris.

Arnaud A.-J. (2003), *Critique de la raison juridique 2. Gouvernants sans frontières. Entre mondialisation et post-mondialisation*, LGDJ, Paris.

Bauman Z. (1993) (1991), *Modernity and Ambivalence*, Polity Press.

Calame P. (2003), *La démocratie en miettes. Pour une révolution de la gouvernance*, Charles Léopold Mayer/Descartes & Cie, Paris.

Das K. (1988), "Social Work and Cultural Pluralism in Québec: Some Unexplored Issues", *INTERculture*, No. 100, pp. 30-52.

Das K. (2007), "Médiation interculturelle?", *INTERculture*, No. 153, pp. 5-7.

de Sousa Santos B. (1995), *Toward a New Common Sense – Law, Science and Politics in the Paradigmatic Transition*, After the Law Series, Routledge, New York/London.

Eberhard C. (2002a), *Droits de l'homme et dialogue interculturel*, Editions des Ecrivains, Paris.

Eberhard C. (ed.) (2002b), *Le Droit en perspective interculturelle. Images réfléchies de la pyramide et du réseau*, special issue of the *Revue Interdisciplinaire d'Études juridiques*, No. 49.

Eberhard C. (ed.) (2005), *Droit, gouvernance et développement durable*, special issue of the *Cahiers d'Anthropologie du Droit*, Karthala, Paris.

---

15. This bibliography covers the studies on which this chapter draws as well as the references quoted in the text.

Eberhard C. (2006), *Le Droit au miroir des cultures. Pour une autre mondialisation*, Collection Droit et Société, LGDJ, Paris (also, forthcoming new paperback by LGDJ/Lextenso).

Eberhard C. (ed.) (2008a), *Traduire nos responsabilités planétaires. Recomposer nos paysages juridiques*, Bruylant, Brussels.

Eberhard C. (2008b), "De l'univers au plurivers. Fatalité, utopie, alternative?", in Dillens A.-M. (ed.), *La mondialisation: utopie, fatalité, alternatives*, Publications des Facultés universitaires Saint Louis, Brussels, pp. 67-104.

Eberhard C. (2008c), "Rediscovering Education through Intercultural Dialogue", contribution to the international meeting of experts on cultural diversity and education, UNESCO/UNESCOCat, Barcelona, 14-16 January 2008, available at: www.dhdi.free.fr/recherches/horizonsinterculturels/articles/eberhardeducation.pdf.

Eberhard C. (2008d), "La responsabilité en France. Une approche juridique face à la complexité du monde", in Sizoo E. (ed.), *Responsabilité et cultures du monde. Dialogue autour d'un défi collectif*, Charles Léopold Mayer, Paris, pp. 155-182.

Eberhard C. (2009), "Préliminaires pour des approches participatives du Droit, de la gouvernance et du développement durable", *Revue Interdisciplinaire d'Études Juridiques*, No. 62, pp. 125-151.

Eberhard C., Fernando M. and Gafsia N. (2005), "Droit, laïcité et diversité culturelle. L'Etat français au défi du pluralisme", *Revue Interdisciplinaire d'Études Juridiques*, No. 54, pp. 129-169.

INTERculture (1981), "From an Integrationist to a Cross-Cultural Québec", No. 73.

INTERculture (1988), "Social Work and Cultural Pluralism", No. 100.

INTERculture (1994), "Interculturalism in Quebec: Philosophy and Practices among the NGOs", No. 123.

INTERculture (2007), "Médiation interculturelle?", No. 153.

INTERculture (2008), "Pluralismes d'ici et d'ailleurs", No. 154.

Le Roy E. (1999), *Le jeu des lois. Une anthropologie "dynamique" du Droit*, Collection Droit et Société, Series Anthropologique, LGDJ, Paris.

Le Roy E. (2004), *Les Africains et l'Institution de la Justice*, Dalloz, Paris.

Macdonald R. A. (2002), "Normativité, pluralisme et sociétés démocratiques avancées. L'hypothèse du pluralisme pour penser le droit", in Younès C. and Le Roy E. (eds), *Médiation et diversité culturelle. Pour quelle société?*, Karthala, Paris, pp. 21-38.

Ost F. (2009), *Traduire. Défense et illustration du multilinguisme*, Fayard, Paris.

Ost F. and van de Kerchove M. (2002), *De la pyramide au réseau? Pour une théorie dialectique du droit*, Facultés universitaires Saint Louis, Brussels.

Panikkar R. (1978), *The Intrareligious Dialogue*, Paulist Press, Mahwah, NJ, United States.

Panikkar R. (1979), *Myth, Faith and Hermeneutics – Cross-cultural studies*, Paulist Press, Mahwah, NJ, United States.

Panikkar R. (1995), *Cultural Disarmament – The Way to Peace*, Westminster John Knox Press, Louisville, KY, United States.

Sauquet M. and Vielajus M. (2007), *L'intelligence de l'autre. Prendre en compte les différences culturelles dans un monde à gérer en commun*, Charles Léopold Mayer, Paris.

Sizoo E. (ed.) (2000), *Ce que les mots ne disent pas. Quelques pistes pour réduire les malentendus interculturels: la singulière expérience des traductions de la plate-forme de l'Alliance pour un monde responsable et solidaire*, Charles Léopold Mayer, Paris.

Sizoo E. (ed.) (2008), *Responsabilités et cultures du monde. Dialogue autour d'un défi collectif*, Charles Léopold Mayer, Paris.

Vachon R. (1981), "From an Integrationaist to a Cross-Cultural Québec", *INTERculture*, No. 73, pp. 2-32.

Vachon R. (1995), "Guswenta ou l'impératif interculturel – Première partie: Les fondements interculturels de la paix", *INTERculture*, No. 127.

Vachon R. (1997), "Le mythe émergent du pluralisme et de l'interculturalisme de la réalité", séminaire sur le pluralisme et société, discours alternatifs à la culture dominante, organisé by the l'Institut Interculturel de Montréal, 15 February 1997, available at www.dhdi.org.

Vachon R. (1998), "L'IIM et sa revue: Une alternative interculturelle et un interculturel alternatif", *INTERculture*, No. 135, pp. 4-75.

Younès C. and Le Roy E. (eds) (2002), *Médiation et diversité culturelle. Pour quelle société?*, Karthala, Paris.

Website: www.dhdi.org.

Training in intercultural competences to accommodate differences in public services – Issues involved

Myriam Jézéquel[1]

The complexity of the situations covered by the reasonable accommodation requirement and the emergence of novel situations argue against a "ready-thought-out" type of training or a catalogue of best practices. Despite the set of highly consensual guidelines[2] that form the framework for living together,[3] front-line and second-tier staff have great difficulty in analysing the situations that require accommodation and in justifying what they consider to be non-negotiable. Moreover, the accommodation requirement is not an exact science and social values are in a constant state of flux. What help can we give them in managing conflicts of values, balancing contradictory interests and reconciling competing rights? What guidance can we give them in negotiating accommodations or refusing what is non-negotiable? What advice can we give them on striking a fair balance between legal requirements and compliance with their institutional mandate? In short, what is the best intercultural training strategy? This article puts forward some points for analysis and proposals for action

---

1. Consultant in diversity management, Ph.D. (Sorbonne-Paris IV). Author of several articles and handbooks on reasonable accommodation and conflicts of rights and values in intercultural relations.

2. The main ones being: equality between women and men, separation of Church and State, primacy of the French language, protection of rights and freedoms, justice and the rule of law, protection of minorities, and rejection of discrimination and racism.

3. "Au Québec pour bâtir ensemble. Énoncé de politique en matière d'immigration et d'intégration", 1990; "La gestion des conflits de normes par les organisations dans le contexte pluraliste de la société québécoise", report of the Conseil des relations interculturelles, 1993; "Le pluralisme religieux au Québec: un défi d'éthique sociale", report of the Commission des droits de la personne, 1995; "Droits des femmes et diversité", report of the Conseil du statut de la femme, 1997; "Un Québec pour tous ses citoyens", report of the Conseil des relations interculturelles, 1997; "Rites et symboles religieux à l'école. Défis éducatifs de la diversité", report of the Ministère de l'Éducation, du Loisir et du Sport, 2003; "Laïcité et diversité religieuse", report of the Conseil des relations interculturelles, 2004; "Réflexion sur la portée et les limites de l'obligation d'accommodement raisonnable en matière religieuse", Commission des droits de la personne et des droits de la jeunesse, 2005; "La laïcité scolaire au Québec. Un nécessaire changement de culture institutionnelle", report of the Comité sur les affaires religieuses, Ministère de l'Éducation, du Loisir et du Sport, 2006.

that emphasise both (1) the different guidelines that should help to resolve conflicts of values and rights, and (2) competences/strategies conducive to concerted action and joint solutions.

1. Developing common guidelines

All too often, the staff of public institutions have to rely on their own practical expertise to manage complex situations of conflicts of standards. The state and the courts leave it to them to devise creative solutions and even set new benchmarks against a background of general principles and compliance with the law. To draw the boundary between what is negotiable and what is non-negotiable, social and health service staff are calling for clear guidelines enabling them to assess the legitimacy or otherwise of granting an exemption from rules of general application.[4] They are also afraid that, with exemptions (or exceptions) ceasing to be exceptional, this might lead to structural changes in the rules of living together.

In this context, management of conflicts of standards is central to the question of living together in a pluralist society. According to this view of "living together", living in harmony does not mean living without conflict or ironing out our differences to settle our disagreements. Rather, this view requires us to have tools to set guidelines for conflicts of standards and inspire diversity management practices.

In response to this need, the task is to formulate a coherent analysis framework that is useful for the work of reconciling rights and negotiating values. Although the specific and complex nature of these conflicts rules out any mechanically applicable formula, it is nonetheless possible to identify the guidelines underlying the way in which conflicts are treated in different players' specific reference frameworks. All too often, conflict resolution is the result of professional practices that exist in competition in society. For instance, would a manager's assessment of a conflict of rights differ from that of a judge? The manager will focus on the best course of action according to his organisation's culture, mission and structure. He will be concerned about how employees respond to the proposed solution or how users perceive a service delivered with certain accommodations. However, in his concern to settle the conflict, he does not have the freedom to ignore the legal guidelines that govern his decision.

---

4. M. Jézéquel (ed.), *Les accommodements raisonnables, quoi, comment, jusqu'où? Des outils pour tous*, Yvon Blais, Cowansville (Quebec), 2007.

The rules for sound management of diversity within an institution are themselves subject to the legal rules governing public freedoms. For his part, the judge is aware that a working environment will have to live with the consequences of his judgment. In interpreting the scope of rights, he may disregard neither the values shared in society nor the different organisations' specific constraints. Consequently, management of living together cannot realistically be confined to a single player, and the grey areas cannot be left to the judgment of a single sector of society.

To sum up, each player gains by knowing the reference framework of the others and by taking on board, and drawing inspiration from, the rationale and tools of other spheres of society. An intersectoral, interdisciplinary and interprofessional approach has the advantage of creative management of conflicts of standards. It enhances the "shared responsibility" of all players for setting collective guidelines. Lastly, fair, creative solutions to conflicts of standards can arise only from the combination of these different guidelines, which is not the same as merely pooling expertise.

For the purposes of this article, I will confine myself to exploring the methods of conflict resolution from different angles: (1) legal: what lessons should be drawn from the arbitration of rights by judges for the purpose of managing conflicts of standards in the intercultural relations context?; (2) standards: what collective values can be applied in order to distinguish the negotiable from the non-negotiable?; (3) procedural: what criteria may justify or rule out a request for adjustment?; (4) institutional: what overall principles and strategies should an institution implement to encourage the proper use and application of negotiated solutions?

Each angle of analysis is illustrated by an example.

1.1. Legal guidelines: the contribution of the law to arbitration of conflicts of rights

Illustration 1: in the name of his religious beliefs, a Sikh teenager at a youth centre refuses to comply when the educator asks him to remove his kirpan in the presence of other young people. On the basis of what principles is the balance of rights decided in the scales of justice?[5] To be

---

5. M. Jézéquel, "Conflit de droits: dilemme pour les juges ou simple mécanique juridique?", *Journal du Barreau*, Barreau du Québec, Vol. 39, No. 10, October 2007, available at www.barreau.qc.ca/pdf/journal/vol39/200710.pdf.

a conflict of rights, the conflict must be between two equally valid and genuinely contradictory rights, namely, it must go beyond the level merely of interests or values. The situation in question sets the young man's right to practise his religion against the right of the other youngsters to security. It requires the educator (and his institution) to negotiate a solution that reconciles respect for both rights. In line with their perspective, judges refuse to rank the rights and freedoms involved. Fundamental rights are equal, indissociable and interdependent. The judge's approach is to weigh up these opposing rights within the well-established charter framework. The legal review starts by defining the scope of the rights involved while seeking a solution acceptable to both parties. When it is necessary to restrict the rights involved in order to balance them, the curtailment of the right must be minimal and proportional to the aim pursued (security).

Faced with a conflict of rights, the judge points out that no right is absolute. The restriction of freedom of religion must be "reasonable" in order not to be discriminatory. Hence, an "absolute" ban on carrying a kirpan would be deemed discriminatory if a reasonable limitation of that right were conceivable. It is the circumstances, in the light of the facts, which determine the possibility of ensuring a "reasonable" level of security by allowing, for example, the young Sikh to carry his kirpan sewn up inside a piece of material. But in view of the real "risk" that he might use his kirpan in a situation of confrontation, another option would be to replace the kirpan with a symbolic medallion. The purpose of these "accommodations" is to balance respect for standards of security and respect for the exercise of religion. We should note that, in some cases, a right may be curtailed if the restriction can be justified in a free and democratic society (Article 1 of the Canadian charter), and subject to proper regard for democratic values, public order and general well-being (Article 9.1 of the Quebec charter). Analysis of case law reveals two main models for reconciling rights in conflict. The pragmatic model seeks to balance the disadvantages suffered by each party in the curtailment of their rights, while reconciliation based on principles tends to weigh up "the interest of society", which is reasonable in a free and democratic society having regard to the social context and cultural values.

1.2. Social guidelines: "socially acceptable" negotiated solutions

Illustration 2: a female social worker goes to the home of an immigrant family to assess the urgency of placing a child with a foster family following a complaint of ill-treatment. The father refuses to co-operate

with a woman. What room for manoeuvre does the social worker have? Should this reluctance to negotiate with a woman give rise to an "accommodation" in the child's interest? It should be noted that the realm of the "negotiable" covers situations of conflict of standards which permit exceptions to the application of an operating rule. In short, some cultural requirements are reconcilable with the standards of the majority. The Quebec Health and Social Services Act requires public services to be made accessible in such a way as to take account of their clients' ethnocultural characteristics. However, the adjustment of services and the allowance made for users' diversified needs may be limited by values of the "common public culture" that are considered non-negotiable. In the case in point, the request to deal only with a man, whether cultural or religious in nature, is not reconcilable with the social ideal and collective value of equality between men and women. The Quebec Council on the Status of Women recently drew attention to the discriminatory effect that such a practice would entail for women.[6] In this context, accommodation finds its limits not so much in the infringement of an individual right as in the social harm stemming from acceptance of a sexist demand. In the name of this shared fundamental value, the Quebec Government decided to amend the charter by means of an interpretative clause to ensure that freedom of religion cannot take precedence over respect for women's dignity (except in the case of certain so-called "captive" clienteles, for example, the choice of female or male staff to provide intimate care to patients). The lesson to be drawn from this example is that, in reaching her decision, a female social worker must take account of certain social values having the same binding force as laws, which extends the range of the legal limits.

1.3. Procedural guidelines: from the "reasonable" to the "functional" nature of an adjustment

Illustration 3: a Muslim female nurse wants an exception to be made to the dress code so that she can wear a headscarf and asks to be absent on certain days to celebrate a religious festival. How do we manage this situation of conflict between the employee's religious standards and the institution's operating rules? It should be stressed that freedom of religion requires employers to see to it that organisational rules do not prevent

---

6. *Droit à l'égalité entre les femmes et les hommes et liberté religieuse – Avis*, September 2007, No. 207-06-A, available at www.csf.gouv.qc.ca/fr/publications/?F=affichage& ma=20&choix=2&s=1.

employees from acting in accordance with their beliefs and do not force them to act contrary to their beliefs. On the basis of this principle, the idea that employees should not bear the full burden of an adjustment in the workplace has gradually gained acceptance in law. Religious beliefs and cultural origins were for a long time an obstacle in employment. The burden has now been reversed and it is for employers to make the effort to create an inclusive working environment with organisational practices free from exclusion effects.

A legal assessment will focus on the admissibility or inadmissibility of a request for exemption, while the manager will have to analyse the ways and means of applying it (its feasibility). Within his reference framework, he will be concerned to find a "realistic" solution that does not unduly harm the functioning of the institution or jeopardise the rights of other employees or the safety of users. His assessment criteria are based on the factors identified in case law for determining what constitutes an "excessive constraint": impossibility, serious risk or scale of risk, excessive costs, impairment of the rights and/or morale of other employees, infringement of a collective agreement, interchangeability of staff and premises.

Hence, to verify the feasibility or impossibility of an exemption from the dress code, the employer must disregard personal aesthetic criteria, the preferences of his clientele and the subjective apprehensions of his staff and focus on the "real" risks associated with the wearing of a headscarf. He will be justified in prohibiting it if he can demonstrate, on the one hand, that it is a reasonable condition of employment (a "justified professional requirement") linked with the nature of the work, for reasons of hygiene, public health or safety, and on the other, that he has exhausted all conceivable solutions for reconciling the wearing of a headscarf and the safety requirement.

Regarding the possibility of obtaining leave on religious grounds, the assessment will depend on the institution's "real" possibilities. Can the employee be replaced? Will the working time be made up? Can floating leave be made generally available? Does the post require regular attendance at work or personal follow-up contact with clients? What would the financial implications be? The request could be turned down if replacing the employee required a major reorganisation of working arrangements, generated excessive costs or slowed down productivity.

It should be noted that the "excessive" constraint threshold is to be assessed objectively and in relation to the characteristics of the institution, its ability to carry the burden, its effects on staff, etc.[7]

1.4. Institutional guidelines: the right conditions for sound management of diversity

Management of conflicts of standards will be all the easier in an organisational culture that is "inclusive" and "open to diversity". To reflect such openness, the organisation will take care to distinguish between uniformly equal treatment and equal treatment differentiated according to the specific needs and realities of certain groups or individuals. We should note that differential treatment is not the same as preferential treatment. Furthermore, in order to establish an inclusive culture, the institution, in its choice of negotiated solutions, must take into account the balance of interests involved. If a conflict of standards is to be fairly managed, it is essential that a fair solution should also be seen to be fair by users or employees. In other words, above and beyond management of conflicts of standards, what is at stake is management of how the chosen solutions are perceived. To ensure the desired perception and forestall resistance, the institution should favour co-operation in the search for negotiated solutions and publicise its policy of openness to diversity. Diversity should be defined in the broad sense, as embracing all differences that may give rise to grounds of discrimination. Two-way negotiation should be central to management of standards, the parties being jointly responsible for the solution and there being a possibility of demanding something in return for the solution envisaged. Negotiated solutions should give priority to inclusive measures benefiting all employees or all users. For example, the proposal to establish a meditation room will be all the more favourably received if it is a room open to all those who wish to meditate in silence, rather than a prayer room reserved for the members of a particular religion (even if the request originated from a specific religious group). Even an individual accommodation measure should pursue a collective, unifying interest. Management of conflicts of standards will also gain by incorporating an overall management model geared to flexibility in the organisation of work and service provision. Lastly, it should be stressed that an

---

7. M. Jézéquel, "Accommodements religieux en milieu de travail: jusqu'où?", *Effectif*, magazine of the Ordre des conseillers en ressources humaines agréés et des conseillers en relations industrielles agréés du Québec, Vol. 10, No. 2, April/May 2007, Quebec/Montreal, pp. 32-35.

institution contributes all the more to creating an inclusive environment if it approaches conflicts of standards positively, not as a problem but as an opportunity for integration and diversity. In keeping with this spirit, it will gain by incorporating equality into its operating rules. This involves considering the potentially discriminatory effects of these rules in the light of the characteristics of its existing clientele, formulating preventively a policy on diversity management and working proactively to meet the future needs of the population in the light of society's demographic trends.

2. Developing concerted action and joint measures

We will approach this part by putting forward some proposals for action:

- include the accommodation requirement in the institution's policy on implementation of client services;

- co-ordinate the efforts (consultation and intervention) of the different services concerned in developing mutual understanding of the situation and seeking joint solutions;

- train staff in the different aspects of cultural and religious diversity and the issues involved by jointly working out solutions to accommodation requests;

- develop a method of negotiation and mediation to consolidate intercultural dialogue that incorporates an accommodation procedure;

- support staff in their working practices, their communication of a refusal to grant an accommodation request or the negotiation of compromise solutions (use of professional arguments);

- accompany each refusal of an accommodation request with an appropriate explanation of the organisational constraints or the legal principles rather than arguments based on a knowledge of religion;

- clarify the most problematic situations, for example, those entailing a risk of conflict between religious freedom and women's rights, without trivialising or exaggerating them;

- keep a record of accommodation requests and the solutions adopted;

- carry out a forward-looking analysis of adjustment needs;

- prefer structural change to special treatment, inclusive measures benefiting everyone to piecemeal measures.

Part D – Overview and conclusions

Lessons to be learned

Myriam Jézéquel

1. Introduction

What lessons can we learn from this impressive work, which has brought together a broad spectrum range of views and perspectives from interdisciplinary and cross-cultural exchanges within the Council of Europe? The result is wide-ranging and highly rewarding.

This publication as a whole deals with the general question of the contribution ("added value") that the legal concept of reasonable accommodation (RA) can make to the institutional integration of cultural diversity in relation to the European legal framework.

This question is a major concern of the Directorate General of Social Cohesion at the Council of Europe (Europe's oldest institution) in its work to preserve ethnic and cultural diversity and frame innovative multidisciplinary social policies promoting protection of rights, social cohesion and a better quality of life in Europe.

The approach is founded on the belief that respect for ethnic and cultural diversity based on fair, common and inclusive rules is a mainstay of social harmony and cohesion in a pluralist society (Gilda Farrell).

The general question has been broken down into three specific questions that go beyond individual subject boundaries:

- Part A: replication of RA in the European legal system: what potential does the concept of reasonable accommodation in the European legal area have to bring about institutional change conducive to protecting and promoting diversity?

- Part B: application of RA to other fields: how might the concept of RA be extended to other grounds of discrimination, other beneficiaries and other purposes?

- Part C: transposition of RA to the civic sphere: what does the concept of RA promise by way of new guidelines, collective education in intercultural dialogue and training in new skills?

This brief survey will thus focus on identifying the issues, highlighting the principal approaches and noting the authors' conclusions and proposed solutions.

2. Accommodation in Canadian law: progress and uncertainty (Jézéquel, Bosset)

Before reviewing the possible advantages of this North American concept, it is important to define its many meanings (Bosset) and pin down its various dimensions and scope (Jézéquel) in the approach adopted by Canada's Supreme Court.

An observer of Canadian law will inevitably be struck, and rightly so, by the spread of one particular method of correcting discrimination: reasonable accommodation (RA):

- firstly, in law: in the course of its rulings, the Canadian Supreme Court has continually increased the scope of this concept by broadening its interpretation of the rights protected, extending the list of grounds of discrimination by invoking RA, urging policy makers to introduce rules that are fair to everybody prior to and beyond individual claims, etc;

- secondly, in the public sphere: originally confined to the field of law, RA has gradually spread to the public arena, raising the general question of its scope and meaning. Thus, beyond courtrooms and meetings of legal experts, the concept of RA has been discussed in Quebec's civic sphere in the Consultation Commission on Accommodation Practices Related to Cultural Differences (CCAPRCD), co-chaired by Gérard Bouchard and Charles Taylor and set up by Quebec's Prime Minister, Jean Charest;

- thirdly, in organisations: the pluralist nature of our societies means that public institutions, in particular, gradually have to adjust to the fact that their users are multicultural. These institutions have traditionally been governed by standardised practices, rules and norms reflecting majority characteristics in various areas of everyday life (education, dietary matters, clothing, health, hygiene, etc.). RA holds institutions responsible for reviewing their norms if the latter are likely to disadvantage persons who do not exhibit these majority characteristics or dominant values.

- However, their responsibilities vary according to the nature of the recommended options. Public institutions should therefore be required to:

- correct the effects of discrimination by managing exceptions to the general rule;

- anticipate potentially prejudicial effects of discrimination by means of preventive (and proactive) management of tensions associated with intercultural relations;

- devise from the outset inclusive rules and new practices reflecting society's pluralism by means of participatory management of the full range of diversity, bringing together all those concerned (policy makers and beneficiaries; majorities and minorities).

The tendency of the law to ensure practical equality, coupled with the spread of RA in the public sphere and institutional practices, is a sign that public institutions will have to follow this groundswell if they are to adjust successfully to the needs of the society that they serve.

3. "Reasonable accommodation" in the European legal framework: potential and limitations

3.1. An impressive set of European measures at various levels (Foblets, Basta Fleiner, Ast, Jackson Preece)

Taking European legal arrangements as a whole, it is clear how far European law has come in recognising pluralism and protecting cultural identity. Is there a role for "accommodations" in this legal framework? And what is the potential of RA?

3.1.1. Framework Convention for the Protection of National Minorities (Basta Fleiner)

Is the legal protection of ethnic minorities better served by the legal device of reasonable accommodation or by the Framework Convention for the Protection of National Minorities (FCNM) in European Community law?

Scope

Lidija R. Basta Fleiner draws attention to the different levels of protection of minority rights in the FCNM (respect, protection and promotion). Minority rights are an integral part of the international protection of human rights, since they do not fall within the reserved domain of domestic jurisdiction. They combine socio-economic rights with the right to participate in public life and call for "full and effective equality" without any discrimination, which may in many cases imply additional rights. Full and effective equality is linked to the principles of tolerance, dialogue and mutual respect (Article 6). It is deemed to entail effective participation as a necessary condition of its existence (Article 4, paragraph 2). For such equality to be achieved, states must take positive measures to support national minority identities and the effective participation of national minorities in public life and affairs (Article 15). It requires states to produce a specific result by adopting a "non-exclusion policy", which can extend to special measures such as quotas.

Limitations

Can a further level of protection be achieved? According to Basta Fleiner, the boldness of the Advisory Committee on the Framework Convention (ACFC, the convention's supervisory body) in pursuing a proactive interpretation of the Framework Convention (and particularly Article 15 in terms of multicultural citizenship) might reach its limit, because "although an integral part of universal human rights, minority rights are often handled as a sort of 'special' rights, different and completely isolated from 'general' human rights".

Added value of RA

The author doubts whether incorporation of RA in EU law will strengthen the protection of national minorities, since RA and the FCNM do not share the same "teleology". Although they have many similarities and both create binding obligations requiring states to take positive measures to promote full and effective equality for persons belonging to national minorities, the scope of positive-discrimination measures under the FCNM is broader and more society-oriented than in the case of RA. The FCNM seeks to "have an additional positive impact on the situation of the persons concerned/given community and on a society as a whole". In short, it stands apart through its determination to translate anti-discrimination standards into an obligation to produce a specific result over and above the "best-endeavours obligation" of RA. Given the sophisticated framework of the FCNM, the author doubts whether RA will add anything to the concept of "inclusiveness" that is supposed to promote the participation rights of persons belonging to national minorities.

3.1.2. Council Directive 2000/78/EC of 27 November 2000 (Jackson Preece)

Scope

The "European equality duty" implicitly includes the test of RA in a number of directives on equal treatment. The obligation to provide reasonable accommodation was first enshrined in Council Directive 2000/78/EC of 27 November 2000 establishing a general framework for equal treatment in employment and occupation. Employers must provide reasonable accommodation by taking "appropriate measures" in response to discrimination against persons with disabilities unless such measures would impose a disproportionate burden on the employer (Article 5). Although this directive has frequently been criticised for applying only to a specific category of people (persons with disabilities) and in a limited sector of employment, Jackson Preece shows that it has been backed up by many other directives supplementing or strengthening national anti-discrimination provisions, covering other beneficiaries (women, ethnic/religious minorities, etc.), targeting other forms of discrimination or undesirable conduct (harassment) and advocating positive action to prevent or compensate for disadvantages. Lastly, all these directives are further supported by (for example) Article 14 of the European Convention on Human Rights and Article 13 of the EC Treaty, inserted by the Treaty of Amsterdam.

Limitations

All the anti-discrimination directives allow for differences in treatment for certain minorities. Positive measures to prevent or compensate for disadvantages associated with racial or ethnic origin are interpreted as "positive action" in favour of a specific group. However, this positive action should not be confused with RA. While the former comes under "preferential treatment", the latter is marked by "differential treatment". Positive action arises out of "justice for a group" (disproportionate effect of a rule on a particular group) rather than individual compensation (discriminatory impact of a rule on an individual). One example of positive action is quotas (reserved places) for groups to restore substantive equality between different social groups.

Added value of RA

Traditionally, the concept of RA relates to individual discriminatory intent or the prejudicial effects of a general policy or measure but does not imply "positive action" to protect vulnerable groups. However, in the context of current European legal thinking, RA would tend to contribute to an exchange of good accommodation practice. European law can use the positive measures developed by RA to assist with its anti-discrimination strategies.

3.1.3. The European Convention on Human Rights (Ruiz Vieytez)

Scope

The *Thlimmenos v. Greece* case[1] demonstrated that the right to equality was violated if states, without an objective and reasonable justification, failed to treat differently persons whose situations were different. For Eduardo Ruiz Vieytez, this recognition of "discrimination through non-differentiation" is based on a more pluralist interpretation of Article 14 of the Convention. In this specific case, a religious difference warranted differential treatment leading to a "reasonable accommodation". Although the Court has generally not pursued this line of approach in its subsequent decisions, it has proved that European law is willing to adapt its laws. Similarly, the European Court of Human Rights held that the act of compelling an individual belonging to a minority faith to take an oath on the Gospels without providing for some practical accommodation was a breach of Article 9 of the Convention.[2] In a further judgment,[3] the Court found indirect discrimination against a racial or ethnic group. These judgments uphold the protection of various minorities and the require-ment for states to adjust their rules to secure certain rights set out in the Convention, with due regard for the national margin of appreciation.

Limitations

Despite this progress in the law, the author considers that the European Court of Human Rights has shown greater reluctance and misgivings when reasonable accommodation relates to the fields of religious and

---

1. *Thlimmenos v. Greece*, judgment of 6 April 2000.
2. *Buscarini and Others v. San Marino*, judgment of 18 February 1999, paragraph 39.
3. *D.H. and Others v. the Czech Republic*, judgment of 13 November 2007.

linguistic diversity. According to the author, the commitment to exclusive secularism that prevails in countries such as France and Turkey influences the interpretation of protected rights and further limits freedom of religion in the public sphere.

Added value of RA

Would the introduction of RA add something to an already strong system of protection for personal rights? The author sees RA as "a sound and effective instrument for pushing forward ... democratic pluralisation". "The ideas of complex equality, indirect discrimination and discrimination through non-differentiation" could gain by the interpretative work of the Canadian courts, particularly regarding religious and linguistic diversity, "without the need for costly legislative changes," according to Ruiz Vieytez.

3.2. Similarities and differences in law (Ast and Foblets)

"In Europe, setting aside the employment sector in the case of persons with disabilities, there is no general right to reasonable accommodation," as Marie-Claire Foblets points out. However, the domestic law of some European Union member states recognises such a right,[4] while the case law of the European Court of Human Rights and numerous EU directives cite a duty of reasonable accommodation on grounds other than disability, including respect for freedom of religion.

"Reasonable accommodation" and "reasonable adjustment": a question of terminology

In English, "reasonable accommodation" is also referred to as "reasonable adjustment". Both refer to a "means of applying the equality principle", requiring an institution or state to take "appropriate measures" in a particular context to avoid the same treatment disadvantaging certain persons. In French, the equivalent terms are "accommodement raisonnable" and "aménagement raisonnable".

Examples of reasonable accommodations/adjustments are provided in the case law of the European courts. The European Court of Human Rights has called on a state to introduce an exception to the rule in order that

---

4. M. Bell, I. Chopin and F. Palmer, *Developing Anti-Discrimination Law in Europe – The 25 EU Member States Compared*, European Commission, Luxembourg, July 2007.

a citizen may have equal enjoyment of his rights (*Thlimmenos v. Greece* judgment),[5] while the European Court of Justice has demanded that an alternative solution be found for a candidate in an open competition organised by the Council of the European Communities the date of which coincided with a religious festival (Vivien Prais case).[6] The European Court of Human Rights has required Greek-language secondary school facilities to be made available to members of a linguistic minority to facilitate their access to Greek-language education and fully exercise their right to education (*Cyprus v. Turkey* judgment).

However, while in English the two terms would appear to be synonymous, Frédérique Ast argues that the two terms used in French refer to concepts which, despite having similarities, are not identical. "*Aménagement raisonnable*" gives victims an individual right actively to demand special treatment, going beyond the right to non-discrimination and also encompassing a collective dimension.

Concept of indirect discrimination: a similar use and interpretation?

Can RA be used "to deal with indirect discrimination as effectively as the methods currently used?" asks Foblets.

Indirect discrimination has been prohibited by many legal instruments, notes Ast, such as in the public international law of the League of Nations and by the United Nations conventions prohibiting discrimination, the European Convention on Human Rights and the revised European Social Charter.

The way in which both the European and Canadian legal systems interpret indirect discrimination reflects a similar concern with the exclusion effects of a general rule whose seeming neutrality makes problematical (and conspicuous) not so much any differences as the expression of certain identities running counter to dominant practices. Similarly, both the European and Canadian courts have proved responsive to discrimination linked to the perpetuation of a historical disadvantage or the application of stereotypes to members of vulnerable groups.

An example of the latter concern is to be found in the *D.H and Others v. the Czech Republic* judgment. The European Court of Human Rights

---

5. ECtHR, *Thlimmenos v. Greece*, 6 April 2000, op. cit.

6. CJEC, 27 October 1976, Case 130-75.

compelled the Czech authorities to review school tests skewed towards the majority culture in order to adapt them for Roma children who had to overcome cultural and linguistic disadvantages associated with their constant uprooting.

The role played by the concept of indirect discrimination is extremely broad according to Ast: as a "powerful legal means", it is a "tool for protecting diversity", a "means of detecting exclusory phenomena" and a "means of ensuring social change". In other words, it can be used to protect pluralism through genuine respect for diversity, cultural traditions, ethnic identities and religious beliefs. It can reveal concealed and systemic exclusion effects stemming from certain general norms (despite the limitations of the disproportionate impact method). It arises out of the same pursuit of substantive equality that may even bring about the adjustment of a rule (and the emergence of a differentiated rule) so that the latter complies with the requirements of an "inclusive" society vis-à-vis minority population groups.

Continuous progress or a new course? In continuing down the anti-discrimination path, the European Court of Human Rights may have set its course towards a new balance of interests, overturning our existing social balances and demanding major reforms with regard to social cohesion. Indeed, the European Court of Human Rights took the plunge with its *Glor v. Switzerland* judgment of 30 April 2009, requiring reasonable measures to protect individual rights, as Ast points out.

One more step or one step too many? However, Ast notes greater reluctance by the European courts to extend their interpretation of indirect discrimination too far. The civil law courts "usually prefer to use alternative means, where they exist, to protect specific persons who are deemed vulnerable. Furthermore, the fear of encouraging communitarianism and challenging the law as a general standard are also curbing this process of transposition [of RA] into continental Europe," says Ast. In other words, the Court might fear that one more step in its interpretation of indirect discrimination would be one step too many, onto the banana skin of differentiated rights that have become a right to difference.

Since it is ultimately the courts which decide the scope of the concept, Ast believes "it is therefore the harnessing of the indirect discrimination concept rather than the concept itself which can help pinpoint different shades of responses to the question of respect for diversity. The courts must provide stimuli to this end, calling for the requisite reforms or even revolutions."

Accommodation measures or appropriate measures: the same solution?

When looking for alternatives, the European and Canadian courts also tend to seek, amongst various means of meeting the norm, those measures that will least affect individual rights and freedoms.

In several cases concerning protection of freedom of religion under Article 9 of the Convention (taken alone or in conjunction with Article 14), Foblets notes that "if a law or regulation with an objective and legitimate purpose nevertheless restricts the liberty of certain individuals and … changes to it would avoid such interference without undermining this lawful aim, then this option should be chosen". The same attitude has been adopted by the Canadian courts.

The proportionality test: the same approach?

When appraising a situation, the courts base their approach on a "proportionality test". Where competing rights and interests come into conflict, both the European and Canadian courts use the proportionality test to strike a balance between the means employed and the aims pursued. Foblets remarks that the "requirement for proportionality between the means applied and the purpose sought … plays a role similar to that of reasonable accommodation. It determines the compatibility with the Convention of depriving someone of their liberty."

Furthermore, for the proportionality test the European Court of Human Rights allows states a margin of appreciation whose "scope … will vary according to the circumstances, the subject-matter and its background". "As a result, the reasons given for ostensibly discriminatory measures are generally assessed flexibly, or indeed contingently," Ast believes.

However, "it needs to be determined how exactly [the concept of RA] could offer significant advantages over the proportionality test, by offering ways of overcoming some of the shortcomings in that test," says Foblets.

"Undue hardship" and a "disproportionate burden": to what extent?

As regards the criteria for deciding whether a measure is reasonable or excessive, the European courts share the same doubts and legal uncertainties, according to Foblets, concerning the limits to be placed on the duty of accommodation and therefore concerning the extent of the freedoms to be protected. "How far can persons demanding equal treatment go in exercising their freedoms?" asks Foblets.

The Canadian legal concept of "undue hardship" is matched in European law by determination of a "disproportionate burden" in terms of "financial costs", the "scale" of an organisation, etc. However, in our view, "undue hardship" entails a more sophisticated list of tests for determining adverse consequences for an institution.

The fact remains that Western courts encounter the same challenge in weighing up the various interests at stake. "For example, what actually constitutes a compelling governmental interest (United States) or a legitimate and compelling objective (Canada) that is sufficient to justify refusing a request for an exception?" questions Foblets.

The same scope and conditions?

Although the European Court of Human Rights has adopted a narrower interpretation of religion and shown a greater legal reserve, the same conditions would seem to apply, requiring applicants to prove that they are sincere in believing accommodation or adjustment measures to be necessary.

The scope of reasonable accommodation is broader in North America than in Europe in two respects: it covers all categories of people who may suffer discrimination and applies to both public and private sectors, employers and government.

3.3. Is the concept of RA necessary, desirable and possible?

Beyond the strictly legal framework, a number of authors have analysed certain obstacles to and conditions for the transposition of RA to the European context.

Feasibility: success or failure of transposition?

From the perspective of legal anthropology, Stéphane Eberhard finds that RA has been conceived in terms of a certain view of intercultural relations and the function of the law: "Reasonable accommodation is strongly imbued with a common law logic which perhaps facilitates its acceptance in the United kingdom but renders it rather alien to the continental countries with their civil law tradition." If it is to be separated from its original legal culture, "it seems neither possible nor relevant to transplant the concept exactly as it is" into a legal culture where an idealistic, ahistorical and systemic view of the law prevails. To entertain more pluralist and pragmatic approaches, the European legal system must first "get away from the unitarist, idealist tradition". This comment is, however, qualified by Pierre Bosset, who refers to successful transplantation into Quebec's legal landscape, which has a dual legal tradition.

Philosophically speaking, according to Eduardo Ruiz Vieytez and Emilio Santoro, transposition of RA would make sense only with a political model that accepted a definition of plural citizenship and was based on inclusive social and economic structures. In other words, RA's chances of success in Europe largely depend on support from inclusive policies. Hence the importance of linking the legal concept of accommodation with a political and ethical conception of plural democratic citizenship, which alone is able to open up to otherness and secure genuine recognition of a plural identity. It is, in fact, the political model and ideological background that are likely to determine the application of RA.

Relevance: useful or pointless?

In Tariq Ramadan's opinion, there is no need for further legal instruments in an array of European law that is already sufficiently sophisticated. The problem in adjusting the law to pluralism is not technical (legal) but rather psychological (bound up with prejudices and resistance). Thus the position of the courts (open or closed to pluralism) will determine the position of the law (for or against incorporating diversity) as a result of their interpretation of rights (broad or narrow).

Effectiveness: the nature of the added value

For Jane Wright, the potential of RA lies not in its scope or purpose but in how it may be applied to increase the number of beneficiaries. In this respect, the added value of RA lies in its inclusive approach and its requirement for reciprocity, creating a wider field of beneficiaries and reinforcing the "mutual" nature of accommodation.

4. Preferred types of accommodation: challenges and outlook (Wright, Ramadan, Ruiz Vieytez)

4.1. Reasonable and mutual accommodation

According to Jane Wright, the suitability of RA as a legal tool should be assessed in terms of the objectives of social cohesion, the latter being defined as "the capacity of a society to ensure the well-being of all its members, minimising disparities and avoiding marginalisation" and having social rights, participation and dialogue as its key markers. In this respect, the need for reciprocity is central to RA, since how RA is applied is in large part determined by negotiation between the parties. RA derives from an alternative, inclusive approach that involves all parties, majorities and minority groups (both traditional and new minorities) in a process of negotiation. RA is thus moving onto ground where the FCNM has hitherto shown a reluctance to venture: integration of "new" minorities. The RA model also conveys the idea that minorities are not "passive beneficiaries" of concessions by the majority but stakeholders participating in the decisions concerning them. There is both a vertical and a horizontal dimension to their participation: members of minority communities should be encouraged to engage in dialogue with public authorities and also with members of the majority population. This process results in "mutual accommodation" between minorities and majorities, understood as exchanges between citizens and the state and between residents themselves. A further consequence of this mutual accommodation is that communities' needs are determined through dialogue and negotiation and managed through local grants and resources. Lastly, this inclusive approach fosters mutual understanding through an intercultural dialogue between all segments of society.

4.2. Accommodations for minorities or accommodations for all?

Tariq Ramadan argues for mutual adjustment of legal systems. As for the "Islamic question", he asserts that "between the margin for manoeuvre in the law in democratic societies and the acknowledged flexibility in Islamic legal traditions, it is possible to find satisfactory solutions without amending existing legal frameworks". Regarding conflicts of rights, the author identifies three possible positions, ranging from a firmly closed approach (assimilation of the minority and domination of the majority norm) to inclusive openness (revising the norms for everybody) with a mid-way compromise solution (specific adjustments to the norm or else exceptions). The compromise solution, in his view, is to be preferred. The effort required then depends on our willingness to exploit the "potential creativity of legal interpretations", broaden the legal options for specific problems (rather than becoming hung up on presumed incompatibilities between systems of law), and fill the gaps in our knowledge of Islamic law (rather than exploring the shortcomings of domestic or EU law).

Instead of amending existing legal frameworks, we should change our way of looking at the law rather than altering its scope. Lastly, the author emphasises that a considerable amount of explanation and support is necessary to educate people as to why readjustments are necessary and can benefit everyone.

4.3. Special services or different methods of delivery?

For Eduardo Ruiz Vieytez, the practical issue of access to rights and services by specific groups of people (such as migrants) raises the "ideological tension between the principle of specific social or cultural treatment of minorities (in a broad sense), and the principle of normalisation, by which they are dealt with through the existing general services". The tension between these two approaches is greater than it seems. The author asks whether specific services should be set up for particular groups on the basis of their difference or whether all users should be covered by the same services. Far from being neutral, the option chosen will reveal a view of the principle of equality that is theoretically grounded in either multiculturalism or human rights. In the author's opinion the answer should be to combine the principle of equality with that of different treatment by means of standard institutions for all citizens which nevertheless offer different arrangements (options) for delivering services, on the same footing as those for persons belonging to the majority.

5. Rethinking the politics and developing training strategies: political culture and consultation guidelines

Leaving aside the legal framework, how the concept of RA is received will depend on factors that are social and political (inclusive citizenship policy), institutional (openness to diversity) and personal (occupational background).

5.1. Political basis and normative context: issues, obstacles and conditions for recognising diversity

To be effective, protection of the rights of individuals from minorities cannot depend entirely on the courts, since legal action is justified only in the event of conflict and for the purpose of settling a particular dispute, fairly much regardless of the overall social context and the specific institutional situation. By its very nature, a court battle tends to bring about a polarisation of positions rather than agreement. Moreover, to live in harmony and build a society, a nation cannot rely solely on legal relationships. Lastly, in a pluralist society, mediation of rights should be coupled with a universal discussion of the common values that we as a society wish to protect in law. This means that any legal discussion on the protection of cultural identities must lead to a political discussion of the importance accorded to minority identities. Irrespective of the legal mechanisms concerned, such discussions encourage us to examine the political factors in producing inequalities in law.

Introducing RA: the appropriate political background (Santoro)

For Emilio Santoro, any discussion of RA must be preceded by a discussion of the best political model to guide social integration. The idea of the nation state that prevailed in the 19th and 20th centuries no longer serves as a sufficient basis for a sense of belonging in a society marked by its diversity of identity. If citizens are unable to build a society around agreement on an idea of the "common good", the challenge of plural democracies is to mediate between differences in values and interests on a new basis. This calls into question the legitimacy of majority decision making and any possibility of maintaining national discipline or national myths to cement the majority culture. The neutrality of rules is another illusion. "Only when a nation state is breaking down and coming into contact with alien points of view does the unspoken agreement hitherto taken for granted come more into the light, and often become problematic," says Santoro. Thus the state considers "acceptable" only those differences that mesh with that society's dominant values (such as expressions of personal autonomy). Can the population be reunited on the basis of fresh values? In the author's opinion, the pursuit of a balance between plural and conflicting interests cannot be the responsibility of the courts alone. Nor is it up to the majority to decide on those individual rights that we consider fundamental. Here the potential of RA is as "a tool for constitutional protection, not of multiculturalism or of other cultures, but of individual differences. This technique of government should be used until such time as a new inclusive citizenship project appears on the horizon." Another advantage of RA's individual, casuistic and pragmatic approach is that it avoids turning an individual problem into a political problem or twisting conflicts of interests into a problem of minority relations with the majority or interpreting any assertion of rights by minorities as cultural demands. Settlement of individual problems can lead to new practices that are "flexible and discreet, or even anonymous" and which in the long term may influence citizens' views of harmonious coexistence even before any amendment to our political model.

Bringing about "the democratic management of plural societies" (Ruiz Vieytez)

Continuing this line of thought, Eduardo Ruiz Vieytez and Lidija R. Basta Fleiner suggest that rethinking our model of citizenship is a precondition for introducing an inclusive and participatory democracy. For Ruiz Vieytez, if the task is to "accommodate diversities" rather than "accommodate immigrants", politics must move towards "the democratic management of pluralist societies", which increasingly consist of "culturally diverse citizens". His suggestion is based on the multiple identities that make up any individual in his or her development and integration into the social whole. However, this conception of an individual with complex identities can flourish only in opposition to a state based on a fixed identity in a closed circuit of national affiliation – an exclusive identity that rejects "foreigners" (non-nationals). Consequently, the political basis of any approach aimed at accommodating diversity must be promotion of plural and inclusive citizenship – the main guarantee of fair treatment for all residents, their right of participation and protection of their cultural freedom. Such an approach is also founded on respect for universal rights beyond the rights secured at national level: "it is a question of being able to exercise human rights through one's own identity, and not despite it" (Ruiz Vieytez).

Social/cultural resistance and identity issues (Fournier)

Against the background of the debate in Quebec on the reasonable accommodation "crisis", François Fournier rehearses and analyses a wide range of objections typically used as arguments against pluralism. They all focus on a sense of loss: loss of national identity and erosion of social cohesion, founding values, collective agendas, visions of the future, security and good social relations. Logically enough, the proposed solutions entail more restrictive and non-negotiable measures. On the legal front, the anti-pluralist position advocates rebalancing rights in order to protect and promote the national culture (for example, freedom of religion should give way to gender equality), inserting interpretative clauses into charters in order to assert the predominance of Quebec's values and historical heritage, and setting out "clear guidelines founded on our identity". On the political front, immigrants must sign an integration agreement as soon as they enter the territory, undertaking to abide by and adapt to the host country's values. If these perceptions are not deconstructed and the relevant arguments refuted, any pro-accommodation line is likely to meet a wall of incomprehension and intolerance. The author recommends using social dialogue to explain RA and how it is rooted in the integration model and to explore common values as well as the many factors that rob traditional landmarks of their stability, thus putting immigration in perspective as a source of cultural pluralism.

5.2. Negotiating reasonable accommodation: preventive management and successful practice

Public institutions consist of a great many norms covering manifold aspects of daily life. How should we rethink our training strategies to meet staff training needs with due regard for the law and social reality (types of diversity, new forms of vulnerability, operating contexts, etc.) and with an intercultural approach that simultaneously encompasses knowledge, technical skills and interpersonal skills?

Structuring training around new types of knowledge (Saillant)

According to Francine Saillant, conventional intercultural training needs to be renewed and enhanced by a corpus of knowledge that goes beyond specific cultural characteristics and skills based on communication, cultural mediation and translation to include new knowledge about the multiple factors affecting the lives of immigrants and their families. Thus intercultural training should include immigrants' specific health conditions (mental health, signs of post-traumatic stress), socio-economic vulnerability factors (poverty, isolation, adaptation problems), cultural factors (for example, immigrants' resistance to using public services) and some knowledge of the right to equal treatment (right to equal access to services; definition of accessibility). The author suggests broadening our view of diversity itself to take in diverse lifestyles and values, and therefore the intrinsic plurality of modern societies, and see difference "as multidimensional (open to dimensions other than, but including, the ethnic dimension) and to be situated in multiple locations (in institutions and public services, in the groups served)". This knowledge, mainly in the fields of anthropology, intercultural relations and health, should form the basis of training designed to meet the needs of public health and social services whose role is to reduce difference-based inequality and vulnerability.

Drawing up guidelines and analysis tools to negotiate reasonable accommodations and settle tensions (Jézéquel)

There is no off-the-shelf training that enables a person to feel at home with complexity, devise creative solutions, identify the nature of the needs being expressed or interact flexibly without losing sight of the purpose of norms. However, to meet the needs voiced in the field, appropriate intercultural training ought, in my opinion, to provide analysis tools and explain the various guidelines by which staff should be governed when negotiating or settling conflicts of rights or values, since any decision to introduce adjustment measures, whatever their extent, requires staff to assess individuals and problem situations in far greater depth than can be covered by a programme of enhanced (new) knowledge. To enable staff to manage/come to terms with diversity and not simply judge its complexity, training should supply them with information on assessment criteria (methods of assessment), guidelines (legal, political, social and institutional) and action/communication strategies for negotiated and concerted solutions. The task is to agree on a fair and useful framework of reference for mediating rights and negotiating values in a context where the specific and complex nature of the situations rules out any automatic application of a formula.

Developing intercultural dialogue skills (Eberhard)

"The logic of reasonable, mutual, accommodation relies on a capacity for dialogue," says Stéphane Eberhard. Hence the importance, in his opinion, of rethinking the framework and functions of intercultural dialogue, the role and status of dialogue facilitators, and the benefits and forms of a dialogue that is genuinely intercultural. In short, he invites us to go beyond a dualistic view of dialogue ("me and the other person") and move from a logic of confrontation to one of exchange, with all that this entails by way of learning. The author recommends enhancing the status of "intercultural mediators" in institutions. The importance of their role stems from their ability to identify common ground and stumbling blocks in dialogue for the purpose of calming tensions and achieving mutually satisfactory solutions. He argues for shared expertise, whereby an institution or other places with specific knowledge (community services, places of worship, etc.) would pool their individual support structures. He urges us to avoid over-politicisation by taking a human and pragmatic view of intercultural society rather than a political one. Lastly, the actual practice of dialogue should not be over-proceduralised at the risk of diluting the responsibility of those involved.

Learning from successful methods of managing diversity (Morariu and Petrei)

Lucia Morariu shows how the application of RA can be improved through good practice such as the Intercultural Mediation programme that has been set up in Belgian hospitals. The programme covers a number of aspects: recruitment and training, types of action, role of professionals within the programme, analysis of personal and institutional problems encountered in a multicultural context, and possible solutions and changes. In describing the implementation of these aspects, the author demonstrates how the programme has made it possible to improve access and quality of care for users belonging to ethnic minorities. Further to this account, Fabrizia Petrei reveals how a hospital in the city of Prato in Italy has endeavoured, through new practices, fresh attitudes and changes in institutional guidelines, to find a solution to a number of critical situations experienced by immigrant women in particular.

6. Social choices and common tasks: appropriate policy guidelines/recommendations for living together in diversity (Jézéquel)

Opening up institutional cultures to diversity means subjecting our mental categories and everyday practices to scrutiny. By way of conclusion, here are a few ideas for consideration or action by the various people concerned.

6.1. Policy

The first idea is to change perspective by switching the burden of adaptation from the user to the institution.

Examples of implementation

- formulate an institution's responsibility to accept and manage (the full range of) diversity in positive terms;

- enshrine diversity among the basic values of an institution's public service mandate rather than confining it to a separate department;

- set up a committee to consider the repercussions/impact of such a policy on public institutions, policies and laws in Europe;

- clarify non-statutory guidelines enabling the public sphere to be renegotiated by means of mutual accommodation.

6.2. Information and communication

The second course is to increase informed demand for change and strengthen support from the persons concerned while ensuring that they understand the implications of accommodation/adjustment measures.

Examples of implementation

- explain the egalitarian model underlying an accommodation policy entailing differential treatment (a plural environment) rather than uniform treatment for all users (a standard environment);

- raise awareness of the need for change through a forward-looking study of demographic trends;

- present the duty of accommodation as a matter of respect for individual rights and a commitment to securing equal treatment;

- borrow tools from the field of mediation and create spaces of dialogue that foster a culture of compromise and a climate of mutual trust.

6.3. Training and support for negotiating reasonable accommodations

The final idea is to enable staff to analyse, negotiate and resolve any tensions between institutional norms and specific user needs by giving them points of reference, guidelines and tools appropriate to their jobs (for example, training in customer service in a multicultural environment for front-line staff).

Examples of implementation

- produce a handbook to help staff draw distinctions between problems of voluntary adjustment and issues of reasonable accommodation, between what is negotiable and what is not, and between majority values and fundamental values irrespective of majority influence, and help them determine whether a demand for or refusal of adjustment stems from a conflict of rights (including fundamental rights), differing cultural values, conflicting interests, etc;

- encourage applicants and the institution to find alternative solutions and consider all the provisions for applying norms rather than changing the norms themselves as soon as they present a limitation.

Sales agents for publications of the Council of Europe
Agents de vente des publications du Conseil de l'Europe

BELGIUM/BELGIQUE
La Librairie Européenne -
The European Bookshop
Rue de l'Orme, 1
BE-1040 BRUXELLES
Tel.: +32 (0)2 231 04 35
Fax: +32 (0)2 735 08 60
E-mail: order@libeurop.be
http://www.libeurop.be

Jean De Lannoy/DL Services
Avenue du Roi 202 Koningslaan
BE-1190 BRUXELLES
Tel.: +32 (0)2 538 43 08
Fax: +32 (0)2 538 08 41
E-mail: jean.de.lannoy@dl-servi.com
http://www.jean-de-lannoy.be

BOSNIA AND HERZEGOVINA/
BOSNIE-HERZÉGOVINE
Robert's Plus d.o.o.
Marka Maruliça 2/V
BA-71000, SARAJEVO
Tel.: + 387 33 640 818
Fax: + 387 33 640 818
E-mail: robertsplus@bih.net.ba

CANADA
Renouf Publishing Co. Ltd.
1-5369 Canotek Road
CA-OTTAWA, Ontario K1J 9J3
Tel.: +1 613 745 2665
Fax: +1 613 745 7660
Toll-Free Tel.: (866) 767-6766
E-mail: order.dept@renoufbooks.com
http://www.renoufbooks.com

CROATIA/CROATIE
Robert's Plus d.o.o.
Marasoviçeva 67
HR-21000, SPLIT
Tel.: + 385 21 315 800, 801, 802, 803
Fax: + 385 21 315 804
E-mail: robertsplus@robertsplus.hr

CZECH REPUBLIC/
RÉPUBLIQUE TCHÈQUE
Suweco CZ, s.r.o.
Klecakova 347
CZ-180 21 PRAHA 9
Tel.: +420 2 424 59 204
Fax: +420 2 848 21 646
E-mail: import@suweco.cz
http://www.suweco.cz

DENMARK/DANEMARK
GAD
Vimmelskaftet 32
DK-1161 KØBENHAVN K
Tel.: +45 77 66 60 00
Fax: +45 77 66 60 01
E-mail: gad@gad.dk
http://www.gad.dk

FINLAND/FINLANDE
Akateeminen Kirjakauppa
PO Box 128
Keskuskatu 1
FI-00100 HELSINKI
Tel.: +358 (0)9 121 4430
Fax: +358 (0)9 121 4242
E-mail: akatilaus@akateeminen.com
http://www.akateeminen.com

FRANCE
La Documentation française
(diffusion/distribution France entière)
124, rue Henri Barbusse
FR-93308 AUBERVILLIERS CEDEX
Tél.: +33 (0)1 40 15 70 00
Fax: +33 (0)1 40 15 68 00
E-mail: commande@ladocumentationfrancaise.fr
http://www.ladocumentationfrancaise.fr

Librairie Kléber
1 rue des Francs Bourgeois
FR-67000 STRASBOURG
Tel.: +33 (0)3 88 15 78 88
Fax: +33 (0)3 88 15 78 80
E-mail: librairie-kleber@coe.int
http://www.librairie-kleber.com

GERMANY/ALLEMAGNE
AUSTRIA/AUTRICHE
UNO Verlag GmbH
August-Bebel-Allee 6
DE-53175 BONN
Tel.: +49 (0)228 94 90 20
Fax: +49 (0)228 94 90 222
E-mail: bestellung@uno-verlag.de
http://www.uno-verlag.de

GREECE/GRÈCE
Librairie Kauffmann s.a.
Stadiou 28
GR-105 64 ATHINAI
Tel.: +30 210 32 55 321
Fax.: +30 210 32 30 320
E-mail: ord@otenet.gr
http://www.kauffmann.gr

HUNGARY/HONGRIE
Euro Info Service
Pannónia u. 58.
PF. 1039
HU-1136 BUDAPEST
Tel.: +36 1 329 2170
Fax: +36 1 349 2053
E-mail: euroinfo@euroinfo.hu
http://www.euroinfo.hu

ITALY/ITALIE
Licosa SpA
Via Duca di Calabria, 1/1
IT-50125 FIRENZE
Tel.: +39 0556 483215
Fax: +39 0556 41257
E-mail: licosa@licosa.com
http://www.licosa.com

MEXICO/MEXIQUE
Mundi-Prensa México, S.A. De C.V.
Río Pánuco, 141 Delegacíon Cuauhtémoc
MX-06500 MÉXICO, D.F.
Tel.: +52 (01)55 55 33 56 58
Fax: +52 (01)55 55 14 67 99
E-mail: mundiprensa@mundiprensa.com.mx
http://www.mundiprensa.com.mx

NETHERLANDS/PAYS-BAS
Roodveldt Import BV
Nieuwe Hemweg 50
NE-1013 CX AMSTERDAM
Tel.: + 31 20 622 8035
Fax.: + 31 20 625 5493
Website: www.publidis.org
Email: orders@publidis.org

NORWAY/NORVÈGE
Akademika
Postboks 84 Blindern
NO-0314 OSLO
Tel.: +47 2 218 8100
Fax: +47 2 218 8103
E-mail: support@akademika.no
http://www.akademika.no

POLAND/POLOGNE
Ars Polona JSC
25 Obroncow Street
PL-03-933 WARSZAWA
Tel.: +48 (0)22 509 86 00
Fax: +48 (0)22 509 86 10
E-mail: arspolona@arspolona.com.pl
http://www.arspolona.com.pl

PORTUGAL
Livraria Portugal
(Dias & Andrade, Lda.)
Rua do Carmo, 70
PT-1200-094 LISBOA
Tel.: +351 21 347 42 82 / 85
Fax: +351 21 347 02 64
E-mail: info@livrariaportugal.pt
http://www.livrariaportugal.pt

RUSSIAN FEDERATION/
FÉDÉRATION DE RUSSIE
Ves Mir
17b, Butlerova ul.
RU-101000 MOSCOW
Tel.: +7 495 739 0971
Fax: +7 495 739 0971
E-mail: orders@vesmirbooks.ru
http://www.vesmirbooks.ru

SPAIN/ESPAGNE
Mundi-Prensa Libros, s.a.
Castelló, 37
ES-28001 MADRID
Tel.: +34 914 36 37 00
Fax: +34 915 75 39 98
E-mail: libreria@mundiprensa.es
http://www.mundiprensa.com

SWITZERLAND/SUISSE
Planetis Sàrl
16 chemin des pins
CH-1273 ARZIER
Tel.: +41 22 366 51 77
Fax: +41 22 366 51 78
E-mail: info@planetis.ch

UNITED KINGDOM/ROYAUME-UNI
The Stationery Office Ltd
PO Box 29
GB-NORWICH NR3 1GN
Tel.: +44 (0)870 600 5522
Fax: +44 (0)870 600 5533
E-mail: book.enquiries@tso.co.uk
http://www.tsoshop.co.uk

UNITED STATES and CANADA/
ÉTATS-UNIS et CANADA
Manhattan Publishing Company
468 Albany Post Road
US-CROTON-ON-HUDSON, NY 10520
Tel.: +1 914 271 5194
Fax: +1 914 271 5856
E-mail: Info@manhattanpublishing.com
http://www.manhattanpublishing.com

Council of Europe Publishing/Editions du Conseil de l'Europe
FR-67075 STRASBOURG Cedex
Tel.: +33 (0)3 88 41 25 81 – Fax: +33 (0)3 88 41 39 10 – E-mail: publishing@coe.int – Website: http://book.coe.int